I0810174

IMAGES
of America

TACOMA'S WRIGHT PARK

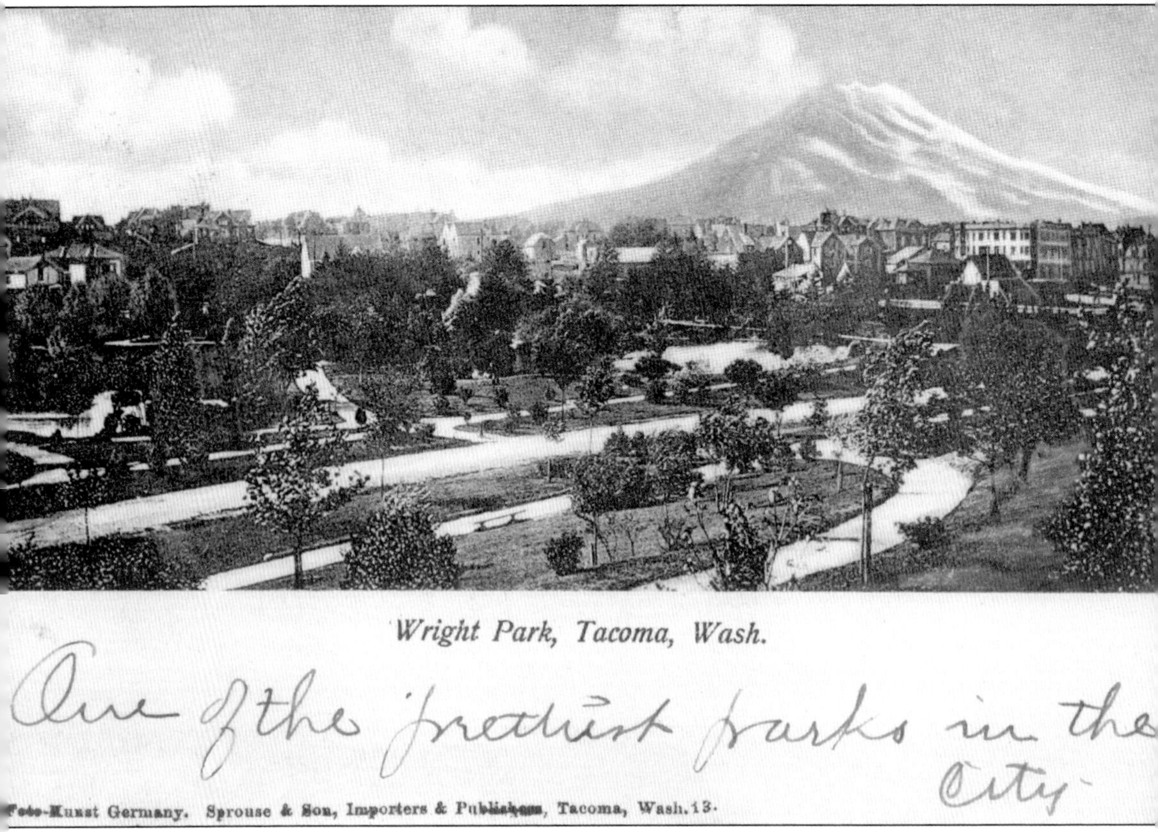

Many people over the decades have shared this sentiment about Wright Park, inscribed on a postcard from 1907. However, the grandeur of Mount Rainier gracing the backdrop is the printer's artistic license; this view actually looks northwest toward the Olympic Mountains, not the Cascades. The moving of the mountain proves that "Photoshop-ing" has been a concept, if not an informal verb, for quite some time.

ON THE COVER: When the Tacoma Land Company donated 27 acres near downtown Tacoma for a city park in 1886, the deed stipulated that the city had four years to improve the property. One of the earliest improvements occurred when the swampy northwest quadrant of the park was excavated and transformed into a lovely little lake. (Courtesy Metro Parks Tacoma.)

IMAGES
of America

TACOMA'S WRIGHT PARK

Melissa McGinnis, Doreen Beard-Simpkins,
and the Metropolitan Park District of Tacoma

ARCADIA
PUBLISHING

ISBN 978-0-7385-5932-2

Published by Arcadia Publishing
Charleston SC, Chicago IL, Portsmouth NH, San Francisco CA

Printed in the United States of America

Library of Congress Catalog Card Number: 2008921575

For all general information contact Arcadia Publishing at:
Telephone 843-853-2070
Fax 843-853-0044
E-mail sales@arcadiapublishing.com
For customer service and orders:
Toll-Free 1-888-313-2665

Visit us on the Internet at www.arcadiapublishing.com

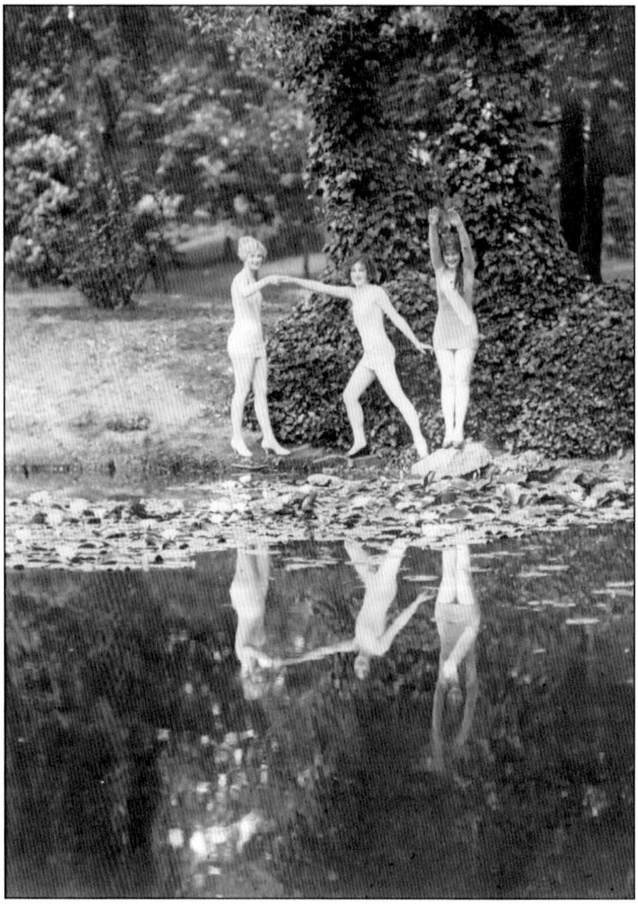

Their names are lost to history, as is the occasion of this photograph, but the enjoyment of these three young women is evident as they pose by the Wright Park pond. Wearing fashionable one-piece swimsuits with banners and matching emblems across the chest, they complete their outfits with high-heeled pumps, leading the viewer to believe that they are not truly headed for a swim.

Contents

Acknowledgments		6
Introduction		7
1.	"An Apparently Unwieldy Piece of Nature"	9
2.	Tacoma's Jewel Box	33
3.	The Wright Park Neighborhood	51
4.	Statues, Monuments, and a Tree Stump	69
5.	Arboreal Splendor	81
6.	Festivals, Concerts, and the Easter Bunny	93
7.	A Walk in the Park	109
Index of Photographs		127

ACKNOWLEDGMENTS

Charles Barstow Wright leads our list of acknowledgments for this photographic history of his namesake, Wright Park, on the northern edge of Tacoma's downtown. His personal generosity as well as his leadership as president of the Tacoma Land Company greatly benefited Tacoma's parklands and other institutions.

In the present day, we recognize the current stewards of Wright Park: the Metropolitan Park District of Tacoma Board of Park Commissioners—Larry Dahl, Ryan Mello, Aaron Pointer, Tim Reid, and Victoria Woodards—and the many employees of Metro Parks Tacoma (MPT) under executive director Jack C. Wilson. We thank MPT communications coordinator Sheree Trefry, in particular, for skillfully and cheerfully preparing the archival images for publication and Terri Walton for her photographic talent. Above all, our fellow citizens of Tacoma merit special recognition for their passage of the 2005 Park Improvement Bond, which has funded the most comprehensive reinvestment in Wright Park's infrastructure, facilities, and features since the park opened to horse-drawn carriages in 1890. Their vote for the importance of the restoration of Wright Park served as the impetus for this photographic retrospective.

Last but hardly least, Tacoma's historic image collections, both public and private, are tremendous, and the enthusiasm with which they are researched and shared among kindred spirits is equally gratifying. We offer a hearty thanks to Jean Insel Robeson, Eric Swanson, Tom Stenger, Jack Fallat of the Annie Wright School, Todd Kelley of MultiCare Health System, Terry Lumsden, the Tacoma Lawn Bowling Club, and the Seymour Conservatory for sharing their personal and institutional photographs. We salute our fellow public servants: Tacoma Public Library Northwest Room staff members Brian Kamens, Robert Schuler, Jody Gripp, Jeanie Fisher, Faye Bloom, and Kathi Aleman, and Washington State Historical Society librarians Elaine Miller and Joy Werlink. Brian Kamens deserves special recognition for his depth of knowledge and singular devotion to the local history of Tacoma.

All images without a photograph credit are the property of Metro Parks Tacoma. Full photograph credit information is provided on page 127.

INTRODUCTION

Wright Park is not Tacoma's first park. That honor belongs to Ferry Park, established in 1883. Nor is it Tacoma's largest, a distinction held by the more than 640 acres of Point Defiance Park. However, Wright Park's slim, rectangular acreage has been beloved for decades as being perhaps Tacoma's most graceful park, a compact oasis of natural yet artfully planned beauty in the heart of town. Bounded by Division and Sixth Avenues and South G and I Streets, Wright Park occupies rolling contours north of the city's downtown core. This urban location is no mere happenstance. Indeed, as is the case with so many of Tacoma's early civic amenities, the history of Wright Park is inextricably bound with Tacoma's selection as the terminus of the Northern Pacific Railway in 1873.

Tacoma's actual origin dates to the late 1860s with the establishment of Tacoma City, a small hamlet of settlers near today's Old Town neighborhood at North Thirtieth and McCarver Streets. These settlers hoped that their locale would become the terminus of the Northern Pacific rails. The railway did indeed choose Tacoma over Seattle, but not the Tacoma City site. Instead, the Northern Pacific chose a site called New Tacoma, in the area that would develop into today's downtown. The two fledgling communities, separated by only a few miles along the Commencement Bay shoreline, eventually joined forces and incorporated as the city of Tacoma in 1884. Between these two early Tacoma town sites was the rough and brambly acreage that would become Wright Park, donated to the young city by the Tacoma Land Company in 1886.

This enterprise was the real estate subsidiary of the Northern Pacific Railway, established in August 1873 to raise working capital for completion of the railroad by selling town lots in Tacoma. Its president, Charles Barstow Wright (1822–1898), was a self-made man from Pennsylvania whose formative business enterprises were helping on the family farm as a child and later working in a general store. Like many ambitious young men of his time and place, Wright took his early business acumen and headed west. In Chicago, he dabbled adeptly in real estate and turned a handsome profit before returning to Pennsylvania, where he expanded his considerable financial prowess to include banking and railroads. By the time he helped select the New Tacoma site as the Northern Pacific's terminus in 1873, he was a wealthy man indeed.

Immediately upon choosing Tacoma, Charles Wright and the Tacoma Land Company began to entertain visions of the appearance of their prodigy railroad town, perched on its forested slopes above Commencement Bay. From the very beginning, the plans and proposals they considered for a Tacoma town site included definitions of acreage set aside for central parkland. The *Weekly Pacific Tribune* of October 3, 1873, although not illustrated, detailed the first plan by James Tilton, the former surveyor for Washington Territory, as including some "27 acres, 1820 feet long by 640 broad . . . proposed as a public park." This is a remarkably close description of Wright Park, more than a dozen years before it was actually created.

The second plan of note was that commissioned by Charles Wright from the nationally prominent landscape architect Frederick Law Olmsted, famed at the time for his work on the design of New York City's Central Park. Olmsted's plan for Tacoma, delivered in December 1873, was very unorthodox, ignoring the usual grid system of city blocks and suggesting instead that the area's sloping topography dictate the city's aesthetic design. The design was not popular, coming at a time of financial constraint for the Northern Pacific and other railroad and business interests. Tacoma/Charles Wright/the Tacoma Land Company—it was hard to distinguish one from another in these early days—rejected it. However, Olmsted's plan, like Tilton's before it, was notable for his generous designation of land not for speculation and profit, but for the creation of parks as public gathering spaces—the lungs of a city, in the parlance of the day.

Charles Barstow Wright recognized the vitality of civic amenities to Tacoma's promotion and development and, in his role as company president, encouraged the Tacoma Land Company to act as an interested party in grants of land for educational and benevolent purposes, parks among them. According to early-20th-century annual report records of the Metropolitan Park District, the original intention of Wright and the Tacoma Land Company had been to set aside a central park tract between South First and South Sixth Streets and Tacoma and Yakima Avenues. An inspection of the actual terrain suggested that situating the park one block farther west would be preferable, and the now-familiar boundaries of what was for a time informally called "the City Park" came into being.

In the language of the original 1886 donation of land, the Tacoma Land Company's terms were that "the said land shall forever be exclusively used as and appropriated for the use of a public park." Furthermore, the grant was contingent upon the following conditions. First, that within two years, the land would be cleared, naturally contoured, and enclosed with "a substantial ornamental fence." Second, that within three years, the land would be seeded and planted with "not less than one hundred and fifty ornamental shade trees." Third, that within four years, "not less than one hundred and fifty additional shade trees" would be planted. The document also stated, "If said land shall at any time hereafter cease to be used for the purpose of a Public park" or if the city shall neglect "to perform within the time and in the manner herein specified . . . then this conveyance and the estate hereby granted shall cease, determine and be null and void."

In other words, the newly minted city of Tacoma, with all the attendant clamor for civic improvements at its often-muddy doorstep, now had a very limited window of opportunity to avail itself of the real estate largesse of Charles Wright and the Tacoma Land Company. The story that follows is a pictorial essay of how this scrappy patch of land came to be downtown Tacoma's venerable original oasis—Wright Park—and introduces those who tended it and the neighborhood that embraced its borders. In essence, the story is also a community's "thank-you" to the Philadelphia philanthropist who never lived in the city of Tacoma, but nonetheless did so much for it.

One

"An Apparently Unwieldy Piece of Nature"

The Tacoma Land Company's donation for Tacoma's city park came with conditions, time constraints, and the challenge of crafting an artful retreat from an uneven, sloping acreage that tended to be boggy in its low spots. According to the *Tacoma Daily Ledger* of May 12, 1890, "This land has always appeared to those who were interested in its improvement as an awkward and nearly useless piece of land for park purposes." By 1890, however, Tacoma prided itself on the progress that had been made in the previous four years since the city received the deed promise from the Northern Pacific's subsidiary.

Not that progress had been easy or certain. Money to afford the relatively simple terms of donation stipulated by Charles Wright and the Tacoma Land Company was tight. In the requisite period of 1886 to 1890, Tacoma citizens of private means more than once came to the rescue of meeting the land company's deadlines for park improvements by fronting the funds or donating embellishments.

The year 1890 also marked the evolution of the city council committee overseeing work on this park into a more formally appointed and separate board of park commissioners that held stronger advisory powers to Tacoma's city council. This body would now also help the council in managing Ferry, Puget, Point Defiance, and Lincoln Parks, all of which had joined the fledgling park system since 1883. Perhaps most significantly for Wright Park, as the city now frequently called the acreage in honor of Charles Wright, the board ratified the map and plans made for the park by professional landscape designer Edward Otto Schwagerl, who "saw the beauties in what was to others an apparently unwieldy piece of nature," as reported in the *Tacoma Daily Ledger* of May 12, 1890.

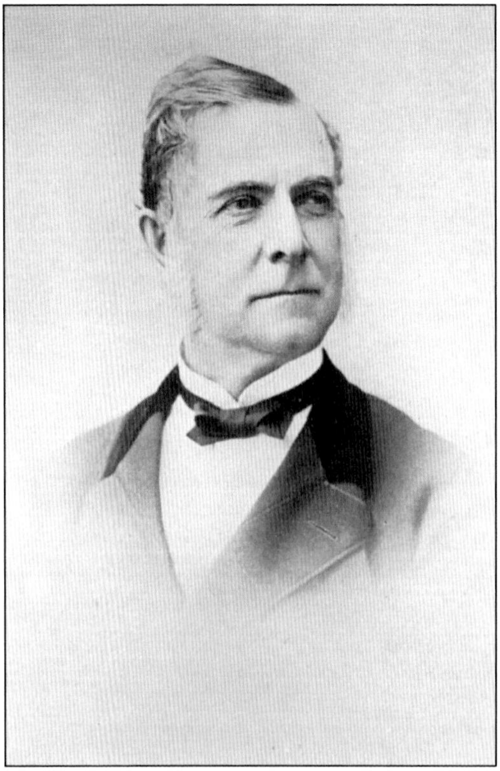

Charles Barstow Wright, president of the Tacoma Land Company, superintended the donation of 27 acres to the new City of Tacoma on May 29, 1886, for use as a park. Though the rough and logged-off acreage would take time and toil to turn into a park worthy of the word, the citizens of Tacoma were grateful. By 1890, they had named the park in honor of Wright.

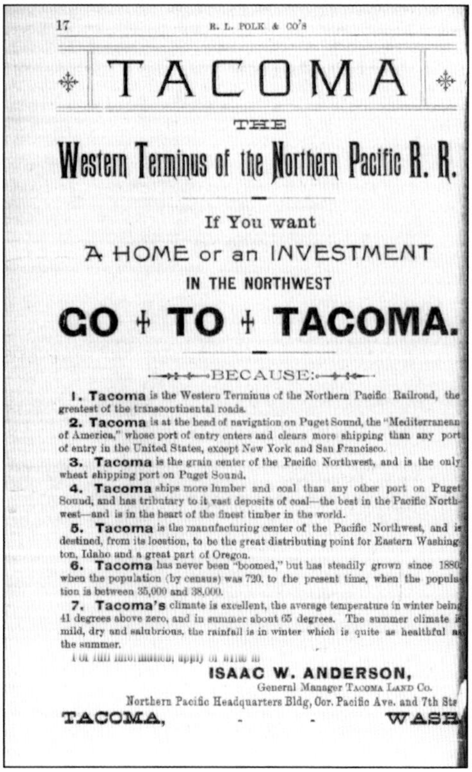

17 R. L. POLK & CO'S

TACOMA

THE

Western Terminus of the Northern Pacific R. R.

If You want

A HOME or an INVESTMENT

IN THE NORTHWEST

GO + TO + TACOMA.

BECAUSE:

1. **Tacoma** is the Western Terminus of the Northern Pacific Railroad, the greatest of the transcontinental roads.

2. **Tacoma** is at the head of navigation on Puget Sound, the "Mediterranean of America," whose port of entry enters and clears more shipping than any port of entry in the United States, except New York and San Francisco.

3. **Tacoma** is the grain center of the Pacific Northwest, and is the only wheat shipping port on Puget Sound.

4. **Tacoma** ships more lumber and coal than any other port on Puget Sound, and has tributary to it vast deposits of coal—the best in the Pacific Northwest—and is in the heart of the finest timber in the world.

5. **Tacoma** is the manufacturing center of the Pacific Northwest, and is destined, from its location, to be the great distributing point for Eastern Washington, Idaho and a great part of Oregon.

6. **Tacoma** has never been "boomed," but has steadily grown since 1880, when the population (by census) was 720, to the present time, when the population is between 35,000 and 38,000.

7. **Tacoma's** climate is excellent, the average temperature in winter being 41 degrees above zero, and in summer about 65 degrees. The summer climate is mild, dry and salubrious, the rainfall is in winter which is quite as healthful as the summer.

ISAAC W. ANDERSON,
General Manager Tacoma Land Co.
Northern Pacific Headquarters Bldg, Cor. Pacific Ave. and 7th Sts
TACOMA, - - WASH.

The Tacoma Land Company promoted the young city's prospects at every opportunity; here they are extolled in a full-page advertisement from the 1890 Tacoma City Directory. By that year, Tacoma's population had grown exponentially, and civic boosters were eager to point to amenities—such as the newly dedicated Wright Park—that would lure additional investment to the city.

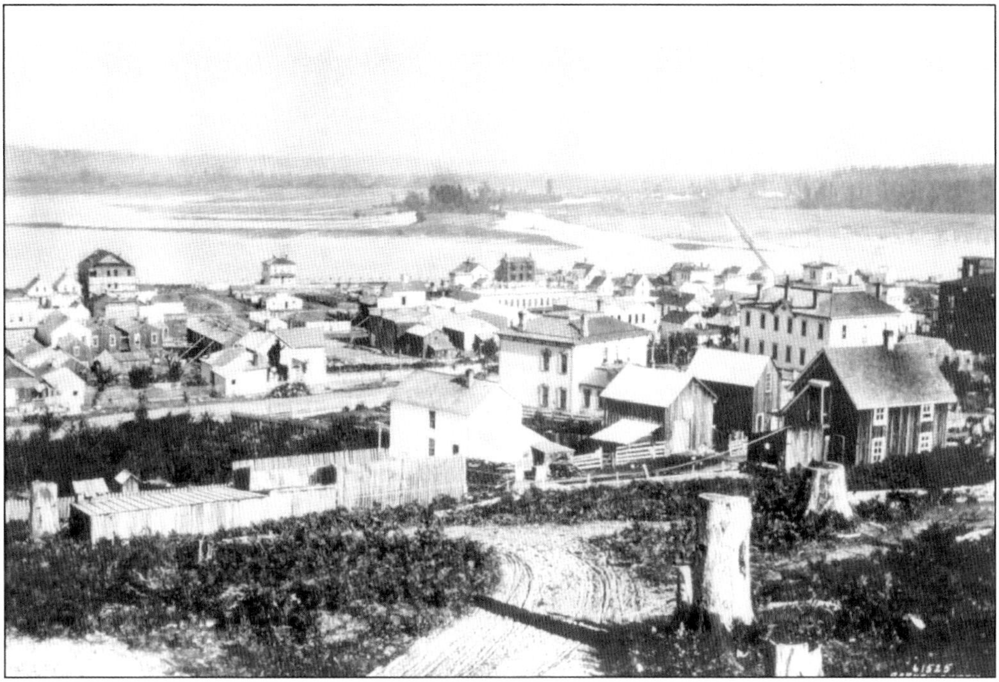

The late-19th-century Tacoma of Charles Wright is captured in these two views, taken approximately 10 years apart. In the *c.* 1881 view above, the vantage point is from the heart of today's downtown, at approximately the 800 block of Fawcett Avenue looking downhill. St. Helens Avenue is the dirt street running left to right across the middle of the image. At the right edge, the two-story white frame structure houses the Northern Pacific's Land Office. Below, Tacoma spreads out below McKinley Hill around 1892. The clock tower of the new city hall, the city waterway, and the old Eleventh Street bridge are distinguishable landmarks. (Both courtesy TPL.)

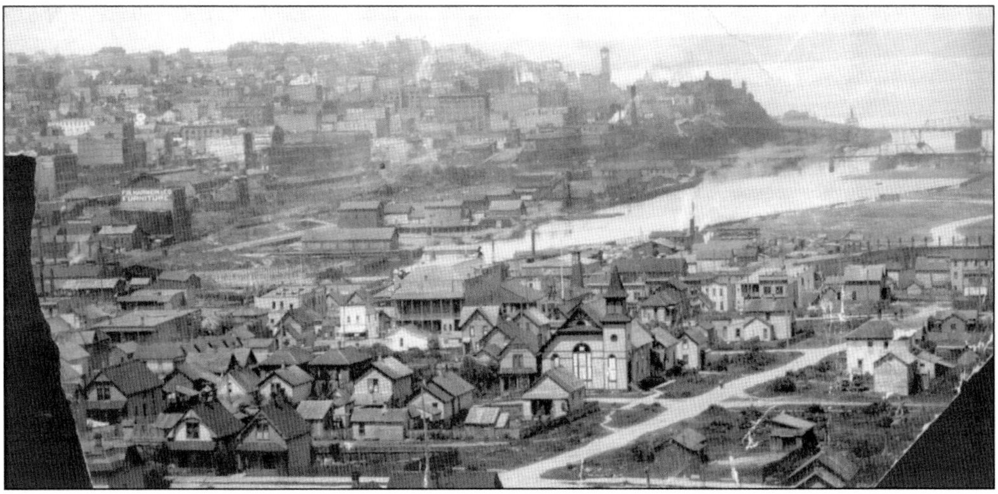

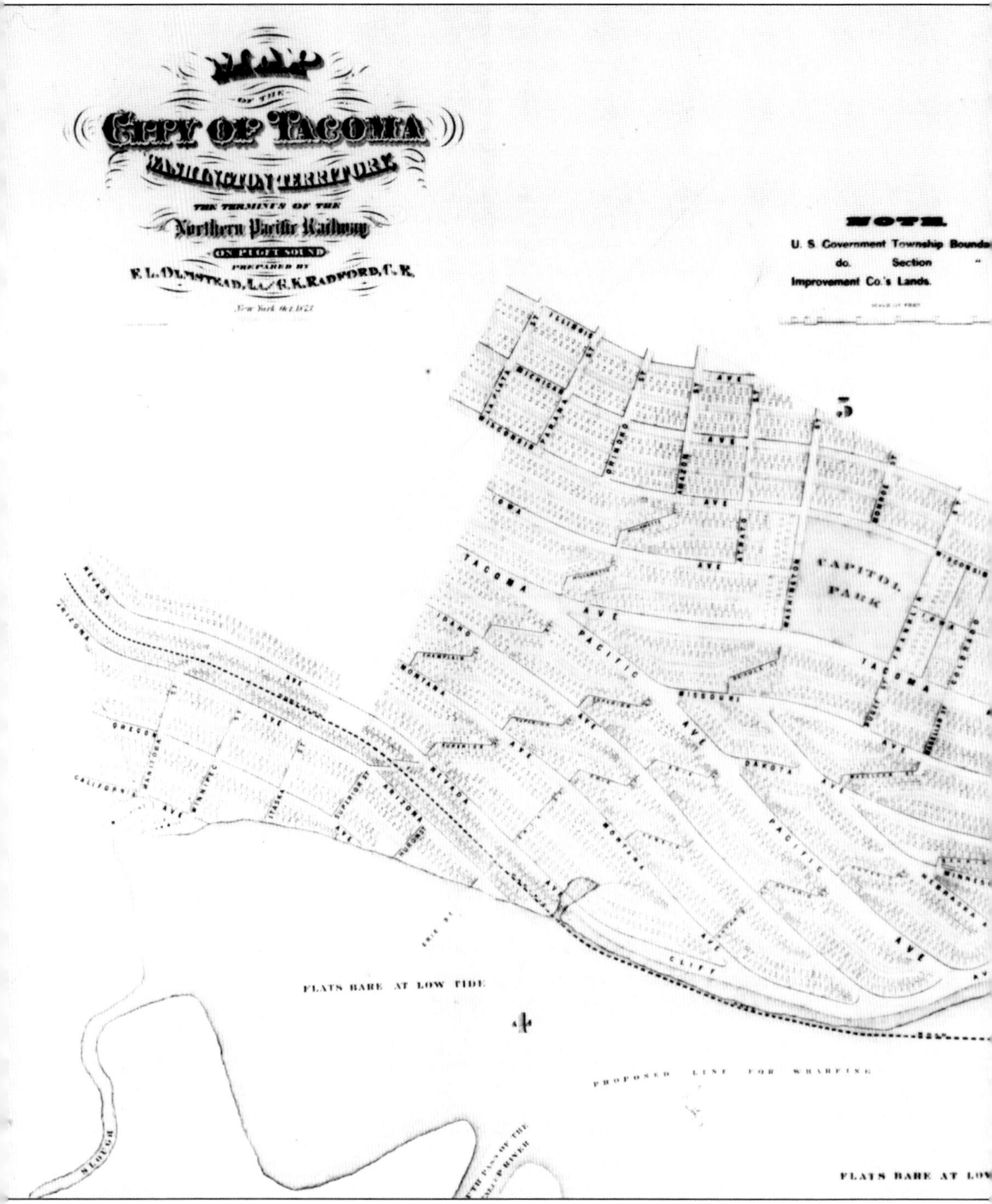

In 1873, Charles Wright invited Frederick Law Olmsted (1822–1903) to submit plans for laying out the city of Tacoma. Hailed today as the founder of American landscape architecture, Olmsted was at the time one of the designers of New York City's Central Park. His concepts for creating harmonious public landscapes were making him increasingly prominent in late-19th-century America. Olmsted submitted this radical city design, with very few square city blocks and several

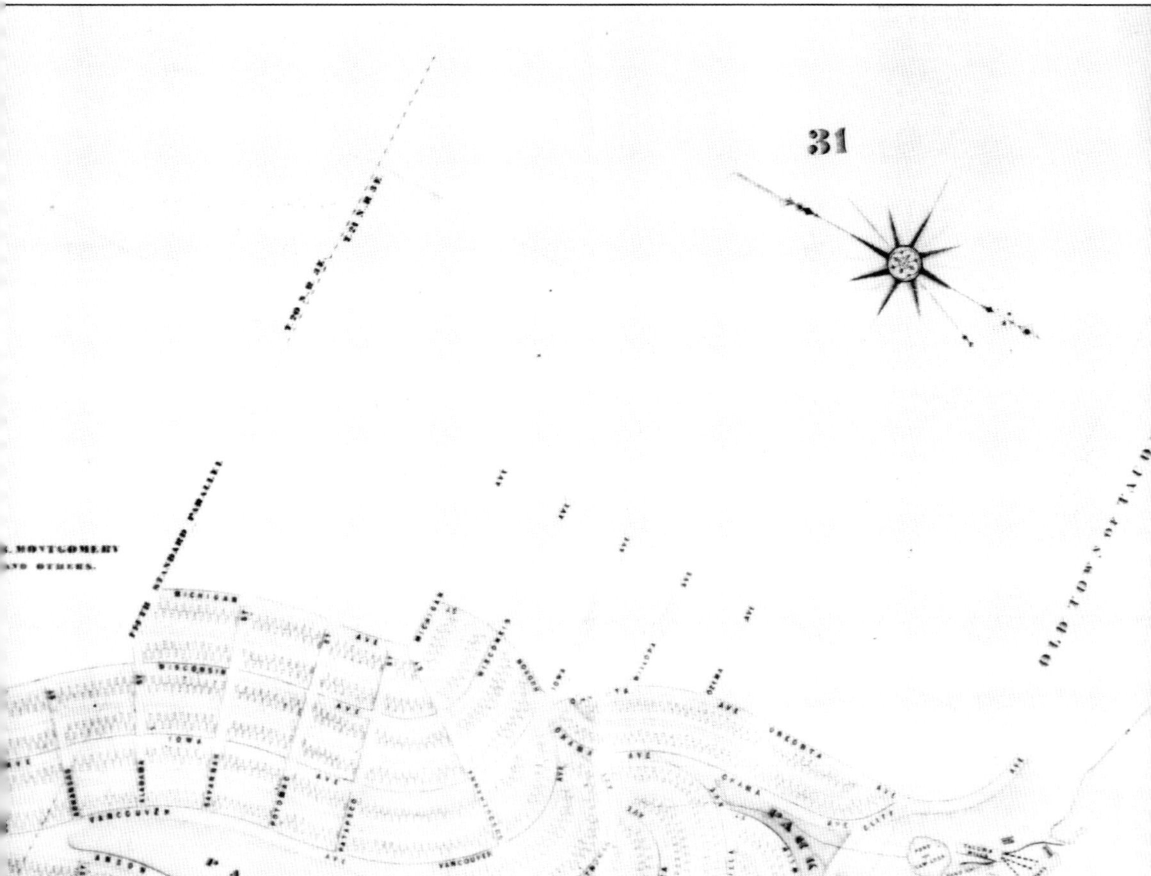

large parcels of park acreage that followed the city's natural topography rather than a grid system. Though Tacoma did not choose to follow this plan, Olmsted's suggestion of land for park creation certainly influenced the aesthetic of those arranging the acreage that was to become Wright Park in the 1880s. (Courtesy TPL.)

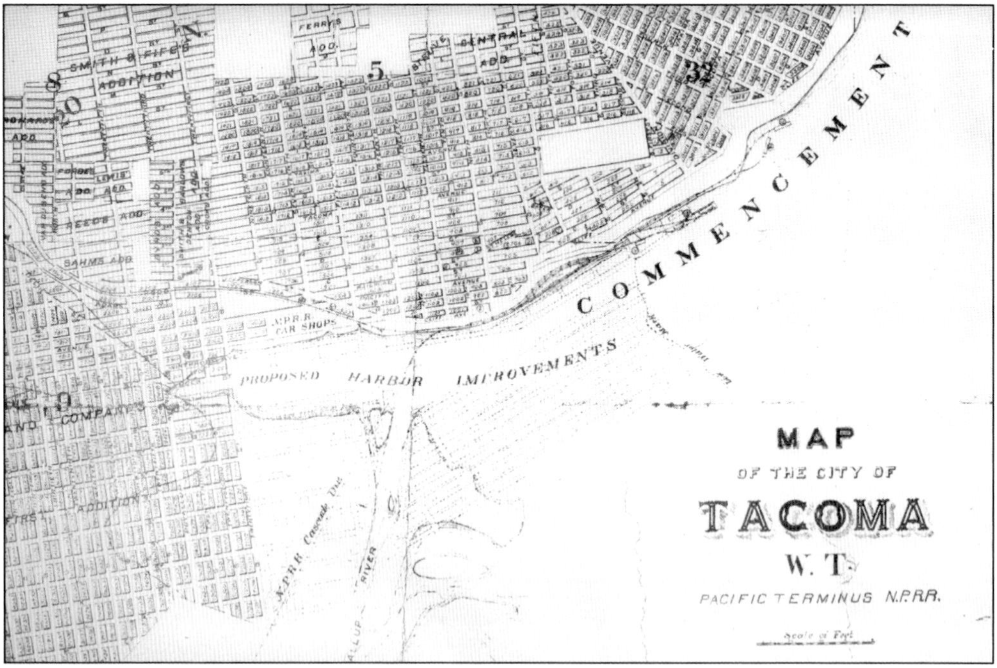

This *c.* 1885 map of Tacoma shows the now-familiar city plan that developed in the decade following the city's rejection of the 1873 Olmsted proposal. The rectangular section of land that Charles Wright and the Tacoma Land Company proposed to set aside for park purposes is clearly visible; the parcels making the park entirely contiguous to Division Avenue were not added to the acreage until 1891. (Courtesy TPL.)

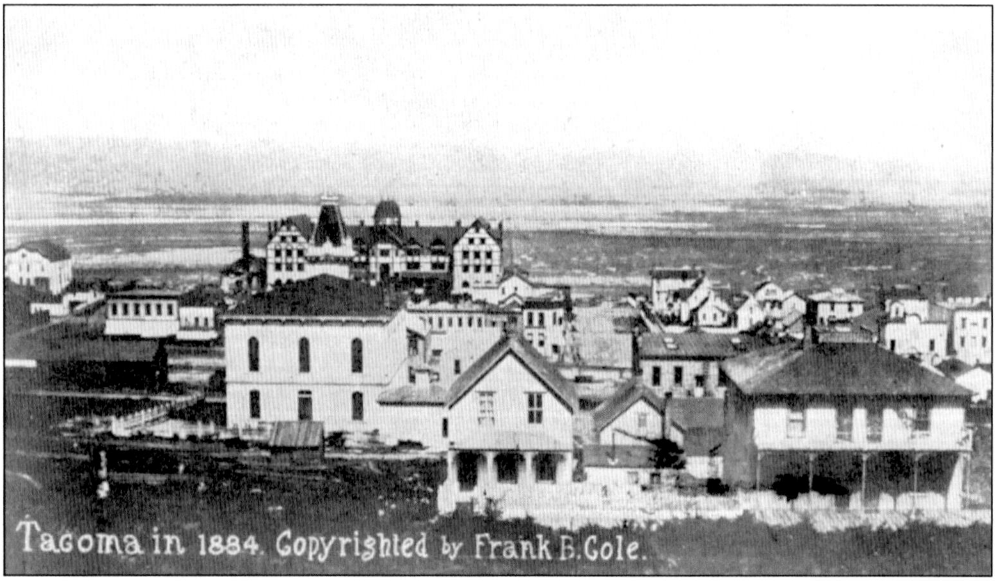

The Tacoma of the 1880s was a study in contrasts. This 1884 view, looking east between approximately South Eighth and South Eleventh Streets from the hill above downtown, shows the simple wood-frame structures of New Tacoma, contrasting with the new and elegant Tacoma Hotel on A Street, another project of Charles B. Wright and the Tacoma Land Company. The tide flats of Commencement Bay lie beyond the hotel. (Courtesy TS.)

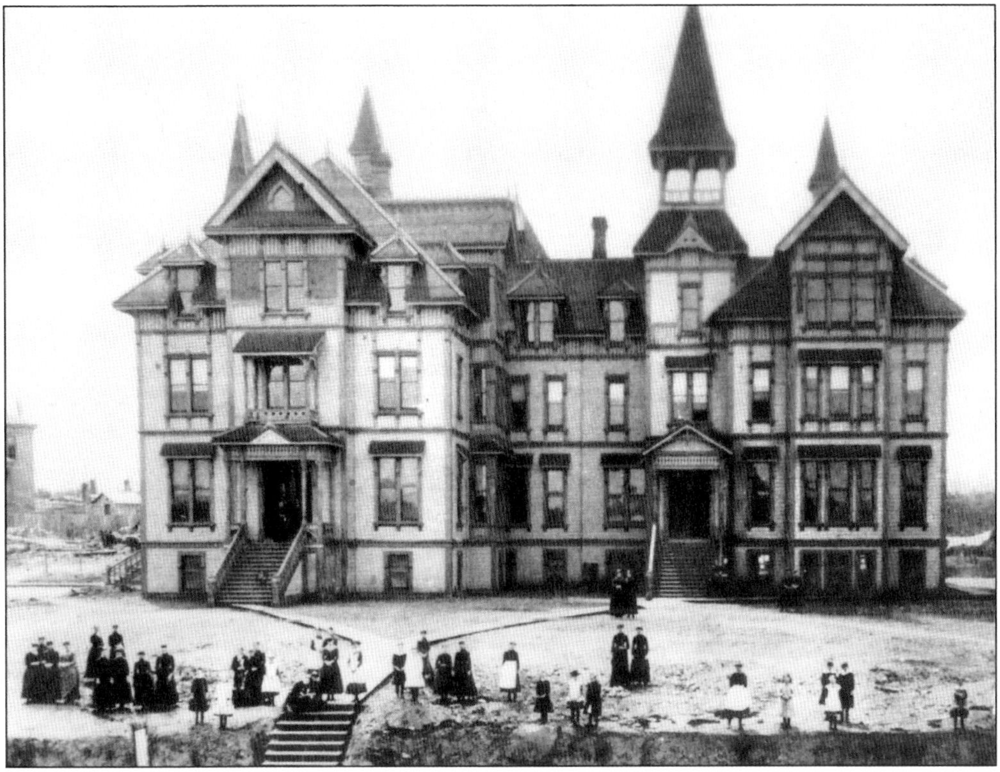

The Annie Wright Seminary exemplified Charles B. Wright's interest in the future of the young city of Tacoma. Named after Wright's younger daughter, the seminary was endowed with $50,000 of his own money. Its original location is pictured here shortly after opening in September 1884; the building stood on the first block of Tacoma Avenue North, on the triangular piece of land across Division Avenue from Wright Park. (Courtesy AWS.)

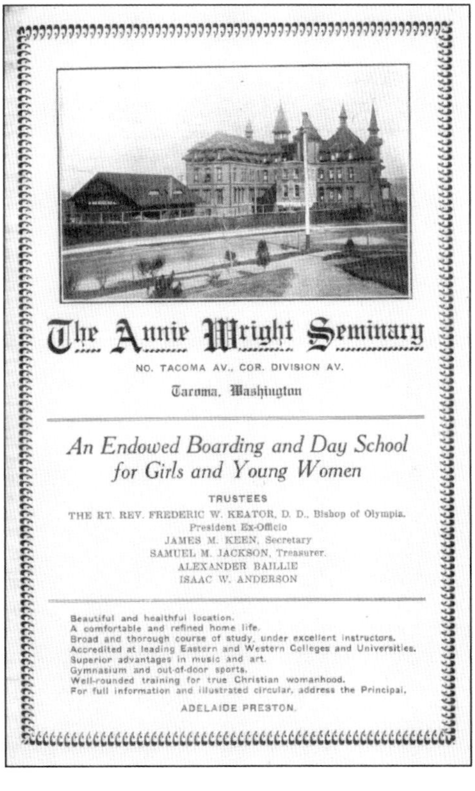

The seminary was advertised in the 1913 Tacoma City Directory with a photograph taken from Wright Park, a small section of which is visible in the foreground. Interestingly, the accompanying photograph included in the advertisement shows the rear of the institution, perhaps to illustrate its new gymnasium at left, as well as its healthful proximity to the park.

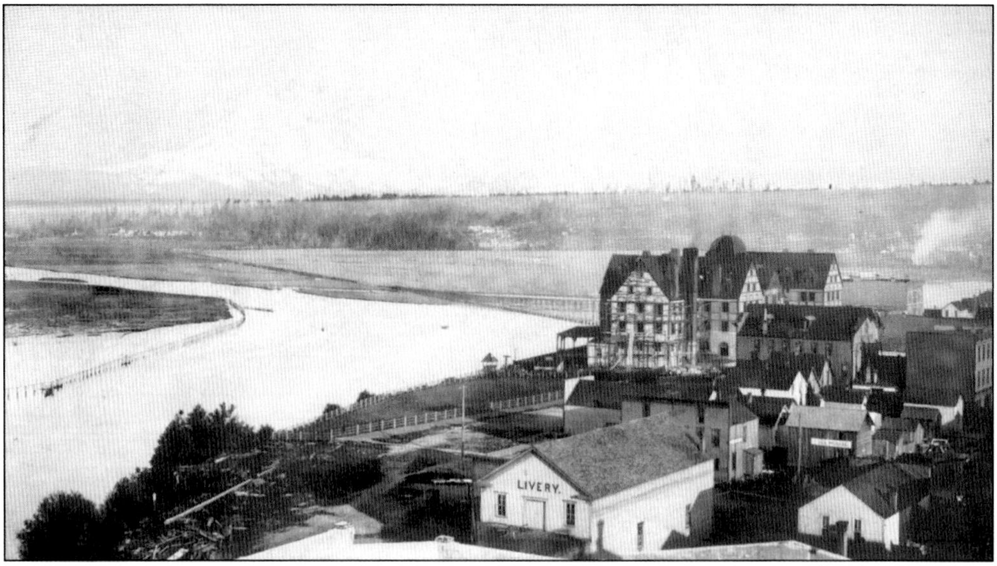

In the early 1880s, Charles Wright, either from his private wealth or in conjunction with donations of real estate from the Tacoma Land Company, also enabled other significant early city amenities. The Tacoma Hotel, shown above about 1884, was a magnificent hostelry for a new city of the modest size and scope of Tacoma. It commanded the brow of downtown's A Street between South Ninth and Tenth Streets until its loss to a catastrophic fire in 1935. The photograph below, taken around 1887, depicts St. Luke's Episcopal Church at its original site on the corner of South Sixth and C Streets (now Broadway), built with a $35,000 donation from Charles Wright. St. Luke's also departed its venerable downtown location; in 1934, it was dismantled and rebuilt at North Thirty-sixth and Gove Streets. (Both courtesy TPL.)

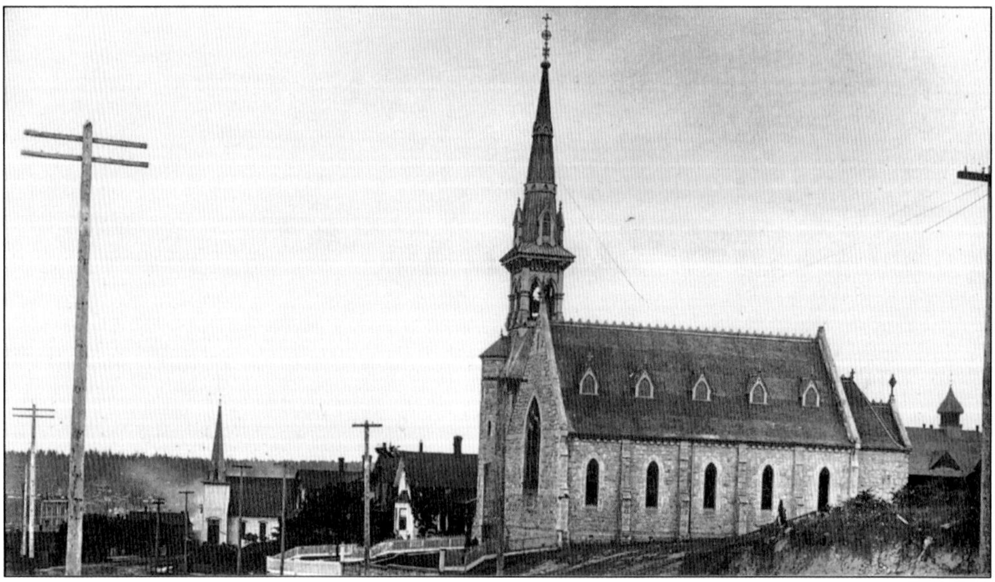

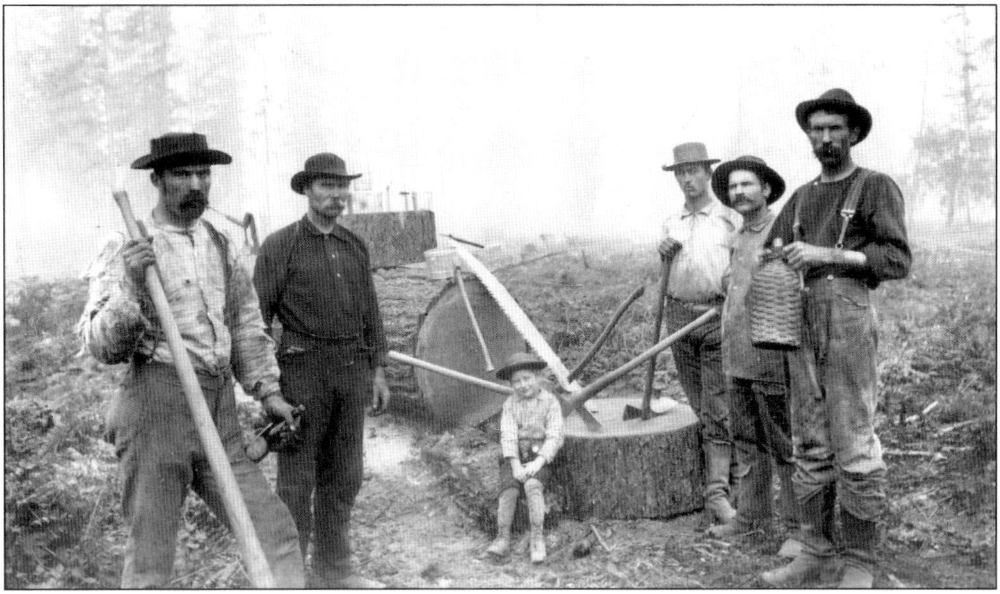

Before donating the acreage that would become Wright Park, the Tacoma Land Company first realized profits from its stands of timber. Here serious and thirsty-looking laborers pause in their work of clearing the land in 1885; note what appear to be tin lunch pails on the rear stump. The next year, the city received the logged-over tract from the company. (Courtesy UW.)

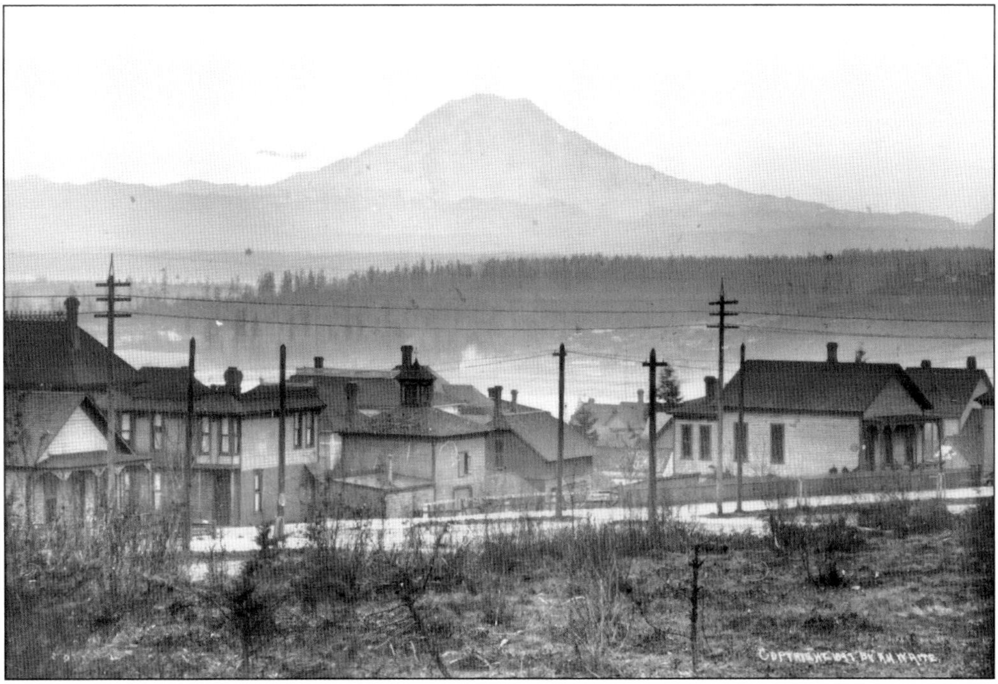

Another view of the early park environs shows Mount Rainier at sunrise from South G Street near Wright Park on December 29, 1895. The wood-frame neighborhood growing up around the park, bordered by South G and South I Streets and Sixth and Division Avenues, appreciated the improvement of the acreage from an otherwise "apparently unwieldy piece of nature." (Courtesy UW.)

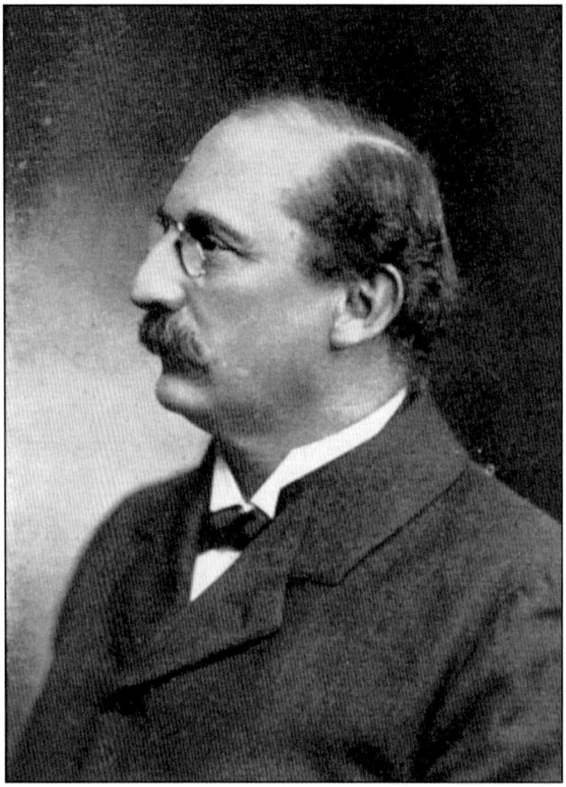

Edward Otto Schwagerl (1842–1910), Bavarian by birth, grew up in Paris and New York City, where both his European and American educations gave him an appreciation for the confluence of art, architecture, and nature. During the 1870s and 1880s, Schwagerl worked in Midwest cities as a landscape designer. From 1890 to 1892, he lived in Tacoma and toiled on the initial plans for both Wright and Point Defiance Parks.

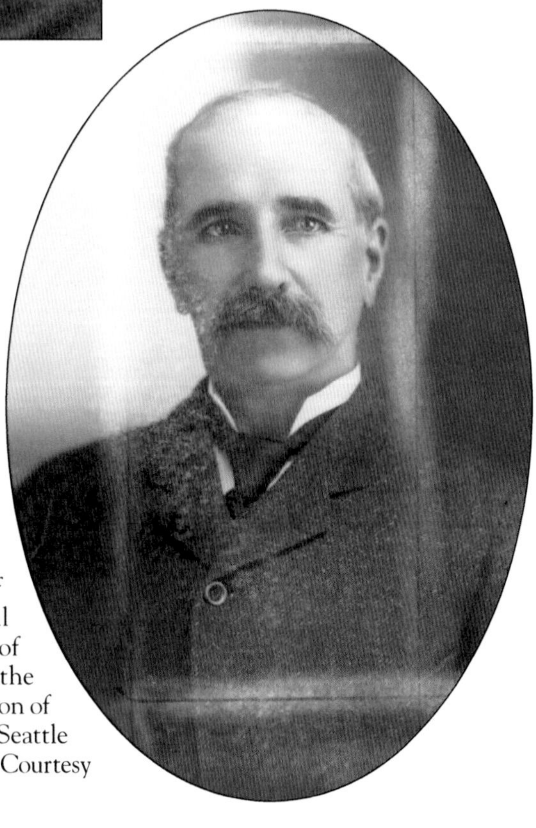

A native of Wales, Ebenezer Rhys Roberts (1854–1918) arrived in Tacoma in 1888 and came to the attention of the board of park commissioners due to his horticultural skills at the private Wapato Lake estate of newspaperman R. F. Radebaugh. In 1890, the board hired Roberts to plant Schwagerl's vision of Wright Park. When Schwagerl left to design Seattle parks in 1892, Roberts took over as visionary. (Courtesy Jean Insel Robeson.)

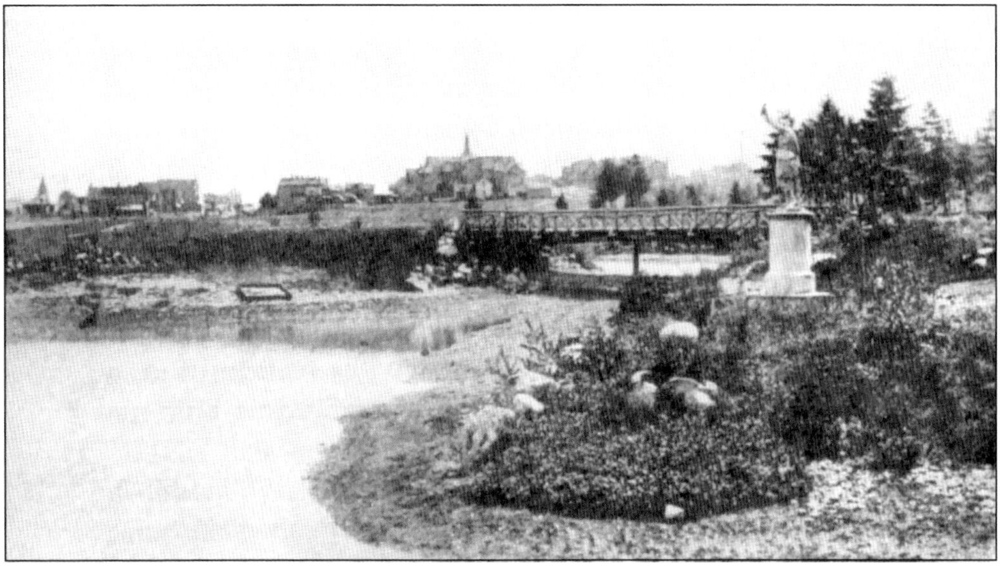

The acreage that Schwagerl and Roberts were charged with designing and planting did not yet have much to recommend it in the early 1890s. Wright Park's natural contouring and tendency to collect rainwater in low spots suggested the creation of a scenic lake feature, seen here under development in 1892. The newly placed statue, the *Fisherman's Daughter*, was one of several gifts of statuary from civic benefactor Clinton P. Ferry.

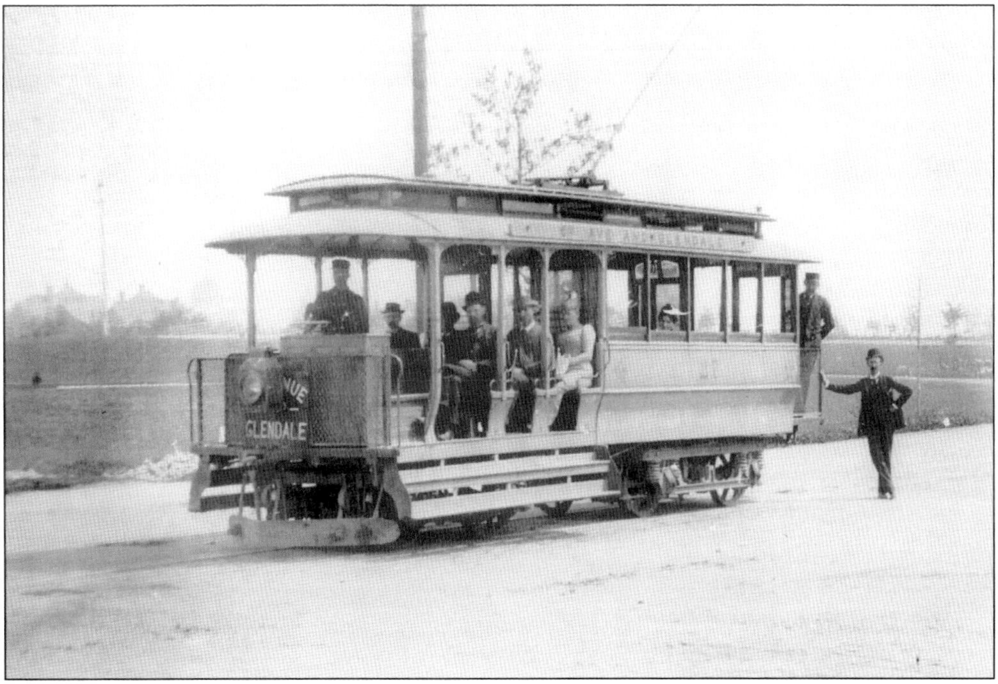

A Tacoma Railway and Motor Company streetcar pauses by a rather barren Wright Park about 1893. Just a few trees can be seen dotting the landscape. Several streetcar companies competed in Tacoma in the 1890s, connecting new residential areas with the downtown core. This Sixth Avenue line took passengers west to a new addition called Glendale, near the intersection with Proctor Street. (Courtesy TPL.)

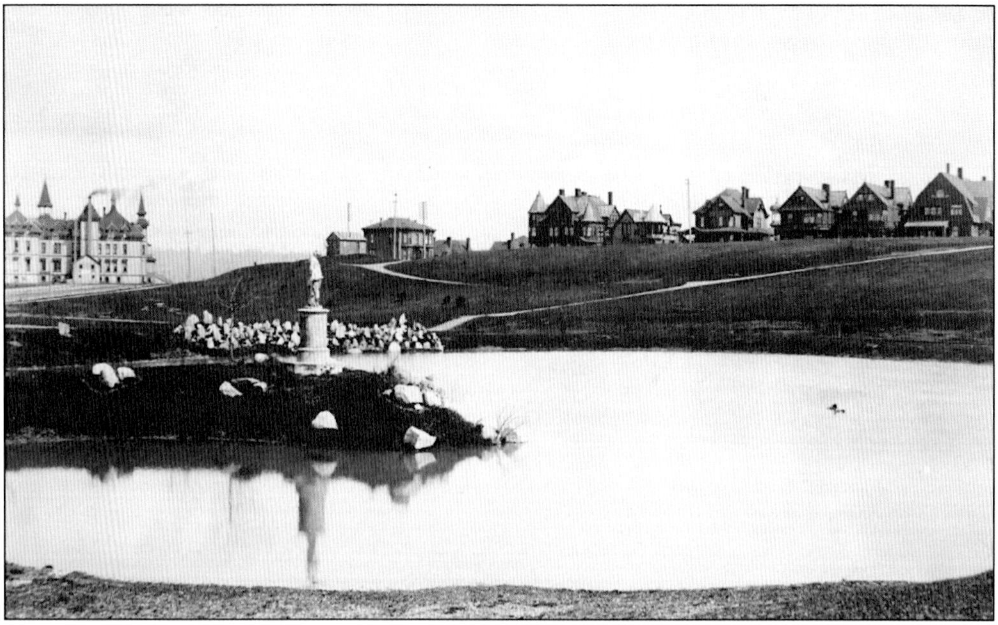

Bird Lake, as the Wright Park pond was called in its early days, and the ornamental *Fisherman's Daughter* statue anchor this view of Wright Park around 1892. In the distance, smoke rises from the main chimney at the Annie Wright Seminary on the corner of Division and Tacoma Avenues, and the grand homes in the 100 and 200 blocks of South G Street dominate the Park Heights neighborhood. (Courtesy WSHS.)

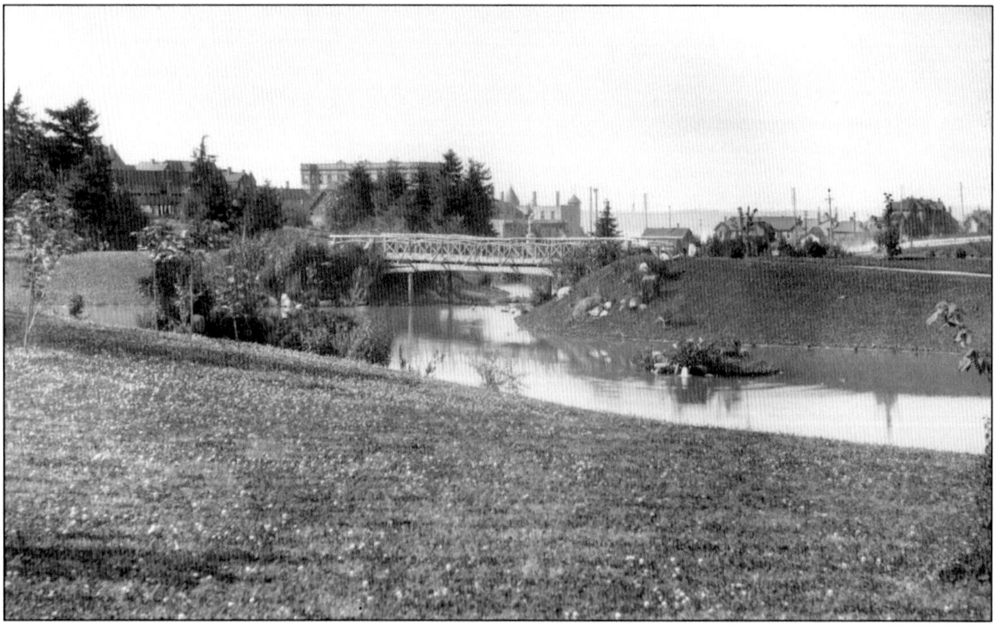

This perspective of Bird Lake, taken in July 1893, shows the rustic bridge built to span the park's water feature. As the lowest part of the topography, the northwest section of Wright Park was inclined to be swampy at the time of the acreage's donation. Landscape designer Edward Schwagerl turned this to an advantage with the creation of a lake in his 1890 Wright Park plan. (Courtesy UW.)

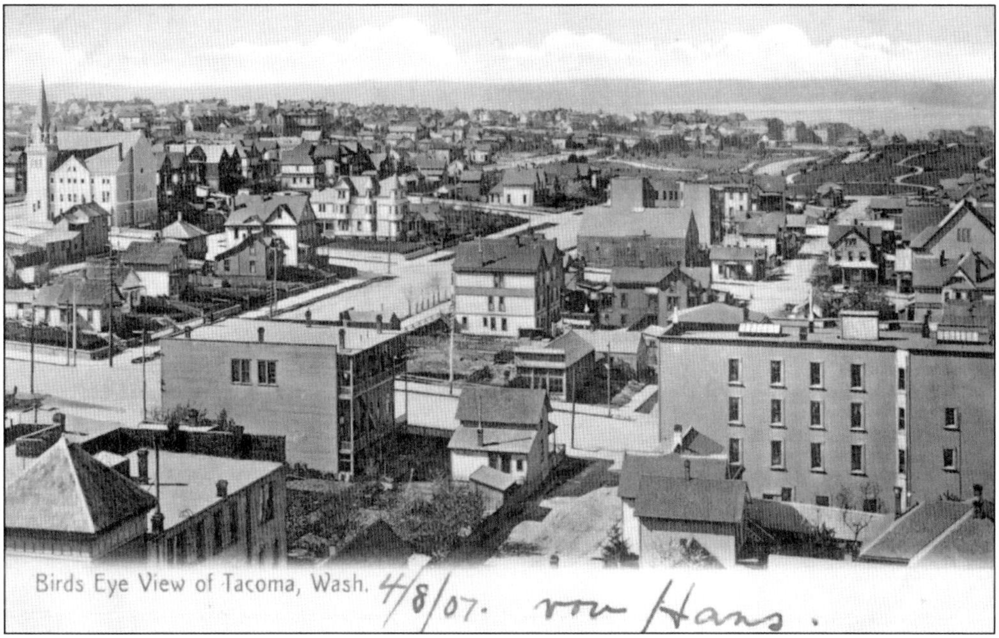

These bird's-eye views from the start of the 20th century give a good sense of the surrounding neighborhoods' embrace of the park, as well as its openness—a decided contrast to today's verdant canopy of trees. Wright Park appears at the upper right corner of the above postcard, dated April 8, 1907, and demonstrates its appeal as an oasis in a rapidly urbanizing yet residential part of Tacoma. The *c.* 1904 image below reveals Wright Park in even greater detail, including two small frame houses standing at the corner of Sixth Avenue and South I Street. The City of Tacoma bought these properties from their owners in 1905, removed the structures, and incorporated the property into Wright Park. (Above courtesy TS; below courtesy WSHS.)

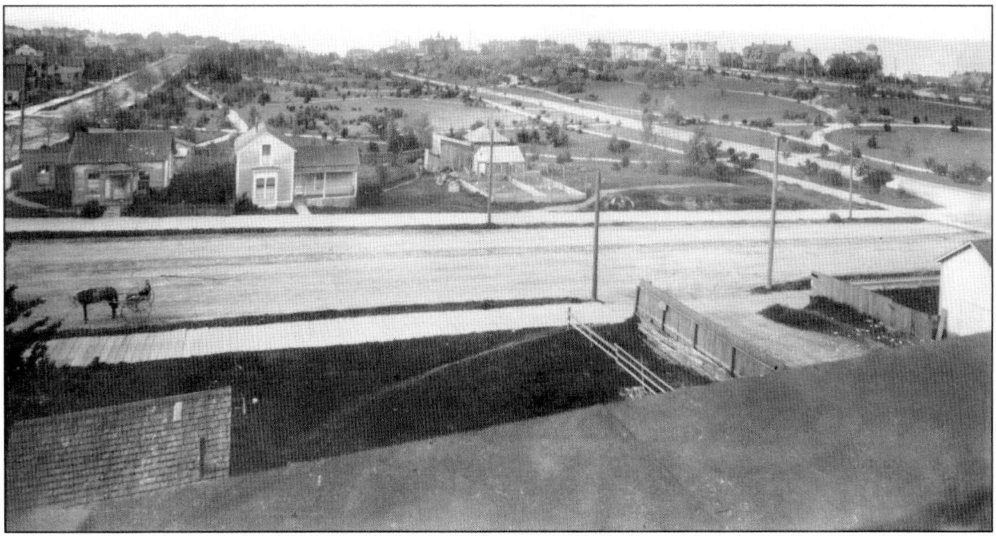

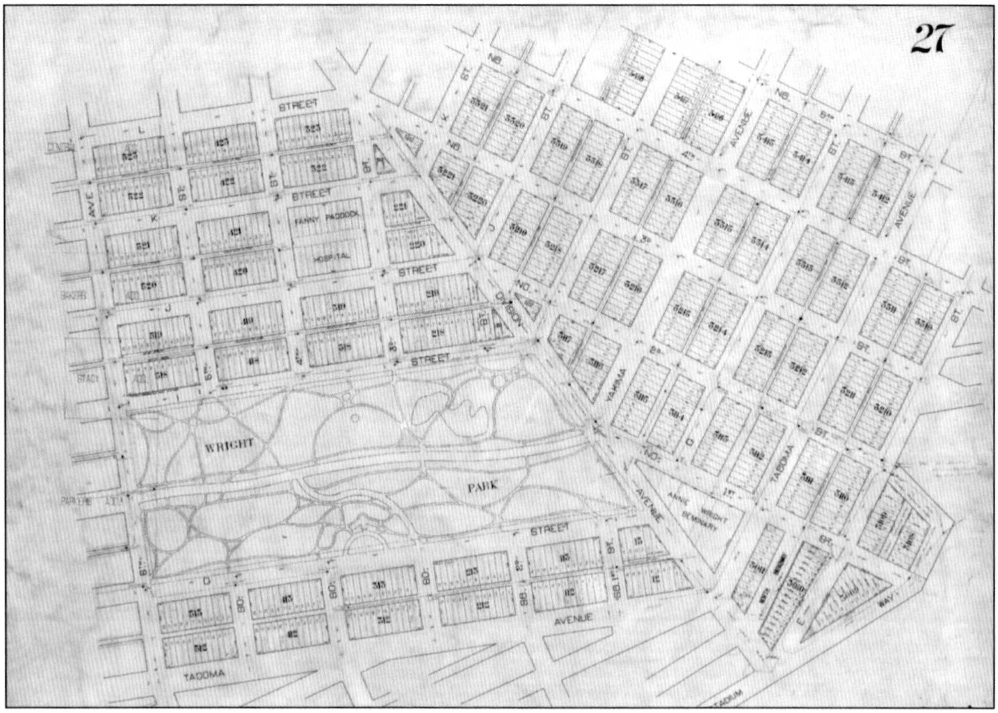

A plan from early city documents suggests the park's layout between 1908, when the Seymour Conservatory was built in the park halfway along South G Street, and 1924, before the Annie Wright Seminary moved to a site farther west on Tacoma Avenue North. Both structures are indicated, as is the site of Fannie Paddock Hospital on South J Street. (Courtesy TPL.)

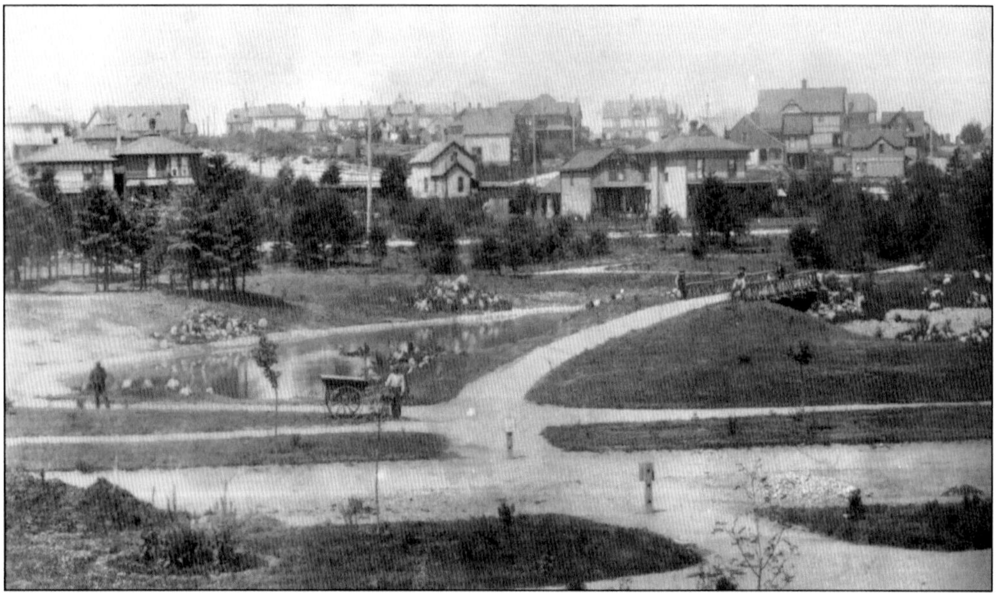

The maturing trees and the groundskeepers who tended them are recorded in this c. 1900 view of Wright Park, with Bird Lake and its bridge in the foreground. The angle is toward the corner of South I Street and Division Avenue, where the First Church of Christ Scientist now stands. The street sloping gradually uphill in the upper left corner is Division Avenue. (Courtesy TPL.)

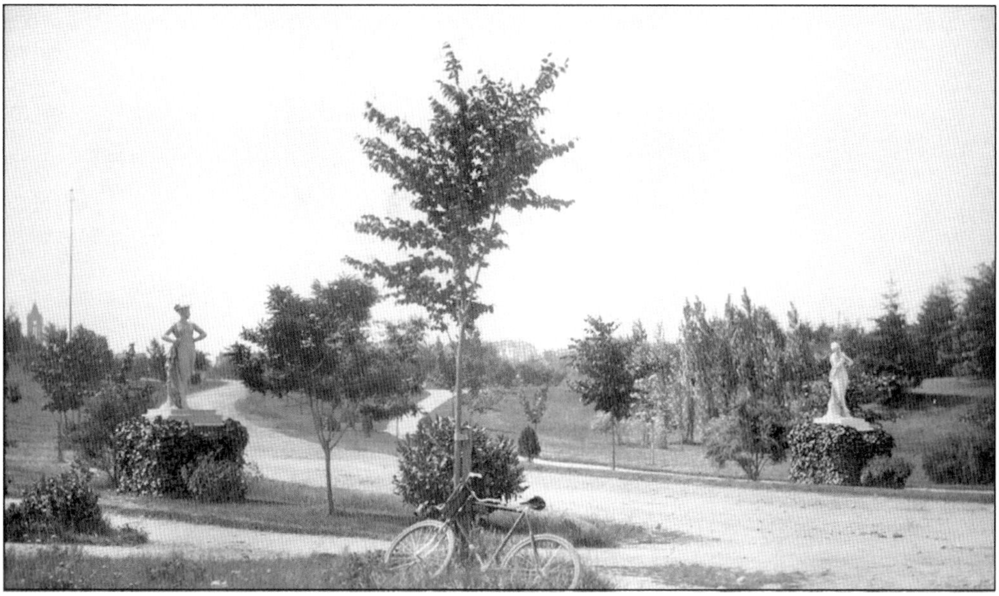

The start of the 20th century saw the evolution of Wright Park's natural and man-made features. In the view above, Yakima Avenue enters the park from Division Avenue, flanked by the dancing maiden statues Clinton P. Ferry imported from Europe in 1891. Note how the dirt thoroughfare of Yakima bends gently as it wends it way though the park, a deliberate effect of Edward Schwagerl's 1890 plan. Below, several species of trees take root around Bird Lake, so called for its creation as an aquatic haven for all manner of winged creatures, including a pair of swans named Victor and Victoria, sent to Tacoma in 1897 from their namesake city on Vancouver Island. The slope behind the lake will eventually become the site of the Seymour Conservatory in 1908. (Above courtesy TPL; below courtesy WSHS.)

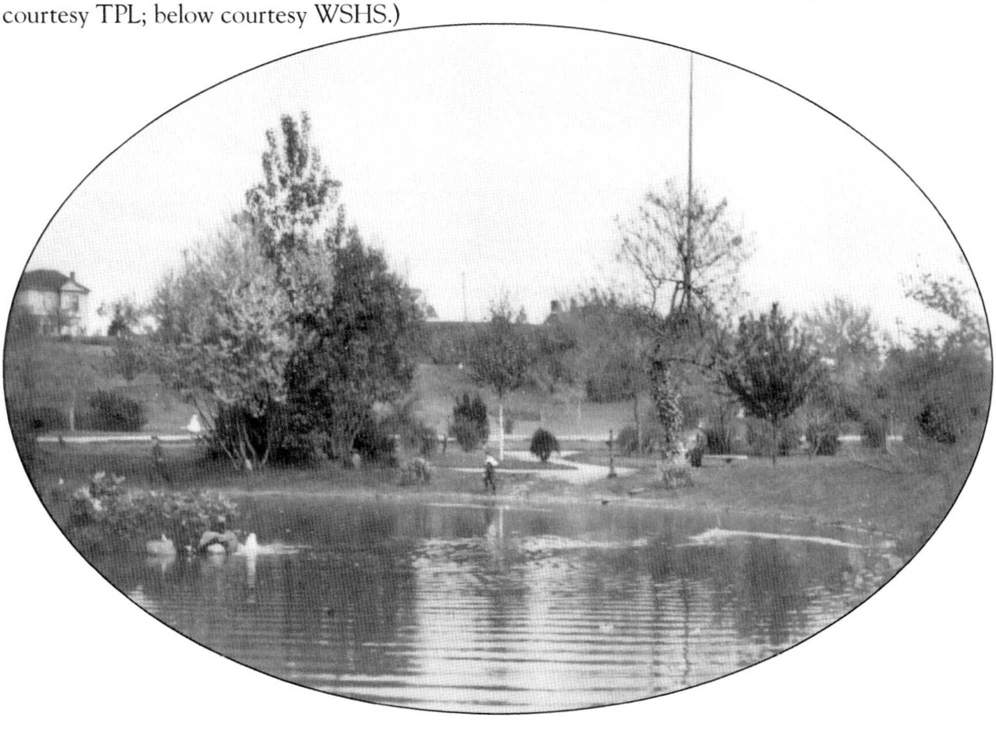

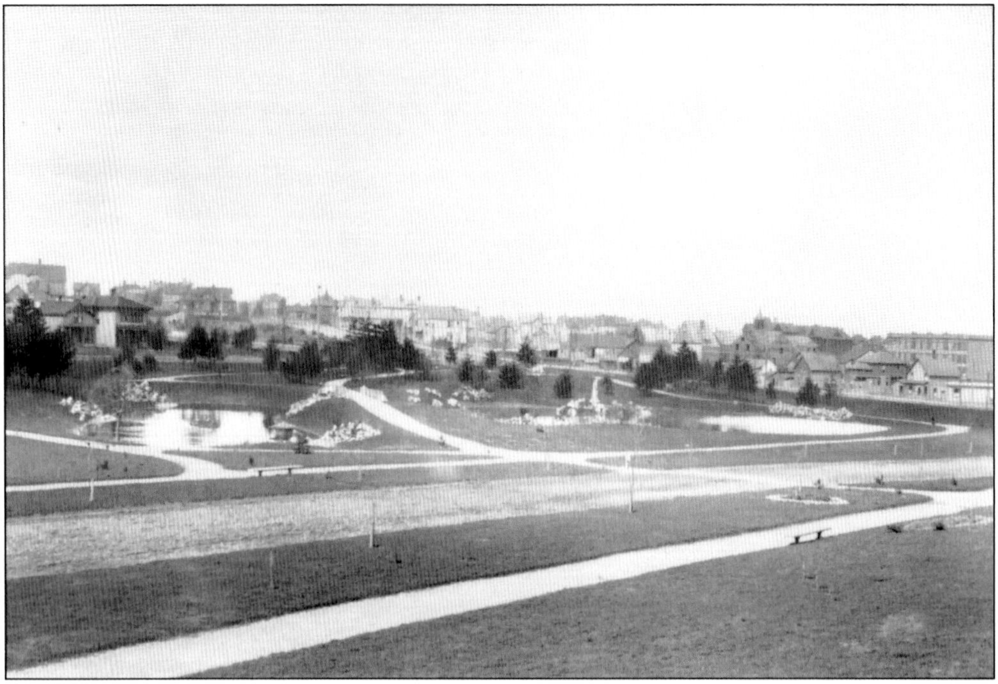

These photographs, from nearly identical vantage points on the South G Street crest of the hill, show the softening of the landscape due to the trees for which the park has long been renowned. Both views look from an approximate point west of the present location of the conservatory, down the park hill, and across Division Avenue to its intersection with I Street. In the *c.* 1895 image above, the built environment dominates the park; however, in the photograph below, taken approximately 10 years later, the park is beginning to command the eye. Yakima Avenue bisects Wright Park from left to right, flanked on each side by parallel footpaths. (Both courtesy TPL.)

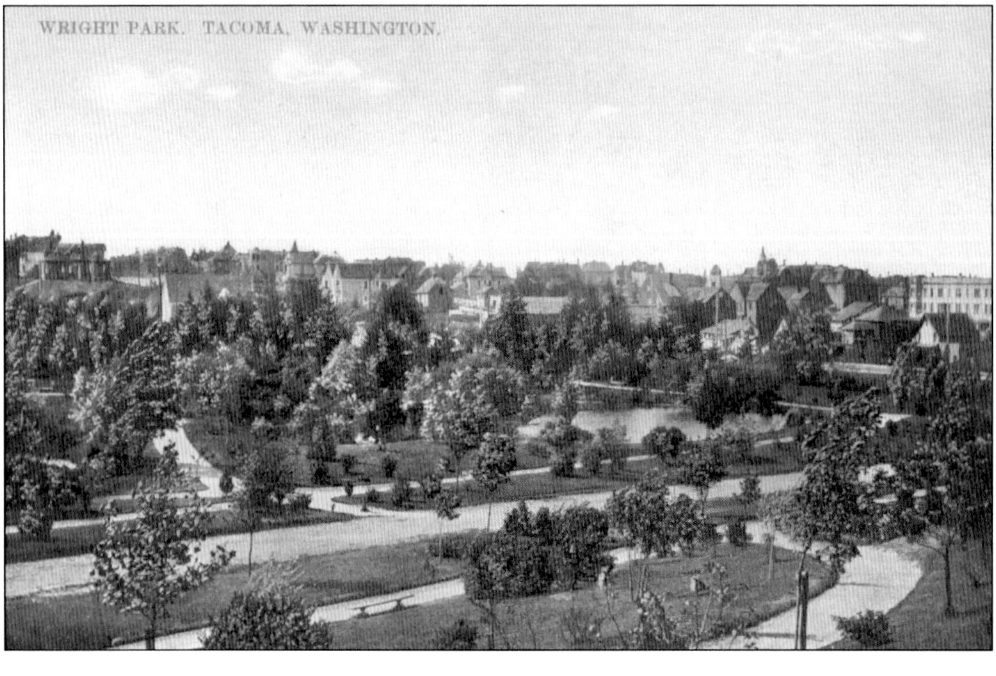

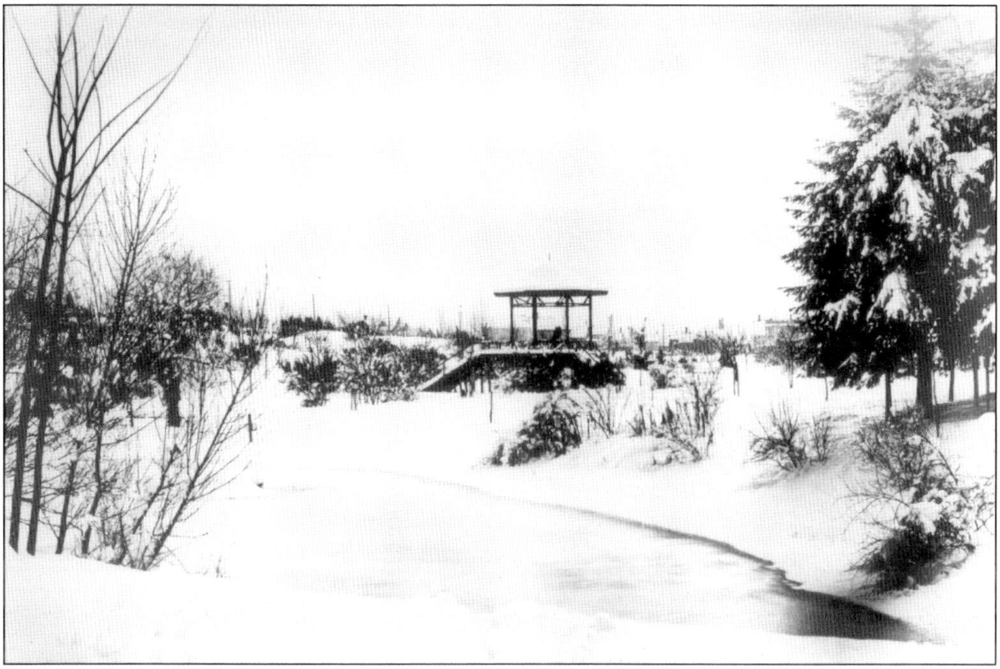

Looking down the park's length in the direction of Sixth Avenue, this view captures the bandstand and Bird Lake around 1895. Then, as now, snowfall of any considerable accumulation sent Tacoma residents to their neighborhood parks to enjoy the wintry scenes. The bandstand was one of the early community recreation features of Wright Park. (Courtesy WSHS.)

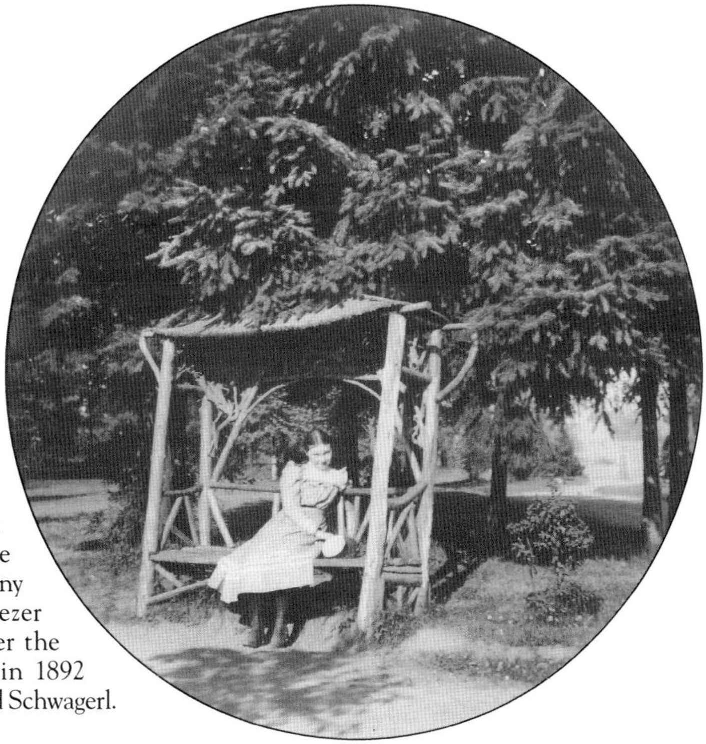

A young girl, identified in an 1890s Tacoma family album as Mabel, enjoys a warm day on one of Wright Park's rustic benches. These benches were among the many amenities added by Ebenezer Roberts when he took over the planting of Wright Park in 1892 after the departure of Edward Schwagerl. (Courtesy WSHS.)

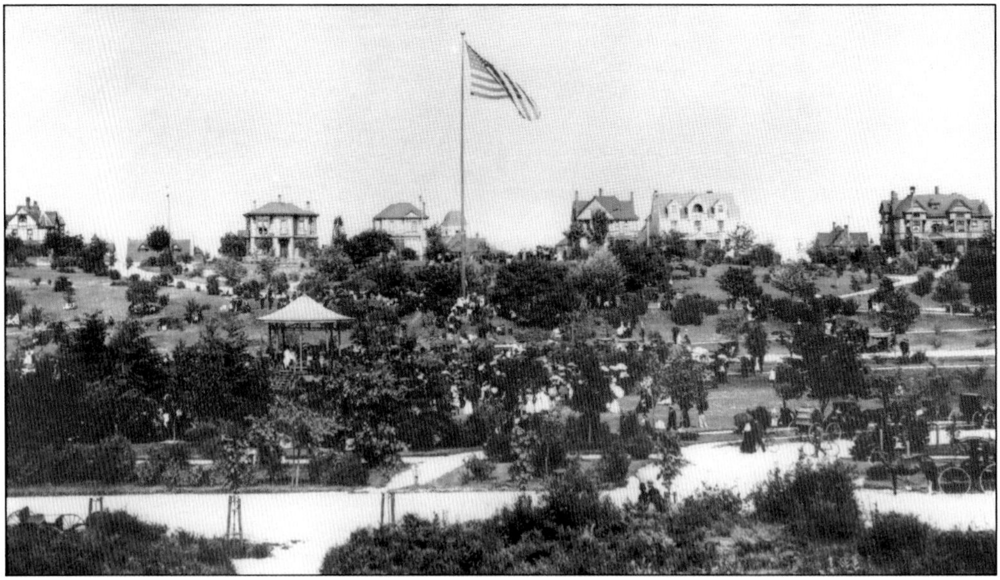

This *c.* 1900 view of Wright Park illustrates its popularity as a gathering space; Tacomans thronged to the locale on foot, by horse and carriage, and on bicycles. Close examination also reveals many women carrying parasols against the summer sun and a crowded bandstand, suggesting a concert or speaker. South I Street crosses the foreground in this view looking toward South G Street. (Courtesy WSHS.)

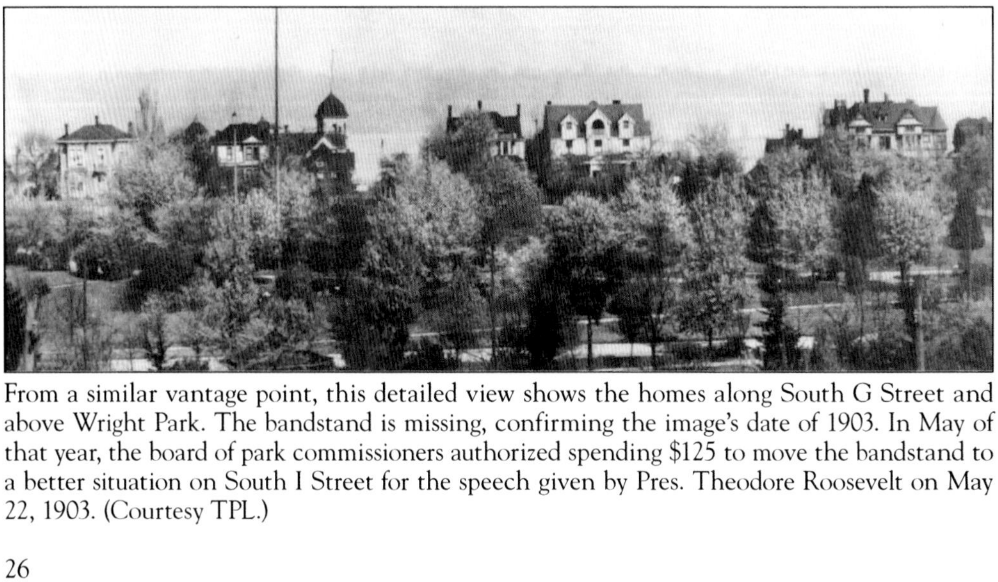

From a similar vantage point, this detailed view shows the homes along South G Street and above Wright Park. The bandstand is missing, confirming the image's date of 1903. In May of that year, the board of park commissioners authorized spending $125 to move the bandstand to a better situation on South I Street for the speech given by Pres. Theodore Roosevelt on May 22, 1903. (Courtesy TPL.)

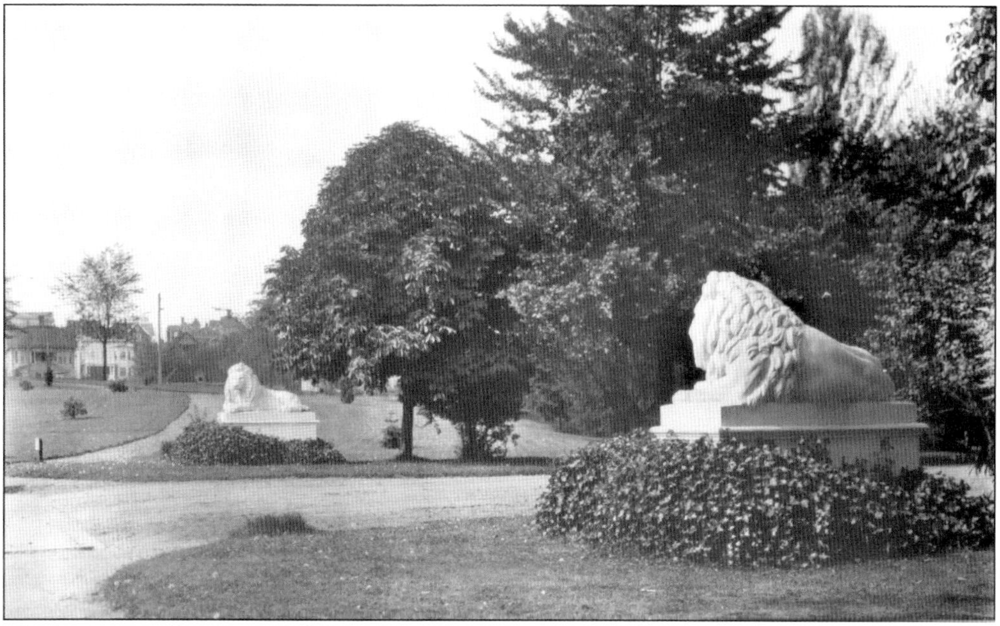

The lion statues have guarded the Yakima Avenue entrance along Sixth Avenue since the 1890s, part of a collection of park statuary brought from Europe and given to the city by Clinton P. Ferry, a wealthy Tacoman who took great interest in the early development of his adopted hometown. The unpaved Yakima Avenue park entrance became the site of the lawn bowling green in the 1930s. (Courtesy UW.)

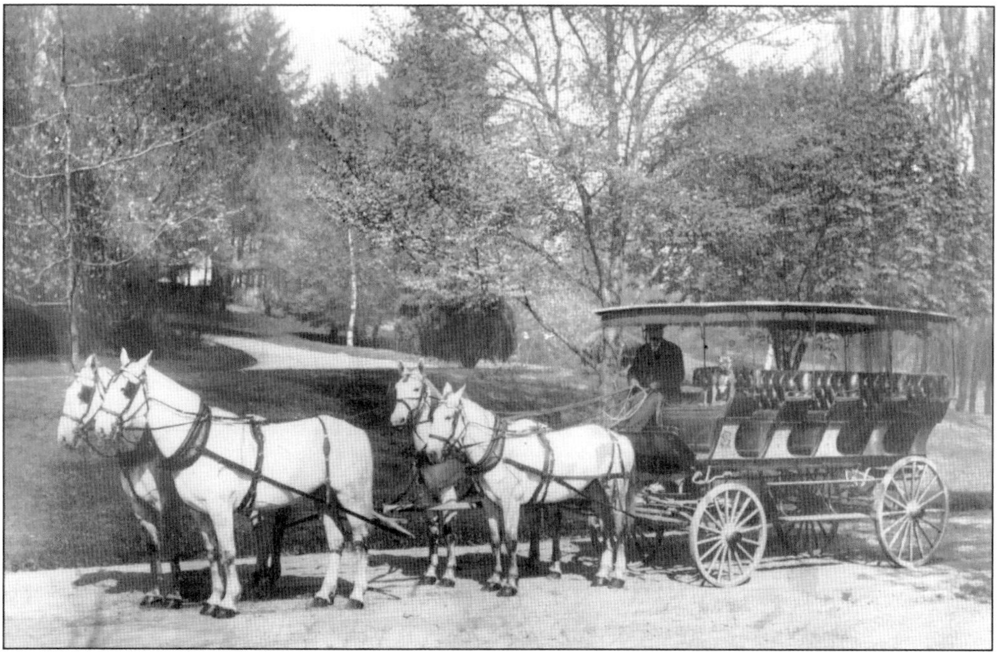

Many forms of transportation brought visitors to Wright Park. The acreage was a popular pedestrian and bicycle route to downtown, and streetcars served the vicinity along both Sixth and Division Avenues. Park groundskeepers used calcium chloride on the dirt roadways to keep the dust down in the dry seasons. (Courtesy WSHS.)

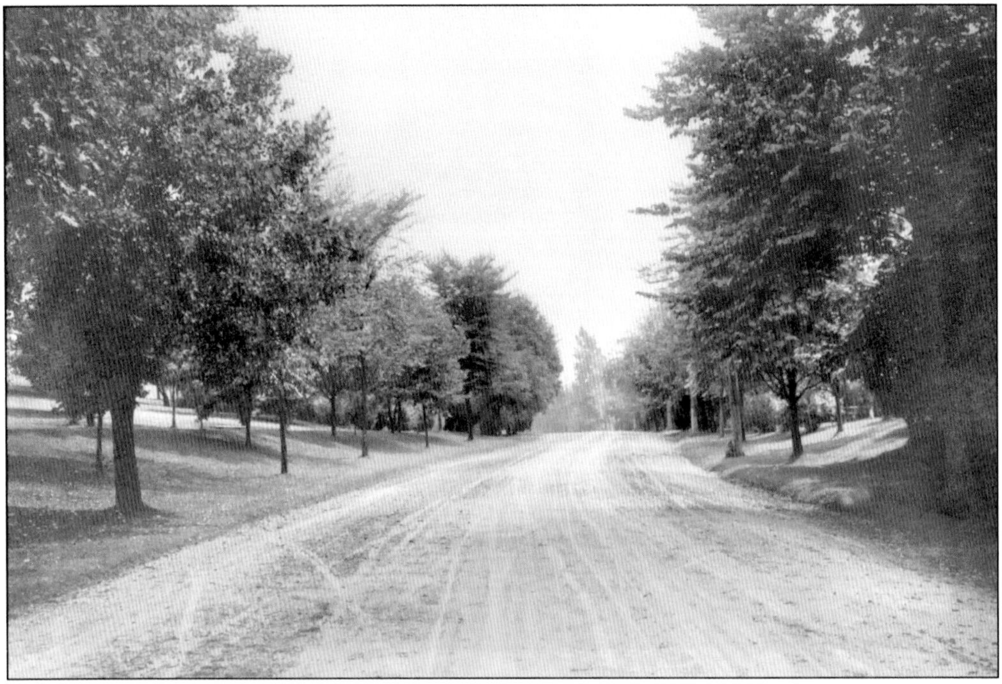

Wright Park's length of Yakima Avenue remained a dirt roadway through the 1920s (as shown above); it likely was never paved. Newspaper accounts dating back to the 1890s record that speed and dust were recurring concerns along the length of Yakima Avenue running through the park, with visitors driving their carriages and later their automobiles at more than the posted leisurely speed limit. This was a major factor in the eventual closure of Yakima Avenue in the 1930s; grass replaced the dirt roadway, and the former level expanse of avenue became home to the playground and sport courts. Below the dancing maiden statues at the Division Avenue entrance bore the whimsical nicknames "Annie" and "Fannie," due to the proximity of the Annie Wright Seminary (now the site of Bruce Titus Chevrolet) and Fannie Paddock Hospital (currently Tacoma General Hospital). (Both courtesy TPL.)

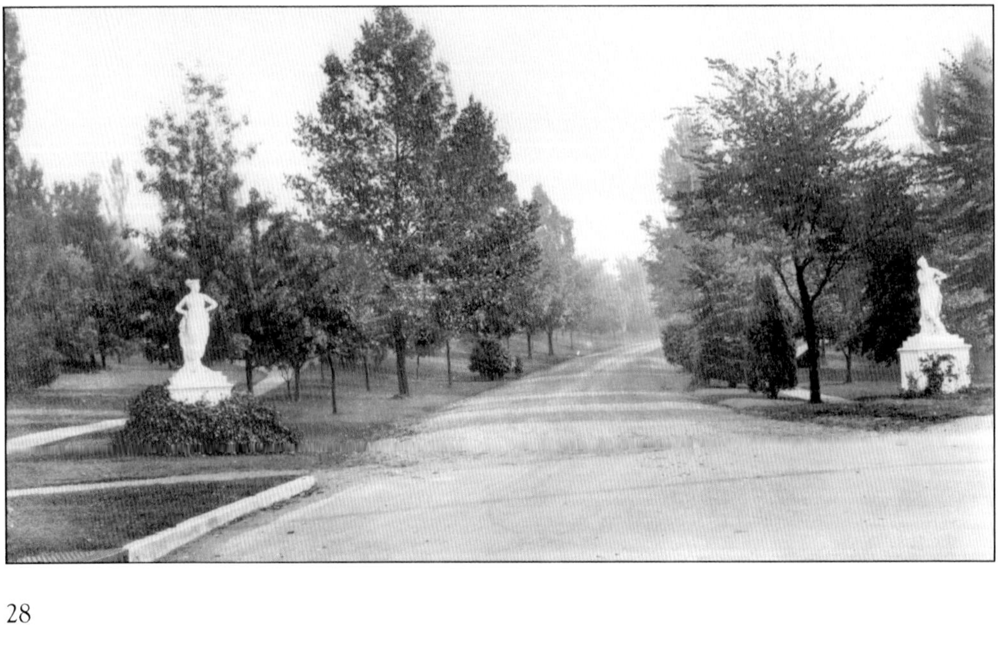

In these two views, unidentified visitors to Wright Park enjoy the often-photographed bridge over Bird Lake about 1910. Rustic features such as the bridge and elevated flower planters were part of the start-of-the-20th-century design aesthetic planned by Edward Schwagerl and actually executed by Ebenezer Roberts. The two men also collaborated on Point Defiance Park in the early 1890s. Even after Schwagerl left Tacoma in 1892 to design public parks and private estates in Seattle, Roberts continued to design and work in Tacoma's expanding park system, soon becoming superintendent of parks. By the time of his retirement in 1908, parks across Tacoma featured rustic bridges, planters, fences, and furniture all bearing Ebenezer Roberts's handiwork and influence. (Both courtesy TPL.)

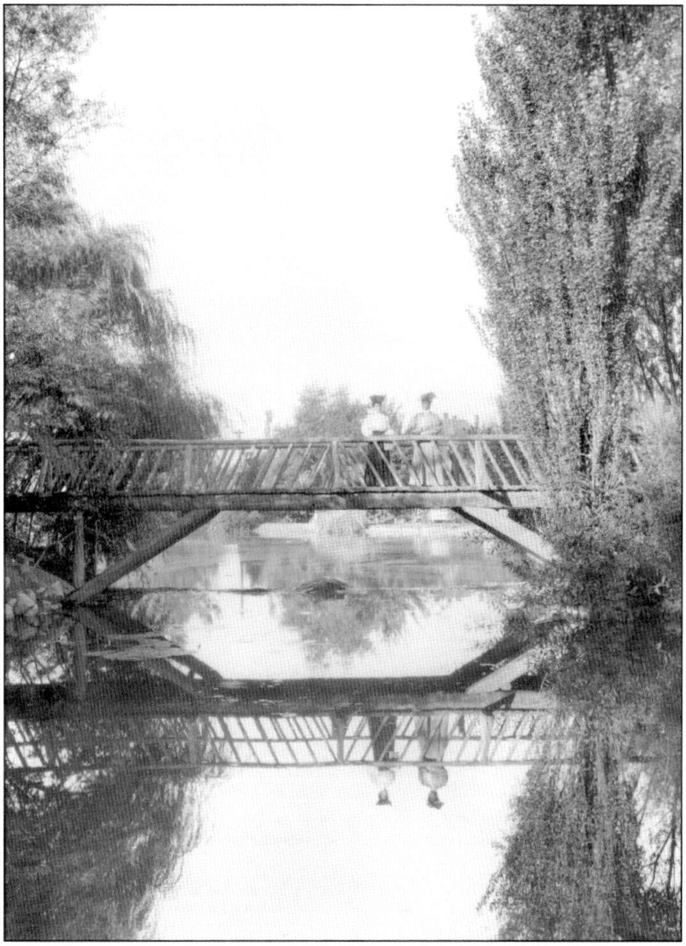

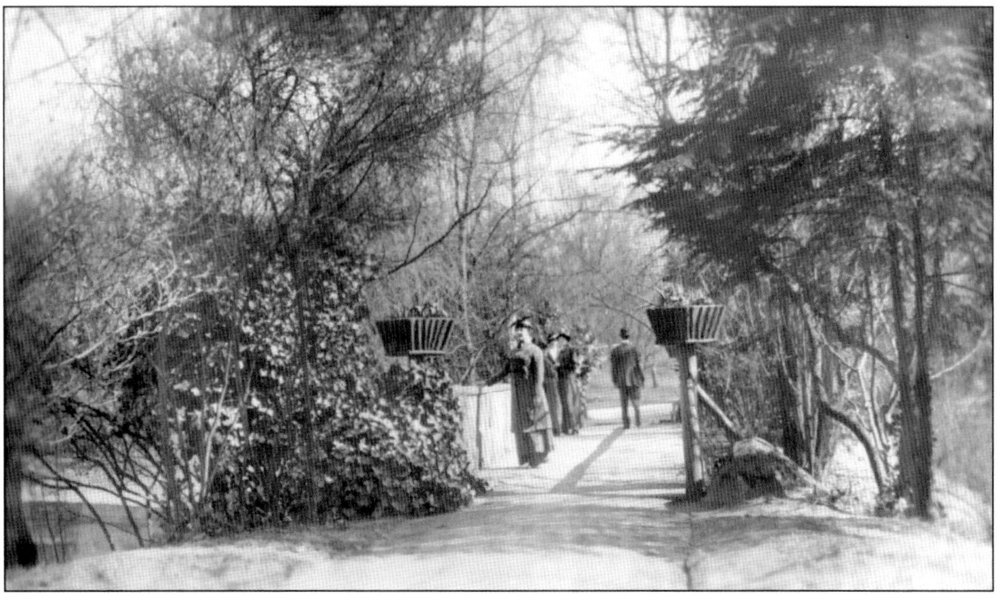

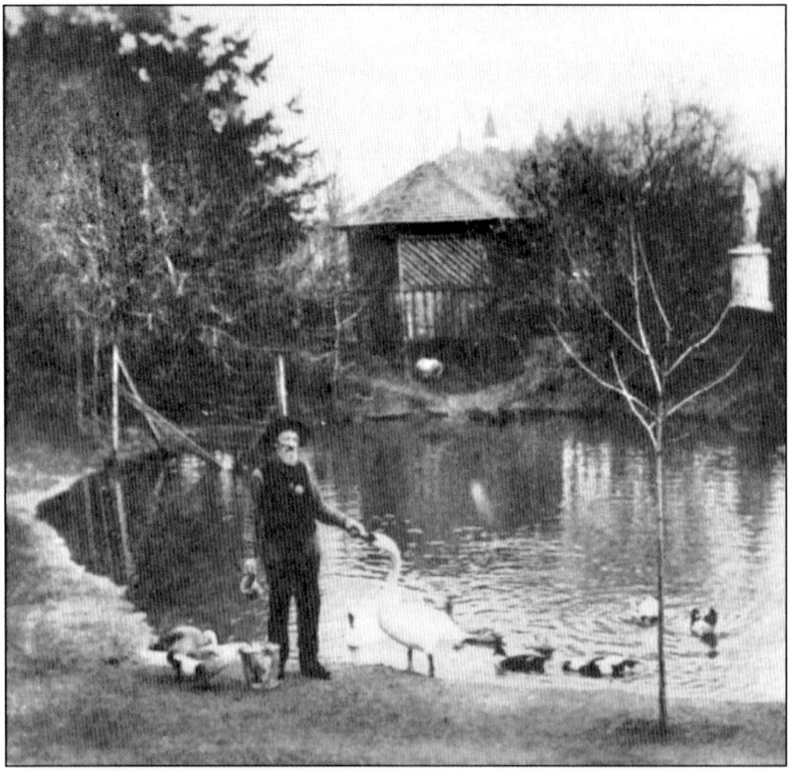

Ignatius Harbaugh tended the swans and other Wright Park water fowl from 1892 to 1905. Here he feeds one of the swans sent to Tacoma from Victoria, British Columbia. The structure visible behind this portion of Bird Lake may have been one of the two "bird houses" designed by Edward Schwagerl in 1890 to shelter the park's swans and other birds.

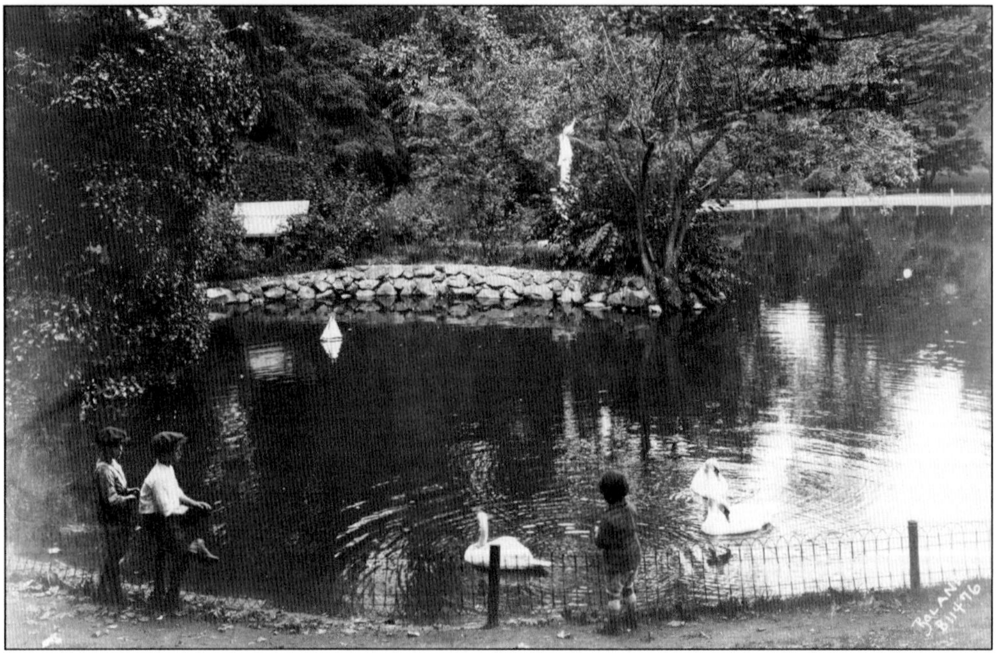

Children enjoy a later generation of swans along the shore of the water, by this time more commonly referred to simply as the Lake or the Duck Pond. The *Fisherman's Daughter* statue, shown in both photographs on this page, stands in its original location on the small peninsula projecting into the lake.

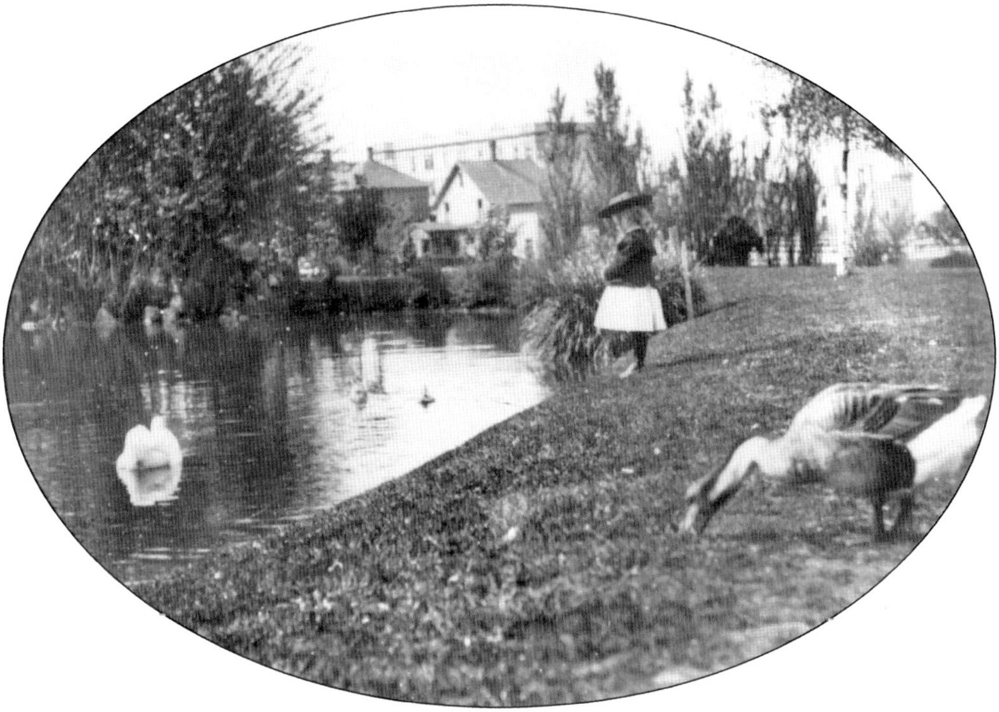

Above, children of the 1890s loved a day in the park no less than their modern counterparts; some would say more. According to the *Tacoma Daily Ledger* of May 12, 1890, landscape designer Edward Schwagerl's Wright Park plan made "especial provisions for the comfort and pleasure of the little folks, with a large playground for children surrounded by walks." In addition, "for the convenience and comfort of the pleasure seekers in the park, pagodas, fruit stands and dairies will be located near the playgrounds so that those who are hungry and thirsty may get refreshments without leaving the park. Swings and other places of amusement are also provided." (Above courtesy WSHS; below courtesy TPL.)

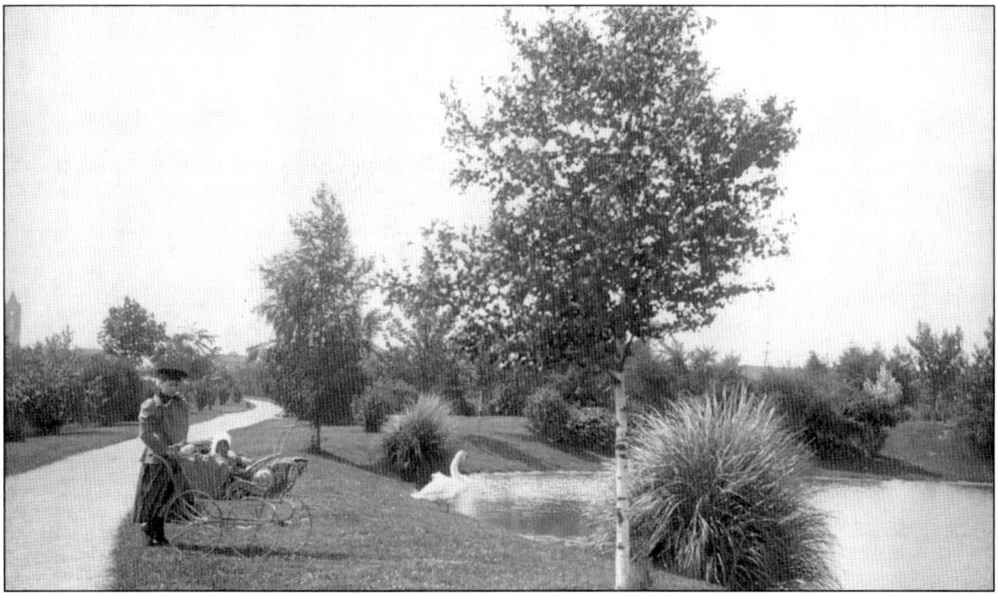

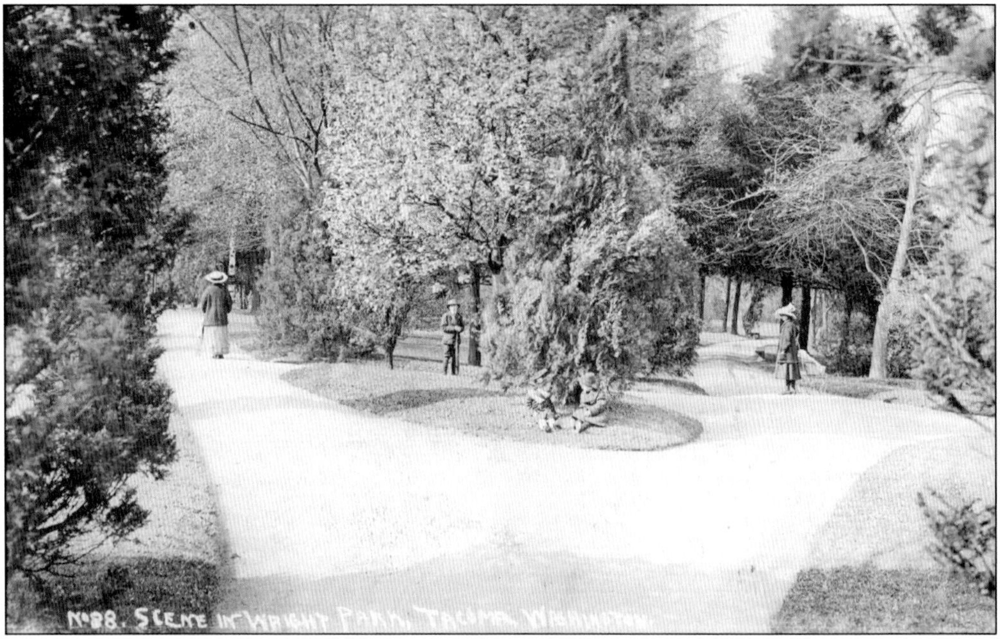

These two *c.* 1914 park postcards show a series of paths and visitors against the background of a rapidly maturing landscape. A 1909 letter from the board of park commissioners described Wright Park as "the only considerable breathing space reserved to the people thronging the central part of this city" and further detailed its responsibility to preserve such space "where the people can get recreation, where children from the congested districts can congregate without danger, and where mothers, nurses and invalids can find a healthful resort during mid-day without being cramped for space or being menaced by shows and their consequent temptations to spend their spare time within the walls of a packed building rather than in the health-giving environments of trees, plants and flowers." (Both courtesy ES.)

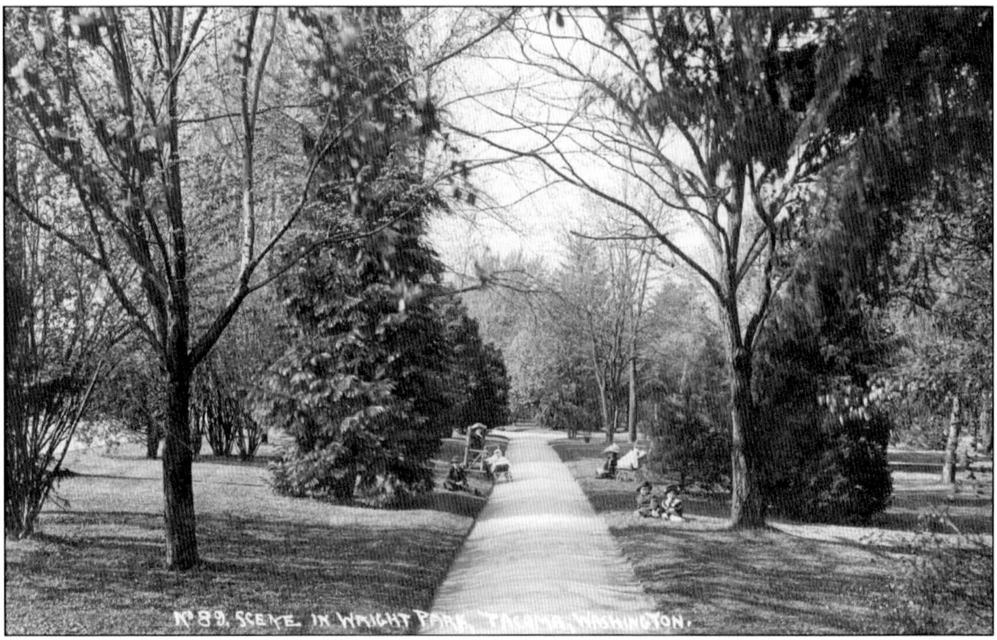

Two

TACOMA'S JEWEL BOX

In 1906, William Wolcott Seymour donated $10,000 to the City of Tacoma to be used as deemed most advisable in beautifying the city. Even though various organizations lobbied the city council for the money, in the end the council recommended that a botanical conservatory be built in Wright Park. Shortly thereafter, in April 1907, the Metropolitan Park District of Tacoma was established to manage the city's parks. The park district followed the advice of the city council and began making plans for a conservatory or palm house.

Four local architects submitted plans for the project. On September 30, 1907, the board chose I. Jay Knapp's design for a graceful glass building with a center dome, two side wings, and an entryway. Construction began in February 1908, and by July, the glass and steel structure was complete. The grand opening had to wait until November 14 to allow park staff to grade the lawns around the structure and arrange the floral displays inside the building.

The opening of the conservatory was held with little fanfare. A notice in the *Tacoma Daily Ledger* simply announced that there would be no formal ceremony. Members of the park board were present to welcome visitors and show them around the building. Even with this inauspicious beginning, the conservatory rapidly became a popular destination for people to enjoy the beauty and variety of plants.

Early official records refer to the conservatory as the Wright Park Conservatory, whereas most newspaper accounts call it the Seymour Conservatory. This discrepancy can be explained by an article written by Nelson Bennett, president of the park board in 1909: "The board had intended calling this structure the Seymour conservatory but owing to the delicate sensitiveness of the donor he has strenuously objected to this. Yet I think it will be known as such just the same." On January 23, 1936, seven years after Seymour's death, the board ordered a plaque acknowledging W. W. Seymour's gift, providing there was no objection from Mrs. Seymour. There was no objection.

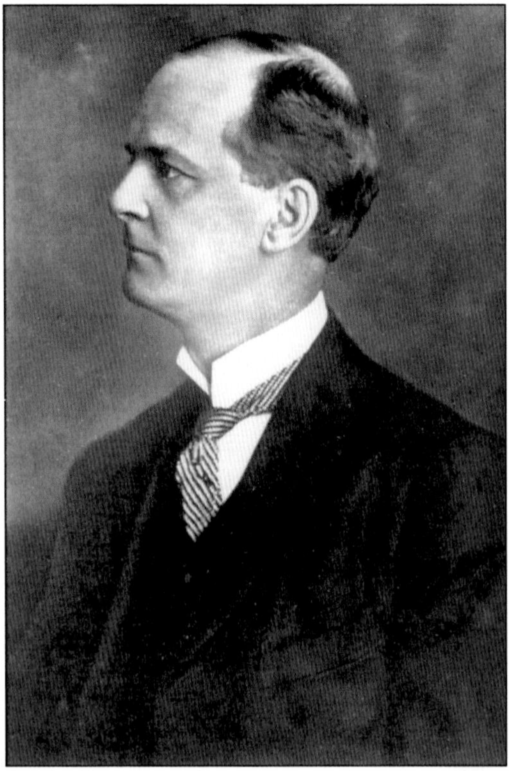

The conservatory's benefactor, William Wolcott Seymour (1861–1929), arrived in Tacoma in 1890. Contemporary articles describe him as an embodiment of the civic-mindedness of his time. He valued the importance of giving back to the community in which he prospered. For a time, Seymour and his wife, Emily, lived on G Street where they could enjoy the beauty of Wright Park daily.

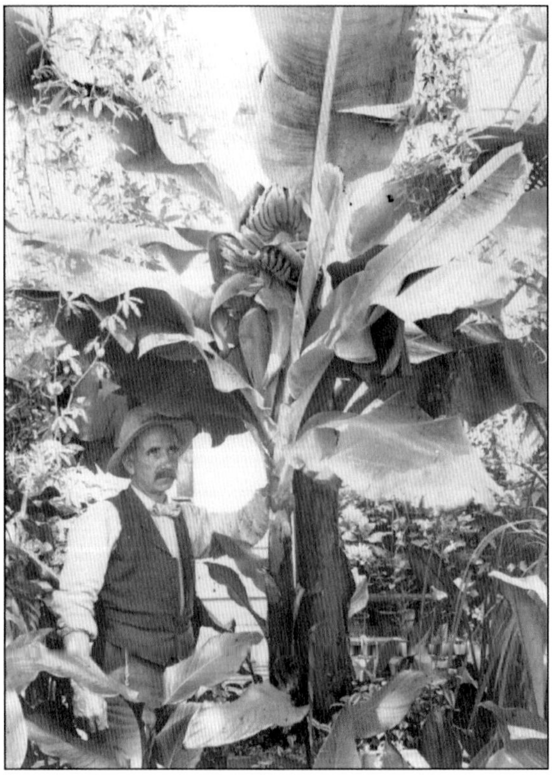

Ebenezer R. Roberts (1854–1918), park superintendent, gardener, and friend of Seymour, deserves much of the credit for the city council's recommendation to use Seymour's donation for a conservatory. Long frustrated with the small greenhouse at Point Defiance Park, Roberts lobbied the city council with beautiful bouquets of flowers to illustrate the value of a botanical conservatory. (Courtesy Jean Insel Robeson.)

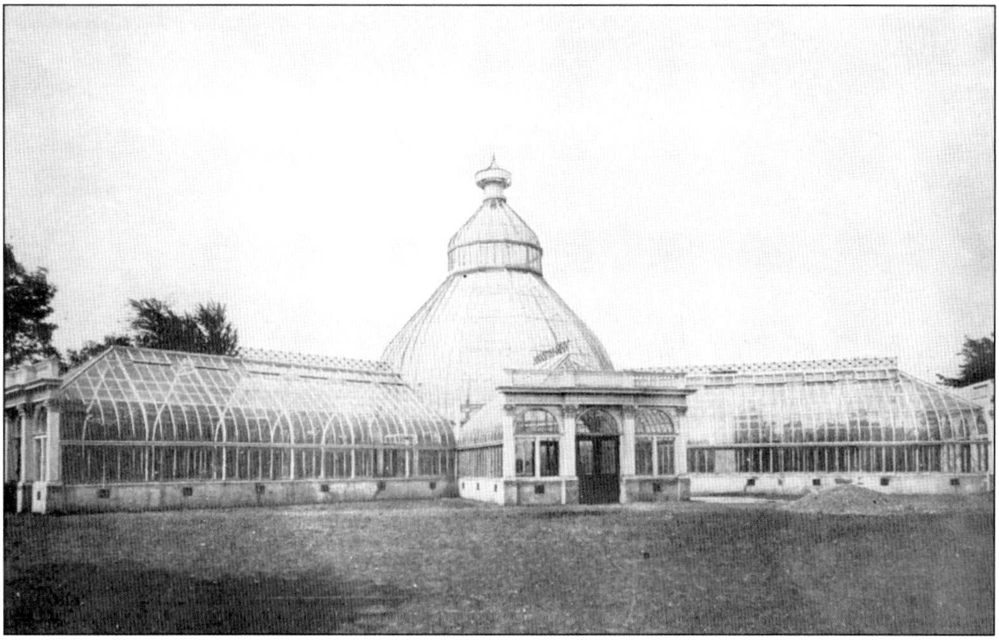

I. Jay Knapp's design included a center dome 45 feet high and 40 feet in diameter with two wings 20 feet wide and 50 feet long and a center portal 20 feet wide and 25 feet long. The base of the conservatory is concrete, but the framework is steel. The decorative entrance facades to the wings were constructed of wood.

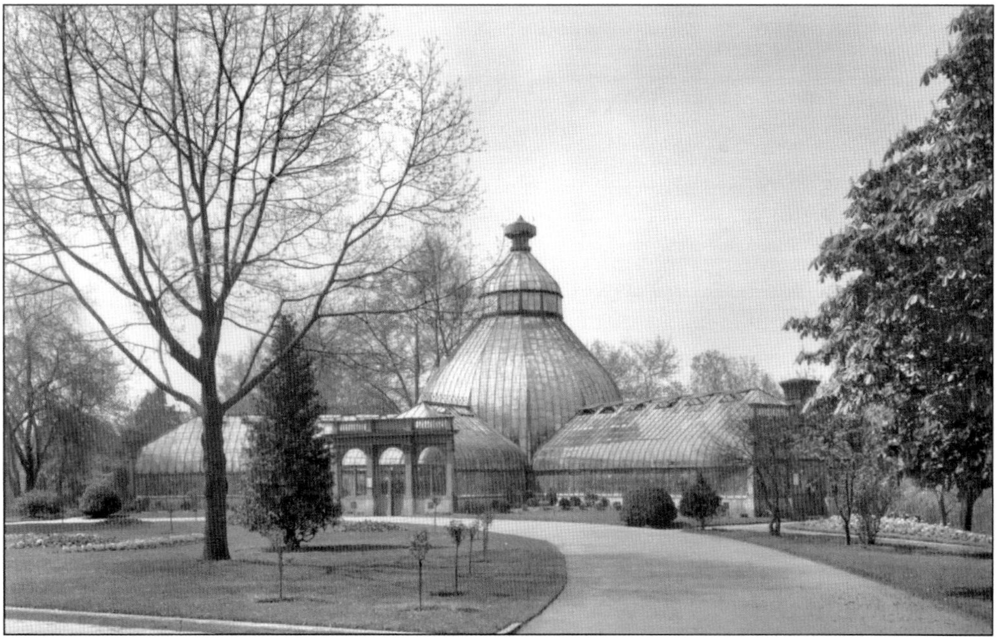

Once the conservatory was completed, park staff began the task of adding a circular drive from G Street to the entrance and landscaping the entrance with trees, shrubs, and flowers. Plans called for the conservatory to house one of the most extensive and valuable collections of rare plants and shrubs in the Northwest. Many of the first plants displayed were cultivated in the Point Defiance greenhouses, just as they are today.

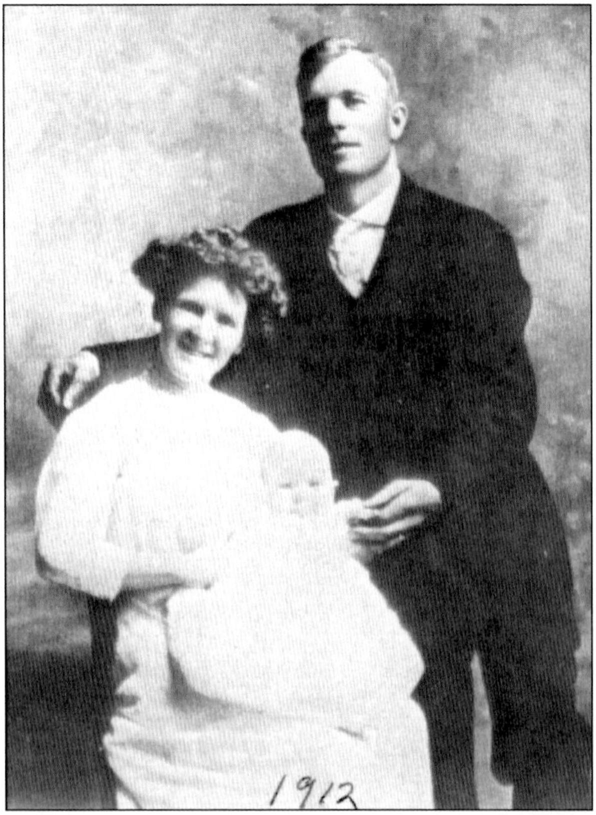

Shortly after the conservatory opened, it became apparent that a specialized knowledge of plants was needed to manage the facility. Gustav Faulk (1876–1962), a park district employee since 1910, was transferred from Point Defiance Park to the conservatory in 1912. Faulk's horticultural training in his native Sweden brought much-needed expertise to make the conservatory bloom. (Courtesy Terry Lumsden.)

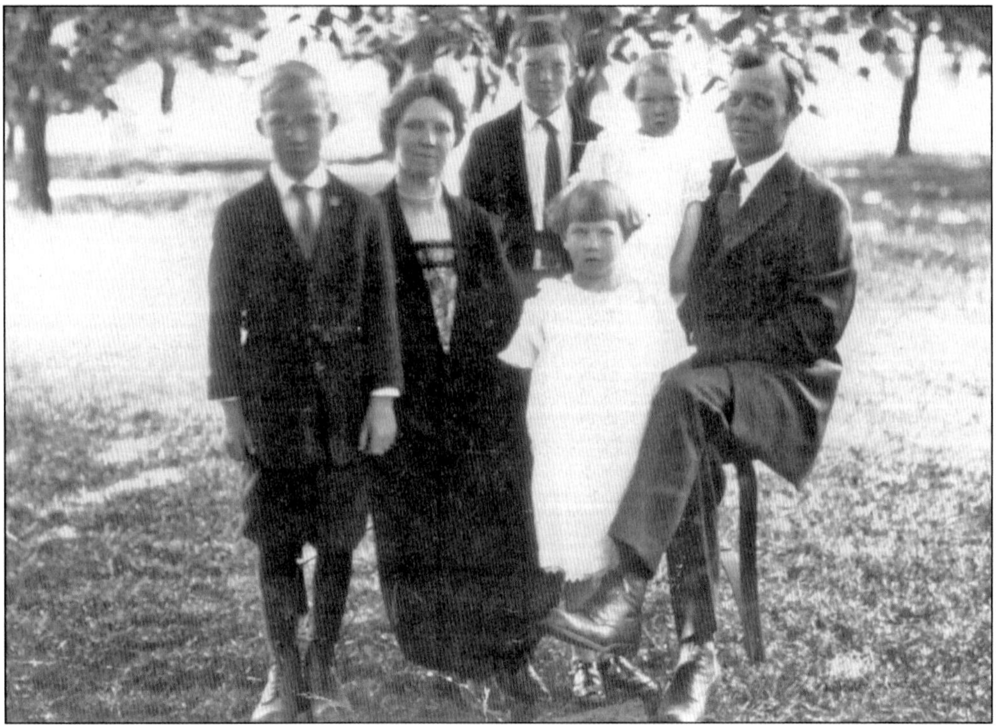

Faulk's love for gardening was only surpassed by his love for his wife, Jennie, pictured here with the couple's four children—from left to right, Lynn, Carl, June, and Arlene. June recalls that her father freely gave advice to conservatory visitors when asked and kept donated plants in a special section so the donors could see them grow. Faulk retired in 1949. (Courtesy Terry Lumsden.)

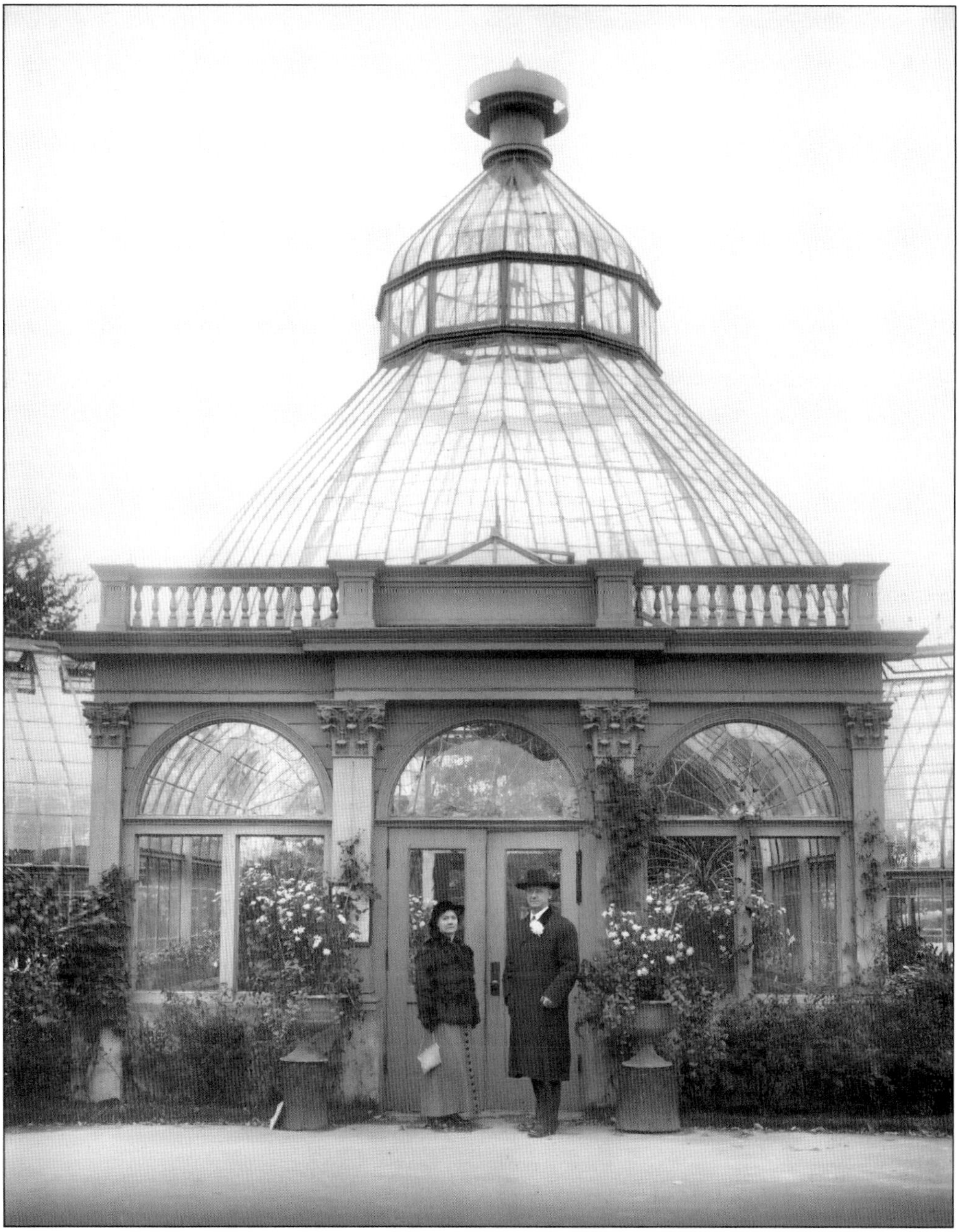

Frank C. Ross and Anna Robinson stand in front of the conservatory on October 13, 1914. Ross arrived in Tacoma in 1879 and spent most of his career buying, improving, and selling land. Thanks to this photograph, the architectural details of the original wooden facades are clearly shown. The flower-filled urns on either side of the front door only hint at the horticultural splendor inside. (Courtesy WSHS.)

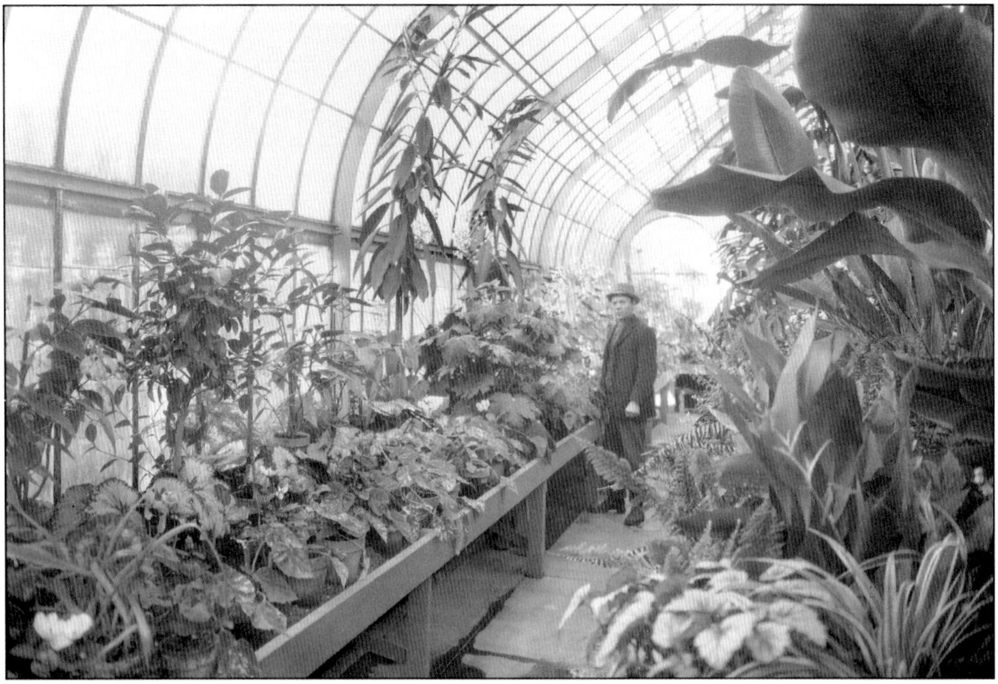

The conservatory's first displays were quite different from those visitors see today. Racks were set up along the walls of the wings to exhibit a variety of potted plants, such as the begonias and cyclamen shown above. Below, an unidentified woman admires the tropical foliage in the central dome. Note that the top glass appears darker than the rest. One method of regulating temperature during the summer months was to whitewash the panes of glass on the exterior to reflect sunlight. When the rains returned in the fall, the whitewash rinsed away. Today cloth is hung over the side wings to keep the building cool. (Both courtesy WSHS.)

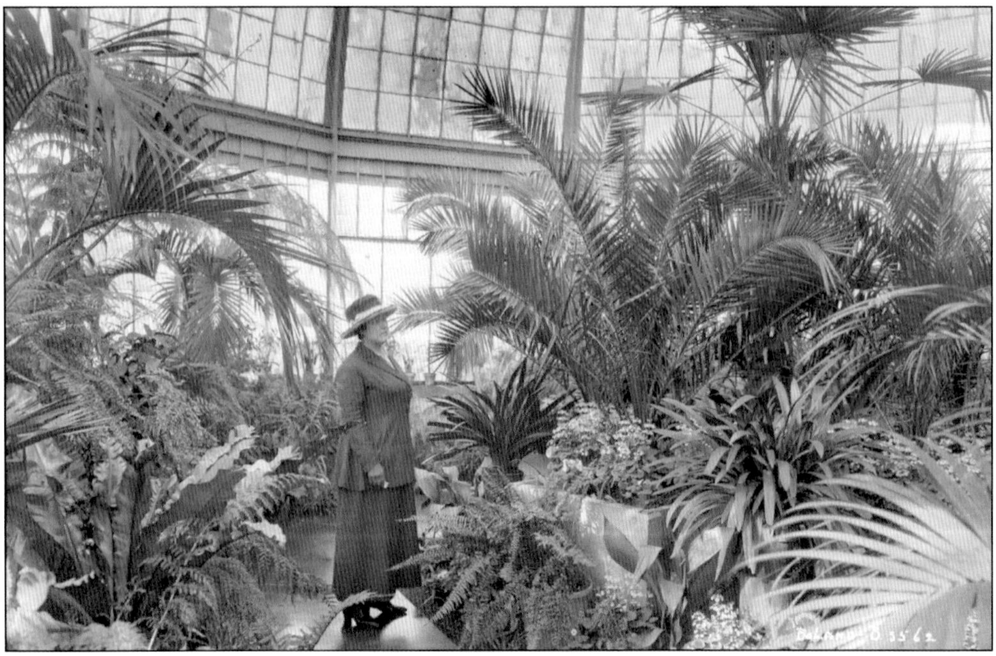

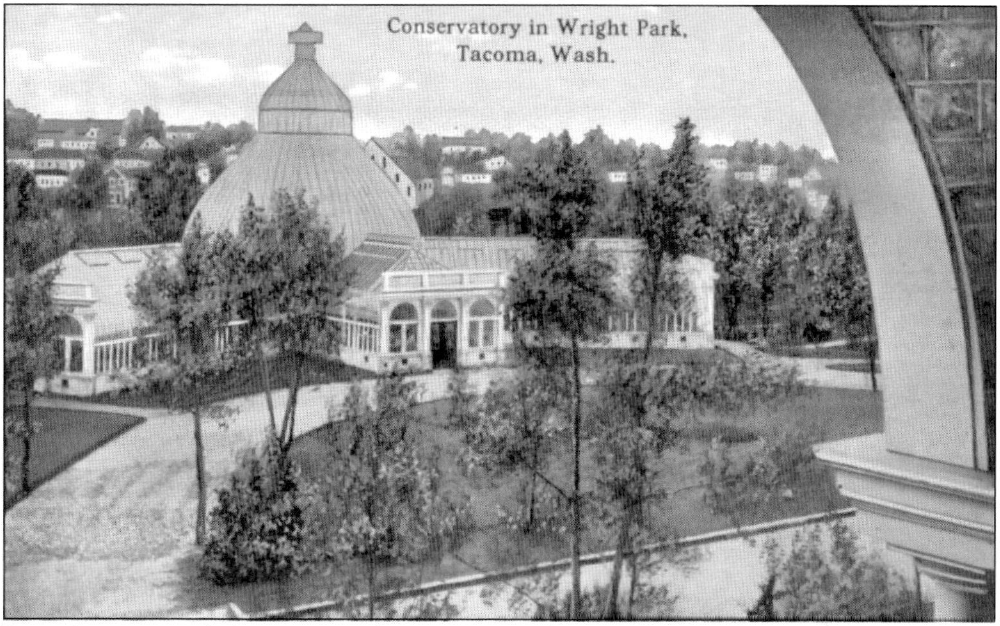

From the upstairs of a home on South G Street, people enjoyed a lovely view of the conservatory. In 1900, prominent citizens called for the narrowing of G Street to slow down traffic. The plan was to enlarge Wright Park by "parking" G and I Streets. G Street was reduced to 30 feet, and the cut-off strips of roadway were planted with grass and trees.

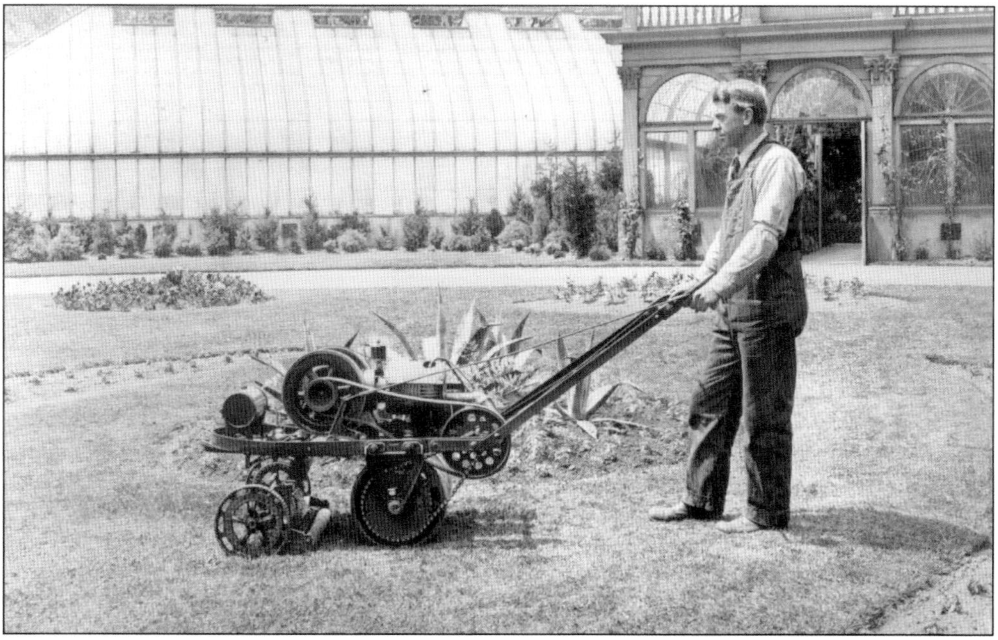

An unidentified park employee mows the grass in front of the conservatory with what appears to be an Ideal Power lawn mower around 1918. The man is wearing striped coveralls to protect his dress shirt, tie, and vest. In its 1913 annual report, the park board proudly announced its discontinuation of horse-drawn lawn mowers.

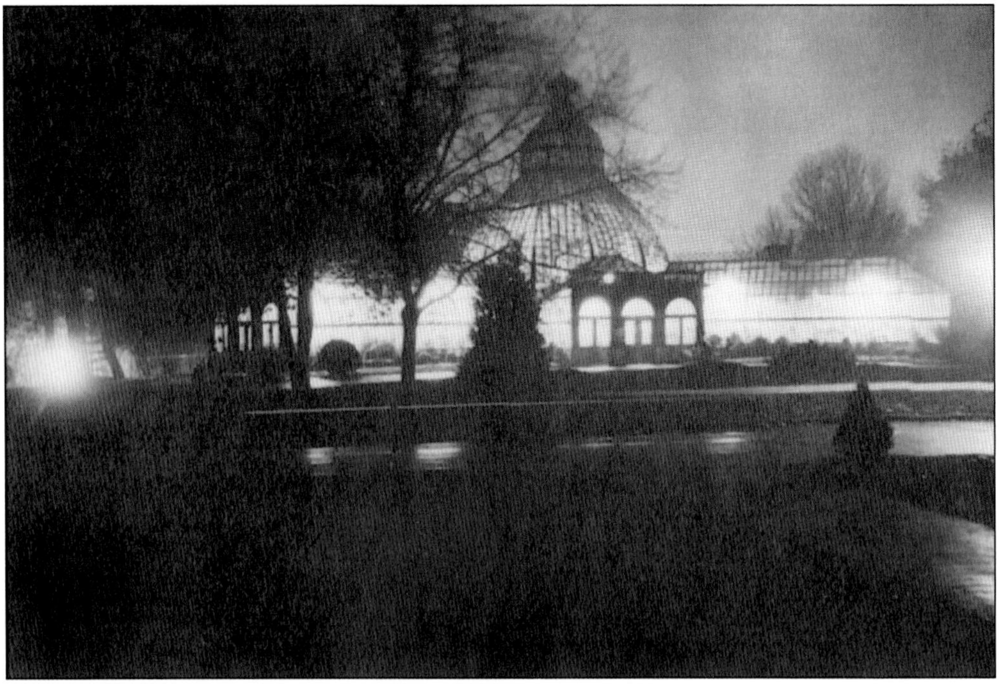

Few early images show the conservatory lit from within. There was an occasion in 1946 when a night-blooming cereus cactus was being featured at the conservatory. The 14-inch blossom started to open at dusk and closed tightly at sunrise. The newspaper announced that the lights were to be left on so that people could look in and see the display.

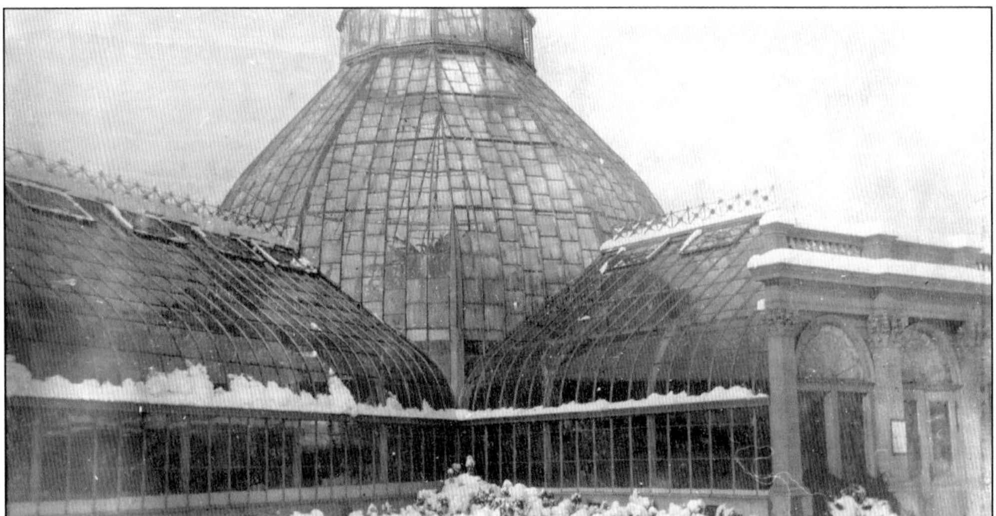

The original plans called for heating the conservatory with an oil furnace. Shortly after construction began, architect and contractor I. J. Knapp suggested changing to a coal-burning furnace with an electric heat circulator. This proposal was approved by the board. Gustav Faulk, the first conservatory manager, remembered walking from his home in South Tacoma during a 1915 snowstorm to check and make sure his plants were safe.

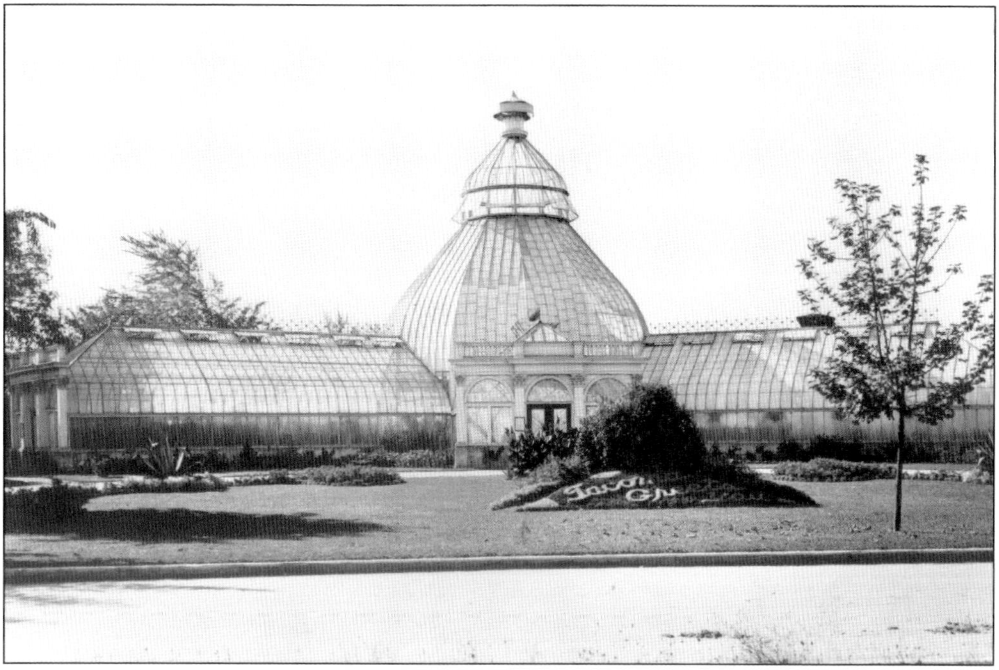

As soon as the conservatory opened to the public in November 1908, it became a popular destination for Tacoma residents and visitors alike. The flowers in the decorative planting mound in front of the building spell out "Tacoma Greets You." Other slogans popular in the early 20th century were "Watch Tacoma Grow" and "You'll Like Tacoma." (Courtesy UW.)

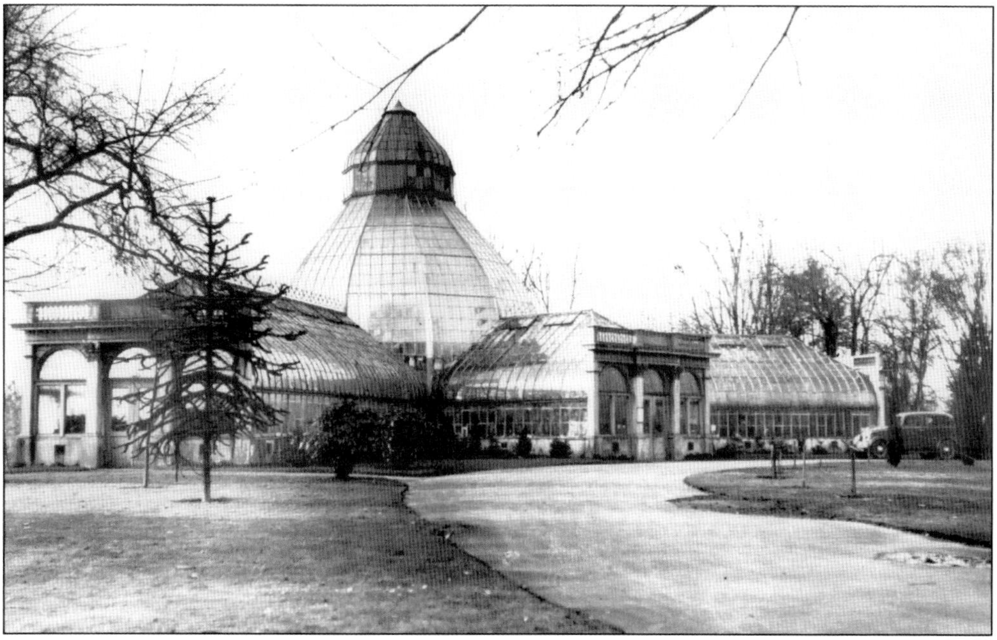

Even though the conservatory's overall appearance has not changed over the years, several modifications have taken place. This early-1930s photograph illustrates the first significant alteration: the metal turbine atop the central dome has been removed and replaced with a copper cap that remains today. (Courtesy ES.)

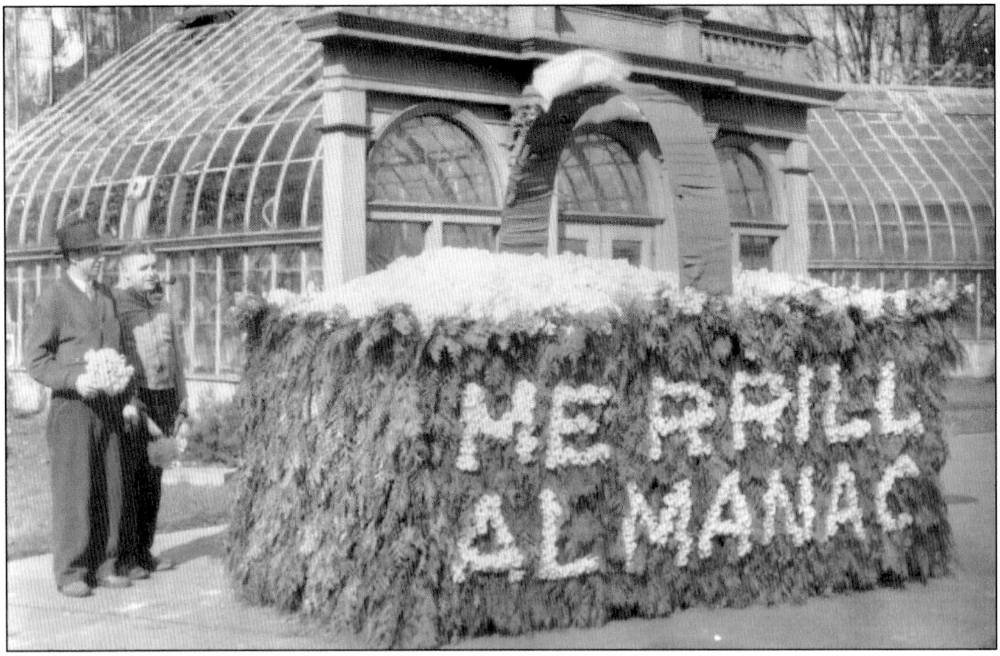

Merrill Almanac's entry in the Daffodil Parade is pictured outside the conservatory on March 23, 1935. This is one of the last images where the facade is still in place on the entryway. Specific details on the removal of the facades have not been found, but the park district did hire John Benthien to rebuild one wing a year beginning in 1935. (Courtesy TPL.)

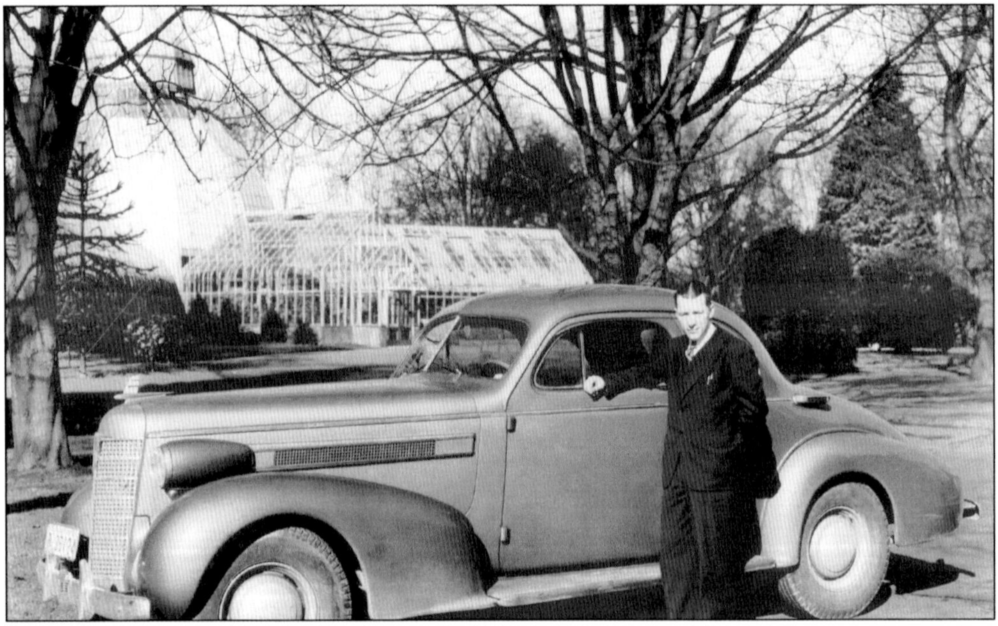

This February 1938 photograph of an unidentified man with an Oldsmobile coupe is just one of many instances where individuals and businesses posed in front of the conservatory. This image, however, also serves to document that the wooden facades have been removed from the building. Also missing by this time is the decorative ironwork along the ridgeline of each wing. (Courtesy TPL.)

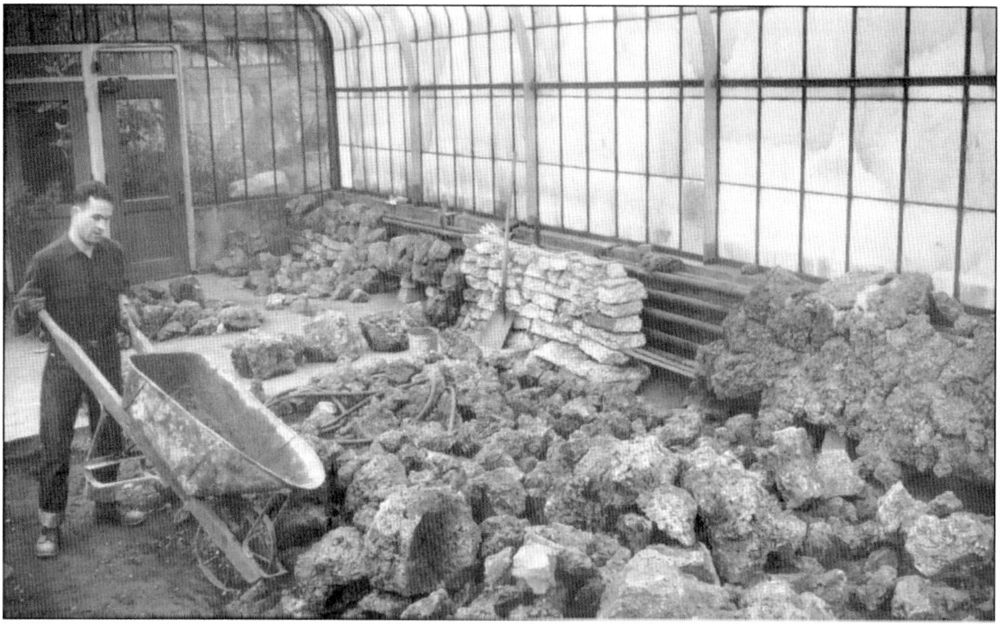

In 1940, Clarence Deming (1912–2003), a park district employee working in the Point Defiance Park gardens, was reassigned to work with Gustav Faulk at the conservatory. When Faulk retired in 1949, Deming was placed in charge. One of his first acts was to significantly change the interior of the structure by tearing out the original concrete walkways and rebuilding the interior with granite, slag, and other rocks. (Courtesy TPL.)

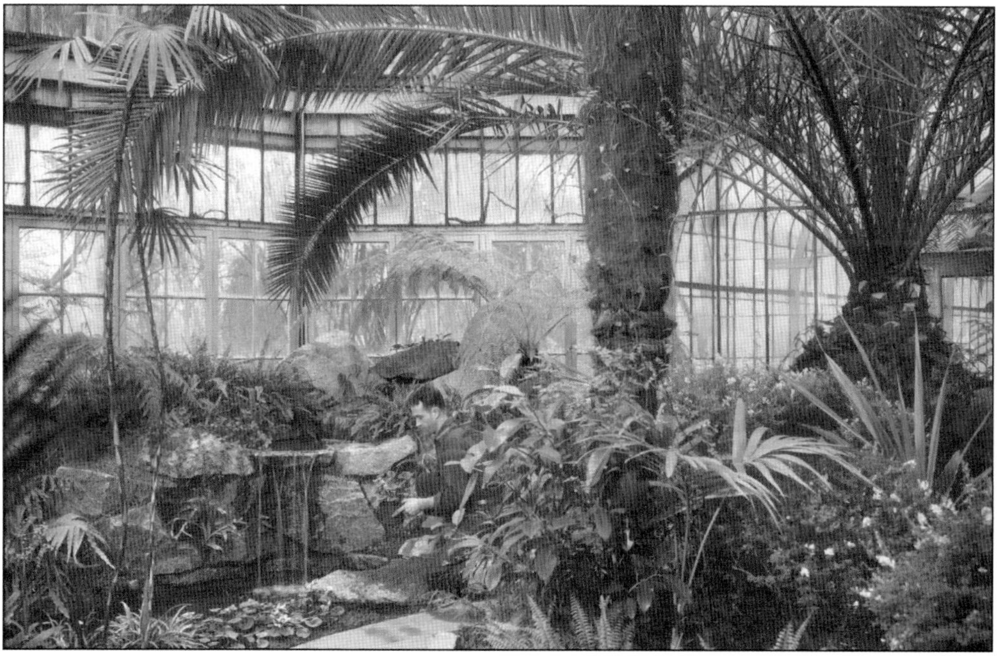

Early interior photographs show counters for potted plants running along the exterior walls of the wings and a large central bed for plantings in the dome area. Deming's work changed the conservatory from a straightforward palm house to a lush tropical jungle with curved walks, sculpture, and areas for changing displays. (Courtesy TPL.)

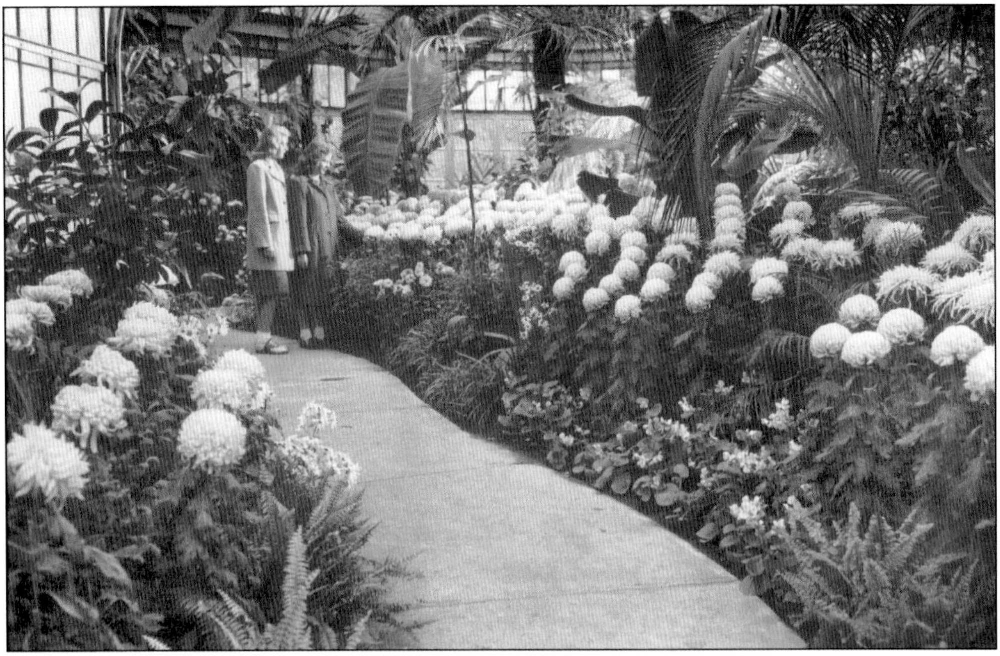

Deming is credited with beginning the seasonal displays that have become a conservatory tradition. Here Lois Holm (left) and Joyce Anderson admire Haven in the Woods, which featured 1,400 exhibition-type chrysanthemums. The "mum" display continues to delight visitors each fall. (Courtesy TPL.)

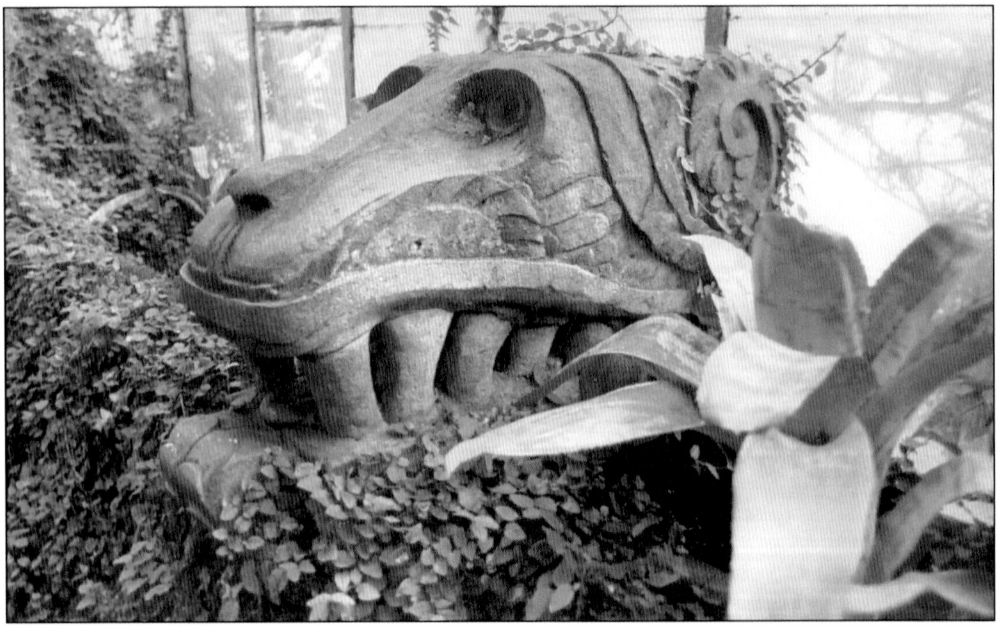

Deming added another dimension to the conservatory when he integrated art into the botanical setting. He designed and built four Aztec- and Maori-inspired statues that are still located in the dome, in the north wing, and two others at the front door. The statues were made of modeled cement over a metal frame, and each reportedly took one day to complete. Deming retired from the conservatory in 1971.

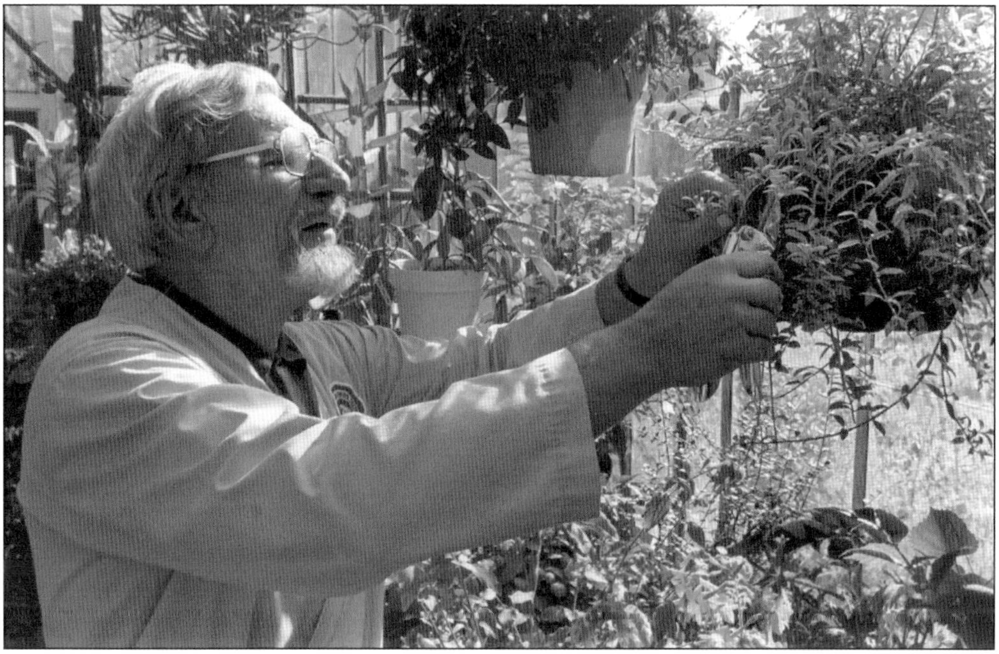

After Clarence Deming's retirement in 1971, the park district appointed Stephen Brightman (1924–1997) to manage the conservatory. Brightman had begun his work with the park district in 1953 at the Point Defiance greenhouse. His education and experience with the Tacoma Garden Club, American Dahlia Society, and American Rhododendron Society made him the perfect candidate for the job. His years at the conservatory can be characterized as a return to more serious horticultural pursuits. Above, Brightman tends to a trailing vine. Below, he is doing what he enjoyed most: talking with visitors such as Carol Gorsuch, answering questions, and providing horticultural advice.

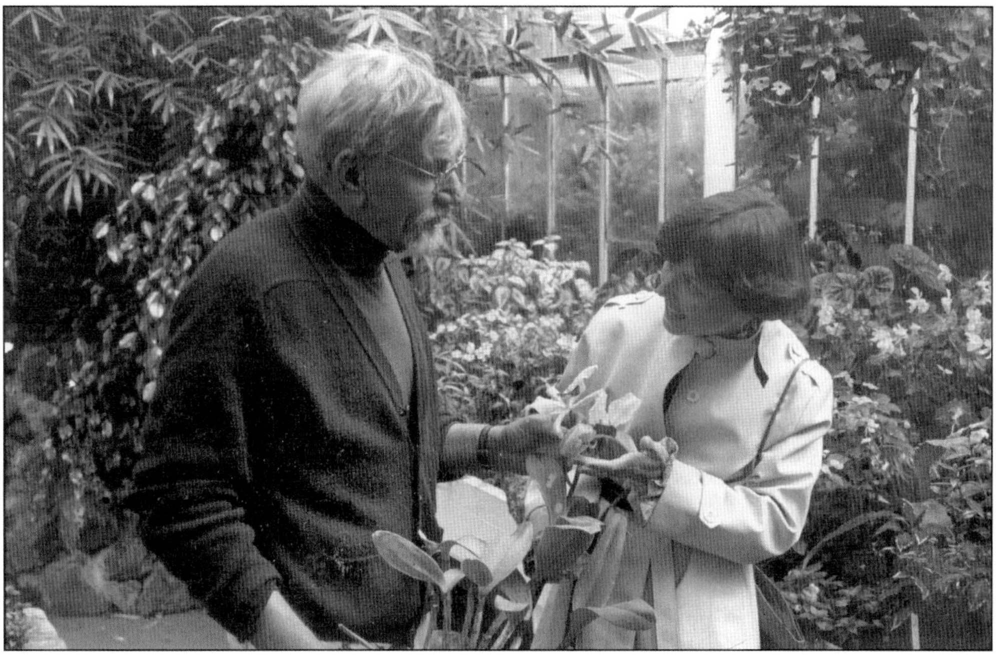

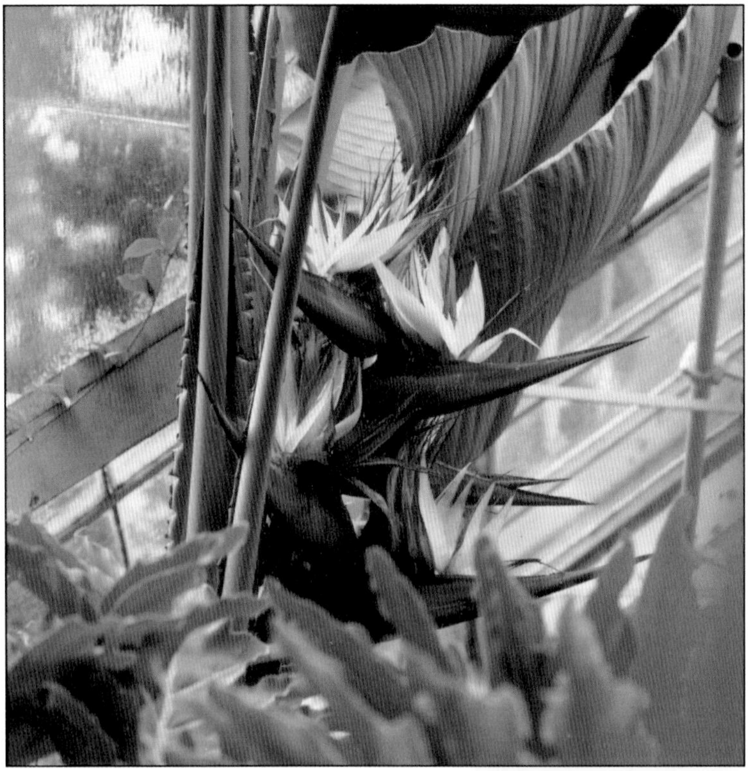

Headlines were made in 1913 when the conservatory purchased a rare bird-of-paradise (*Strelitzia nicolai*). Some 23 years later, the plant made news again when Gustav Faulk reported that it was blooming for the first time. Faulk credited repairs for reducing cold drafts on the plant. This species boasts blossoms with dark blue bases and lighter blue and white petals and can grow 40 to 50 feet high. It is still in the conservatory today.

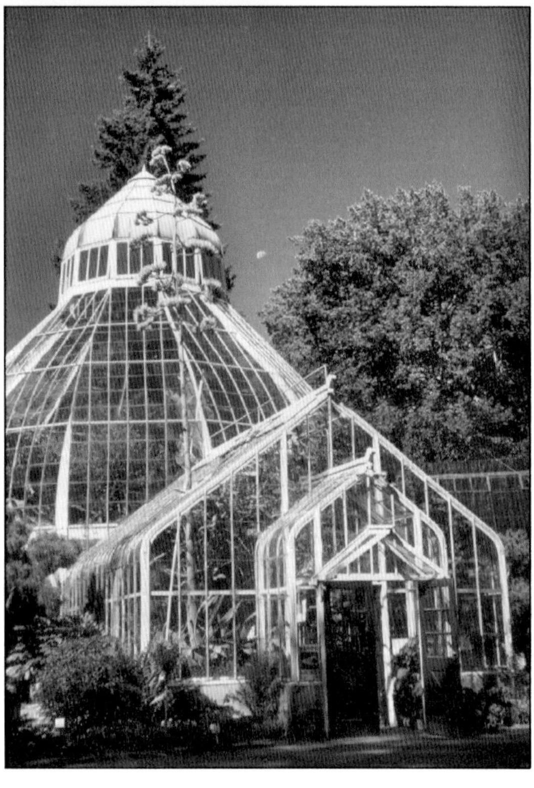

During the summer of 1988, the conservatory's century plant (*Agave americana*) bloomed. For several weeks, it rose four to five inches a day, forcing staff to remove a pane of glass to allow for the growth. Even though the plant died after making this supreme effort, it produced new plants, or "pups," one of which is thriving in the conservatory today.

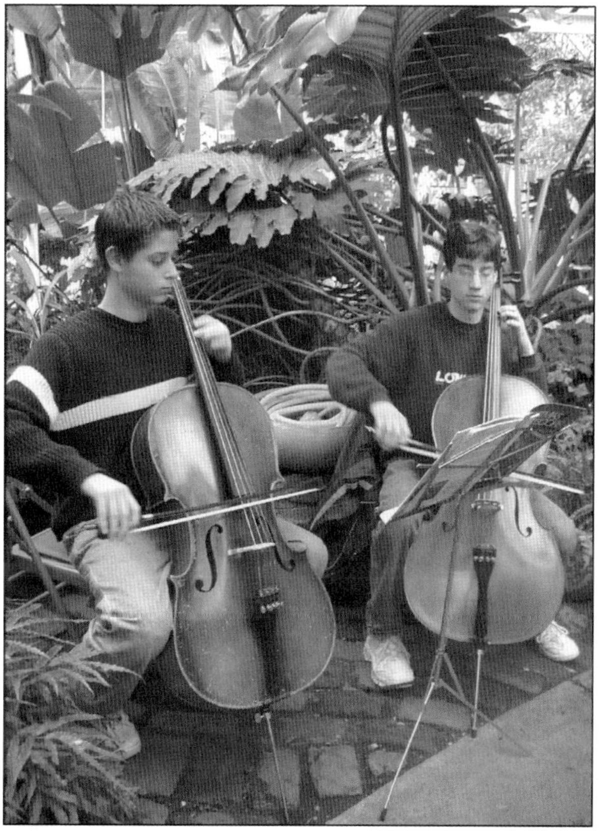

Continuing the tradition begun by Clarence Deming, the conservatory's displays change with the seasons, but even more activities and programs now add to visitor enjoyment. Above, two young men provide the background music for the annual Victorian Holiday Celebration while nestled in the lush greenery of the tree philodendron. Below, a delighted young lady has her photograph taken in the pumpkin patch. Local musicians provide acoustic music on the second Sunday of each month while visitors stroll through the displays.

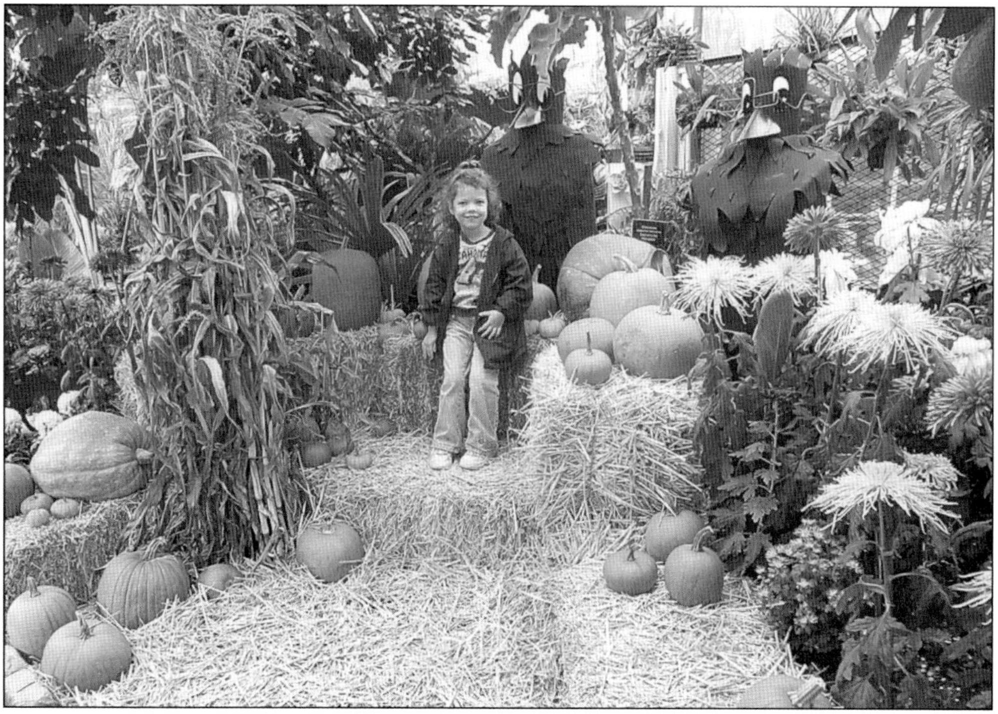

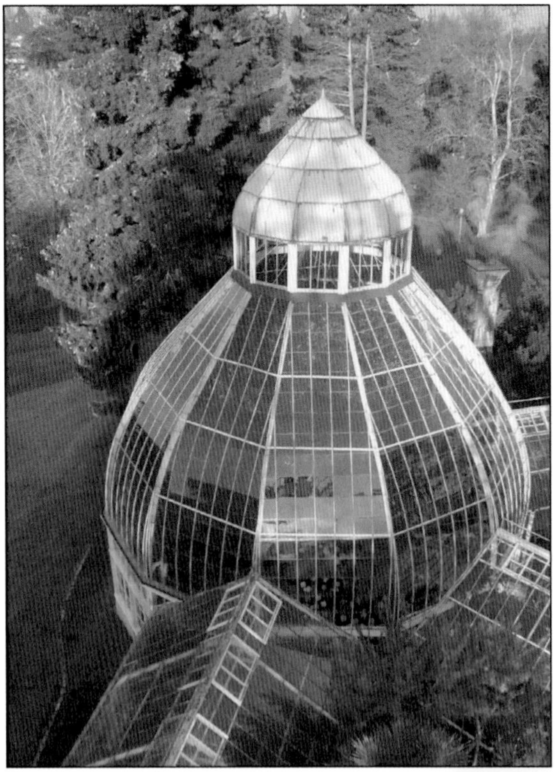

Visitors to the Seymour Conservatory, one of only three Victorian-style conservatories on the West Coast, seldom enjoy this bird's-eye view of the building and its more modern gazebo. The 12-sided domed steel structure and its 3,500 panes of glass are impressive in their own right. The ventilating windows along the ridge of all three wings are visible in the photograph to the left. Just below the copper cap atop the dome, windows allow hot air out to regulate the interior temperature. The small steel-frame gazebo seen below was added in 1992. Donated by Holland Ornamental Iron, it reflects the graceful symmetry of the conservatory and has proven to be a popular location for small weddings and other gatherings.

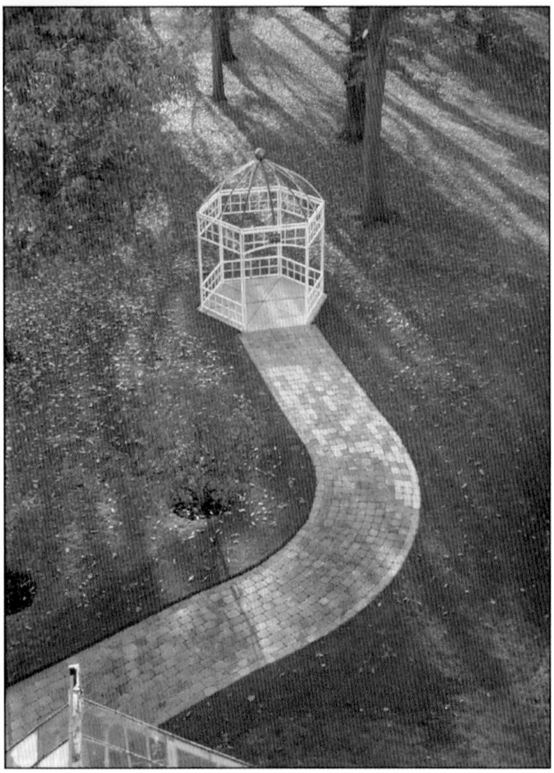

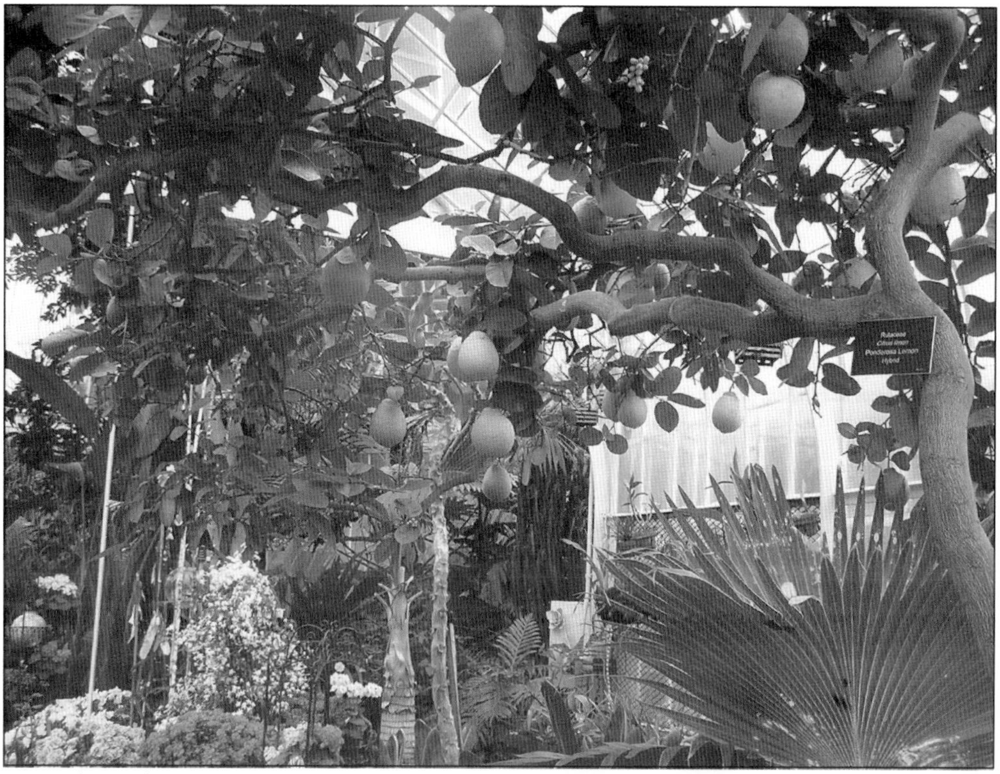

A Ponderosa lemon tree (above) evokes amazement from visitors as they walk in the door. The huge fruits dangle a few feet from the path, beckoning people farther into the conservatory. Between the size of the fruit and the wonderful fragrance from the abundant flowers, it is easy to understand why it is also known as "the Wonder Lemon." The vibrant colors of the rotating floral displays (below) pop out against the backdrop of tropical foliage. Varied fragrances mingle to create exquisite perfume. Plants bloom at different times, providing a unique experience with each visit. In 2008, to commemorate the centennial of the conservatory, special glass displays were added to the rich floral exhibitions. The bowl pictured here was created by the Hilltop Artists in Residence. (Both courtesy Terri Walton.)

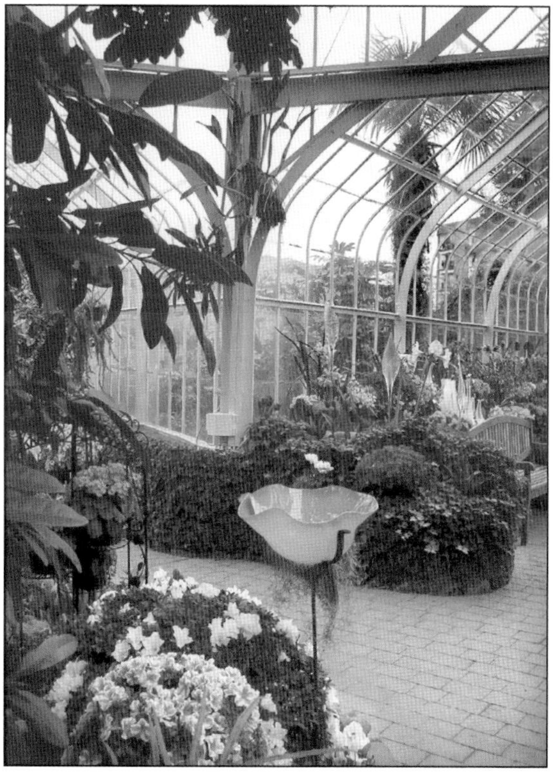

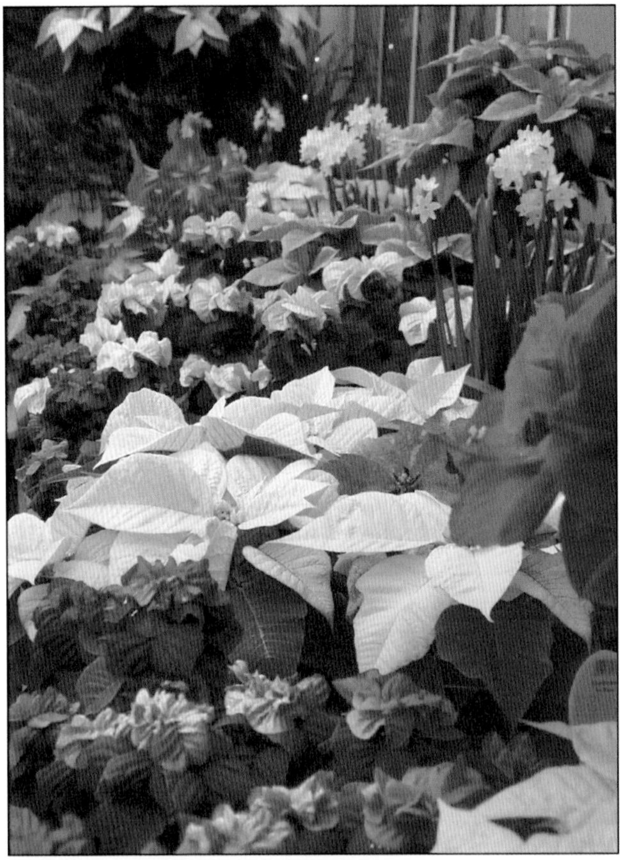

Even after 100 years, the charm of the Victorian-style W. W. Seymour Botanical Conservatory is apparent. Eye-catching colors, fanciful shapes, and exotic fragrances capture visitors' imaginations. Generations have discovered firsthand the wonder of botany and experienced flora from all around the globe, including the poinsettias and paper whites in the annual December display (left). Interpretive materials and other self-guiding tours allow visitors an opportunity to study the collection in more detail. Whether appreciating the floral displays or looking closely at a cymbidium orchid (below), visitors connect with the natural world, thus gaining respect for the environment and a conservation ethic. (Below courtesy Lindsay Keeton.)

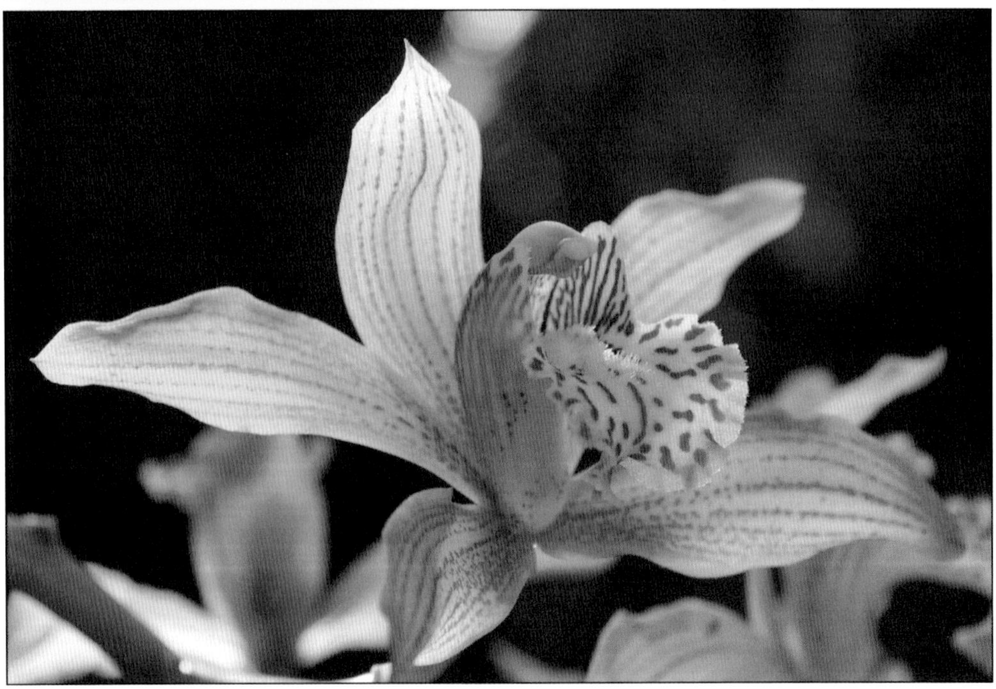

Three

The Wright Park Neighborhood

Once Charles Wright and the Tacoma Land Company made their contingent donation of land in 1886, interest grew in the acquisition of private property surrounding the acreage. Even before the city had completed the requisite improvements to secure the tract's donation, lots fronting the new city park were under construction for homes and small businesses, giving the Wright Park neighborhood its first residential ambience. The district was viewed as a highly desirable part of town, removed from Tacoma's main business thoroughfares and working waterfront and "located in the most healthful part of the city," as described in the 1890 city directory.

Vital community institutions also have a long history in the Wright Park neighborhood; several of these are also beholden to Charles Wright's benevolence for their origins. The Annie Wright Seminary—situated on land donated by the Tacoma Land Company, endowed with funds from Wright's personal fortune, and named for his daughter—educated several generations of young girls and women in the neighborhood from 1884 to 1924 before relocating farther west on Tacoma Avenue North. Charles Wright financed the construction of the original Episcopal St. Luke's Memorial Church, which stood from 1883 to 1935 on a lot given by the Tacoma Land Company at Sixth Avenue and South C Street (now Broadway). The Fannie C. Paddock Memorial Hospital made its initial footprint in the Wright Park area in 1889, thanks to Charles Wright's encouragement of a donation of South J Street property by the Tacoma Land Company; today MultiCare Health System's neighborhood presence has grown to be considerable.

Many institutions of religious observance established an early presence on the streets bordering Wright Park, including the synagogue of one of Tacoma's early Jewish congregations. Several stately houses of worship remain to grace the park with their architecture and to contribute their sense of community to the neighborhood. Today home, health, and heritage continue to define the Wright Park locale.

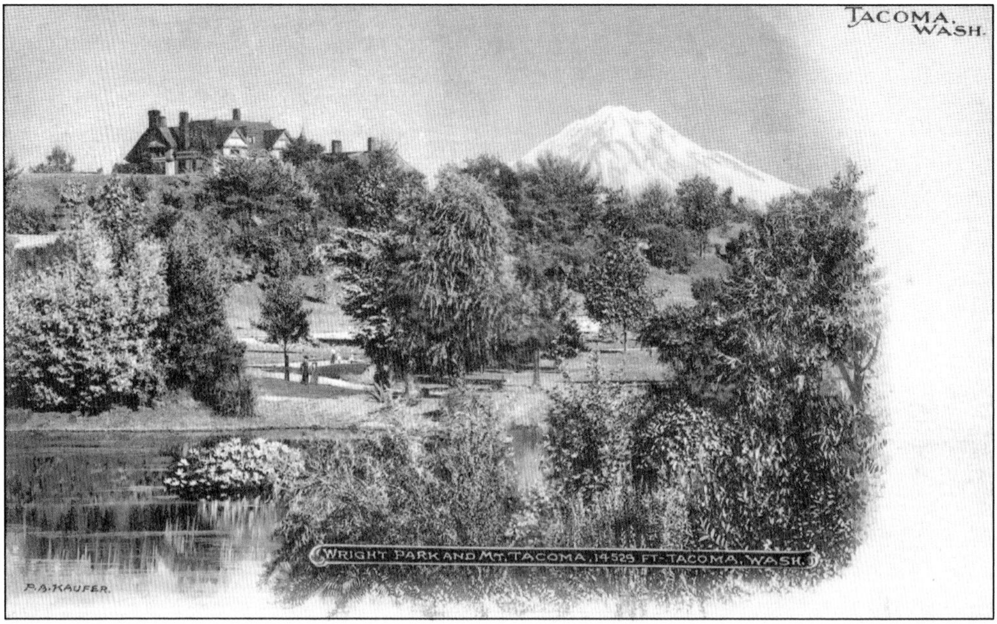

Wright Park became an increasingly popular subject for postcard views as the landscape matured and the setting grew more picturesque. Taken from the lower portion of the park, these early-20th-century views look up the slope toward the homes built along South G Street, an area often referred to as Park Heights between the 1890s and the 1930s. Mount Rainier is at least in its approximate geographical location in the above image (as opposed to the postcard view on page 4). The street running along the lower edge of the image below is Division Avenue, and the faint conical shape at the right edge may be an artist's addition of the conservatory's glass dome. (Both courtesy ES.)

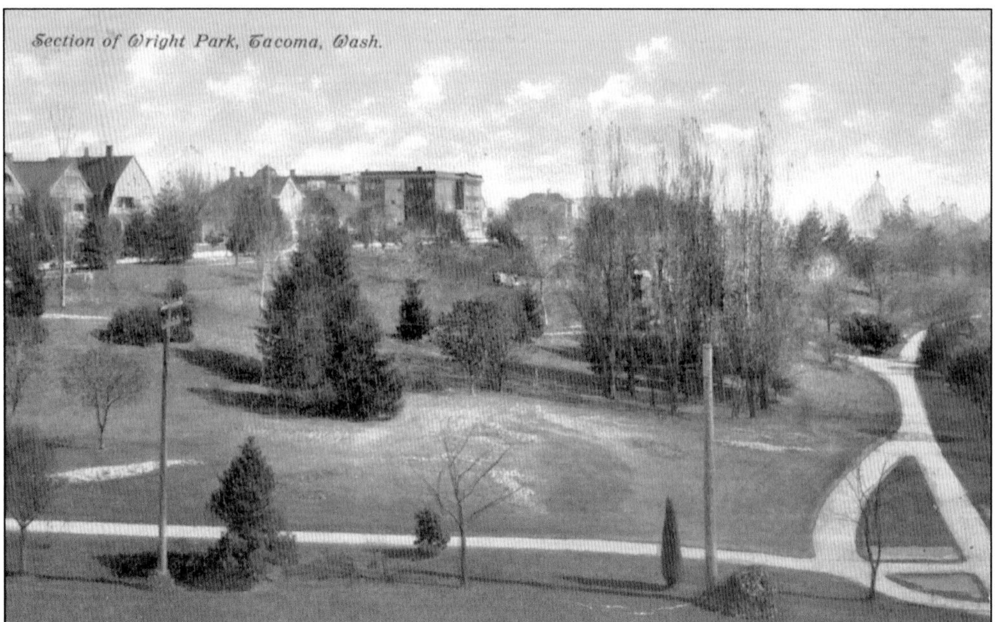

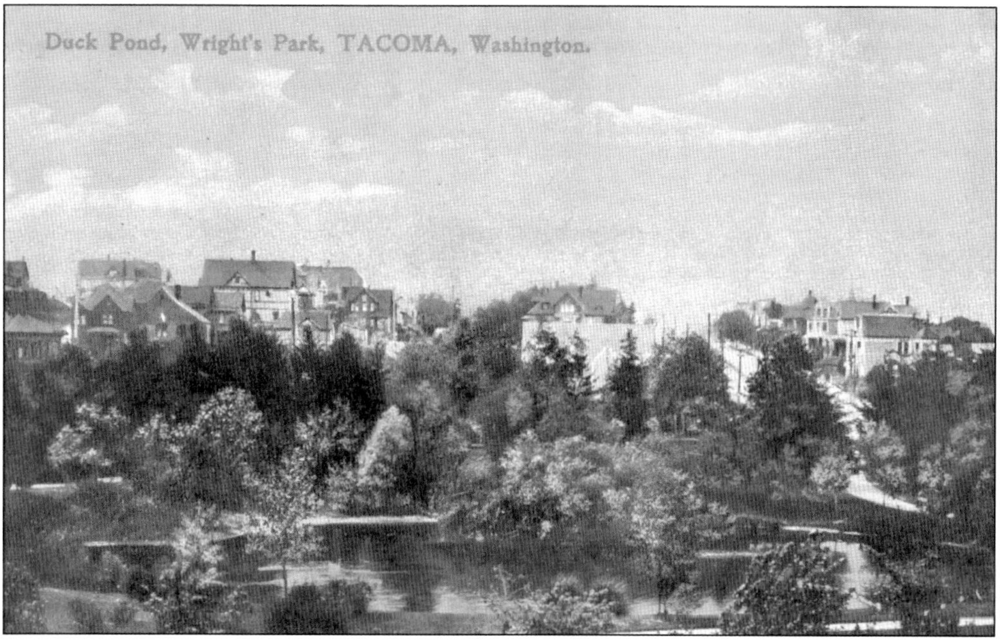

These postcard photographs reinforce the overall residential ambience of the Wright Park neighborhood around 1910. Both views look west from the east side of the park; Division Avenue, seen above, is the thoroughfare partially visible through the trees. Rather indistinguishable among the rooftops above is the 1889 Fannie C. Paddock Memorial Hospital, standing on South J Street. Bird Lake is marked "Duck Pond" above, and the growth of the landscape is significant enough to obscure the bridge and the *Fisherman's Daughter* statue on the lake's small peninsula. The postcard below also places the mountain range correctly. (Both courtesy ES.)

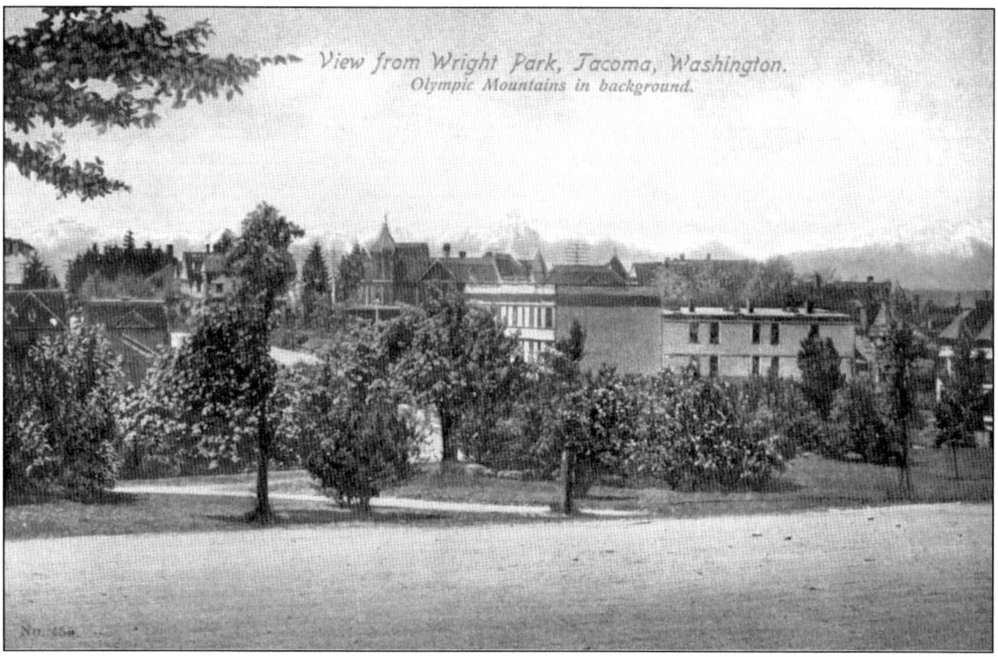

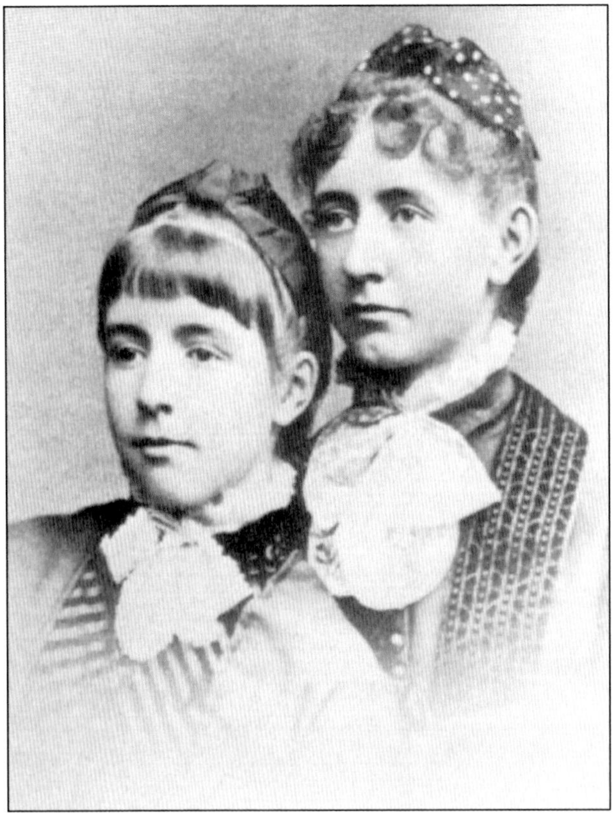

Anne Louise Wright (1863–1904), left, and her elder sister Kate Elizabeth Wright (1861–1881), are pictured about 1880, before Kate's untimely death from tuberculosis at age 19. The seminary located across Division Avenue from the park was endowed by Charles Wright and named in Annie's honor. He laid the cornerstone in August 1883. (Courtesy AWS.)

The establishment of the Annie Wright Seminary was the result of Charles Wright's interest in the future of Tacoma, and his response to requests for assistance in funding institutions of the Episcopal faith in Washington Territory. This view of the seminary shows the entrances facing Tacoma Avenue North at the corner of North First Street. The school and its outbuildings occupied the entire triangular block. (Courtesy AWS.)

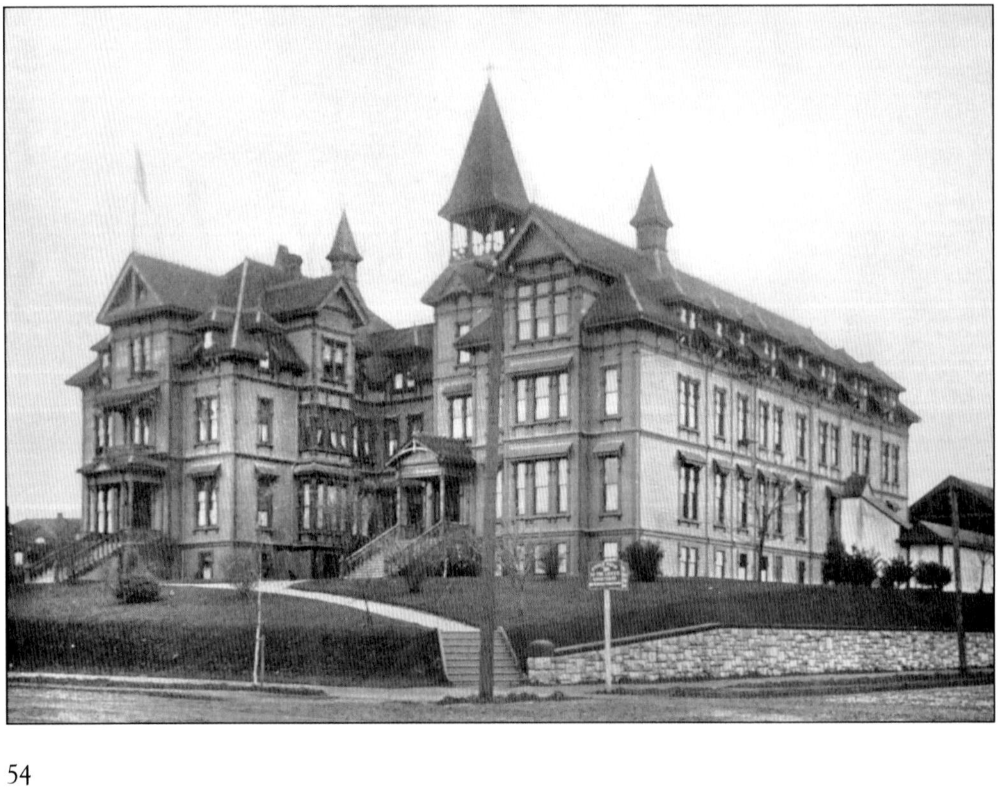

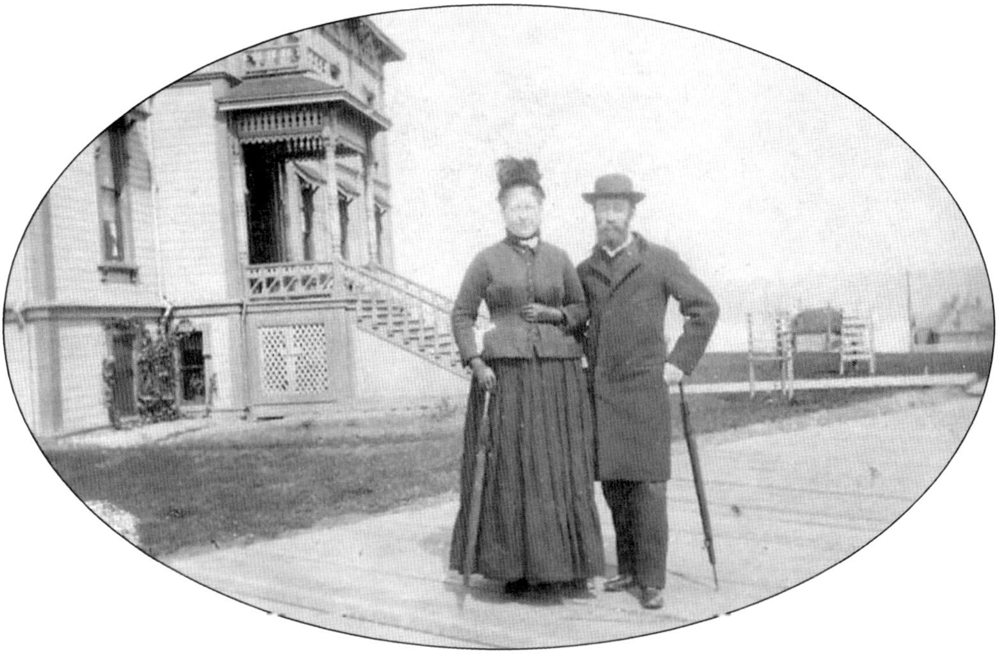

An unidentified man and woman stand with umbrellas outside the Division Avenue entrance to the Annie Wright Seminary about 1890. Note the faint view of Commencement Bay and the outline of Northeast Tacoma behind them. This side entrance would have led to Wright Park. (Courtesy AWS.)

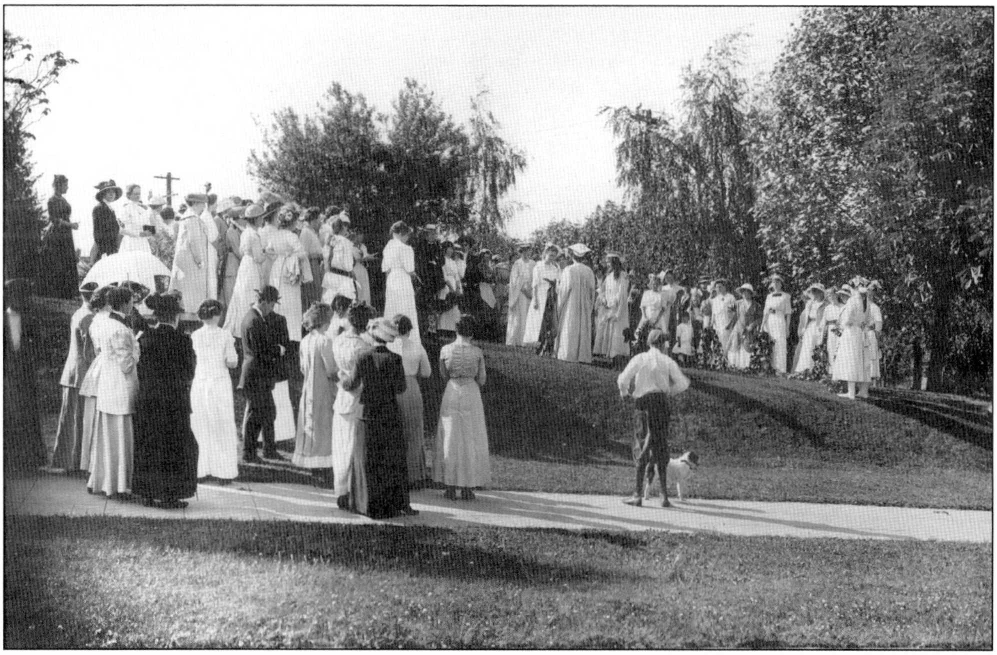

For many decades, a beloved Annie Wright tradition has been the planting of a tree by the school's senior class. In this c. 1910 view of mostly girls and women, the tradition appears to be under way in Wright Park, just off Division Avenue, rather than on seminary grounds. Note that sidewalks in the neighborhood are now hard surfaced. (Courtesy AWS.)

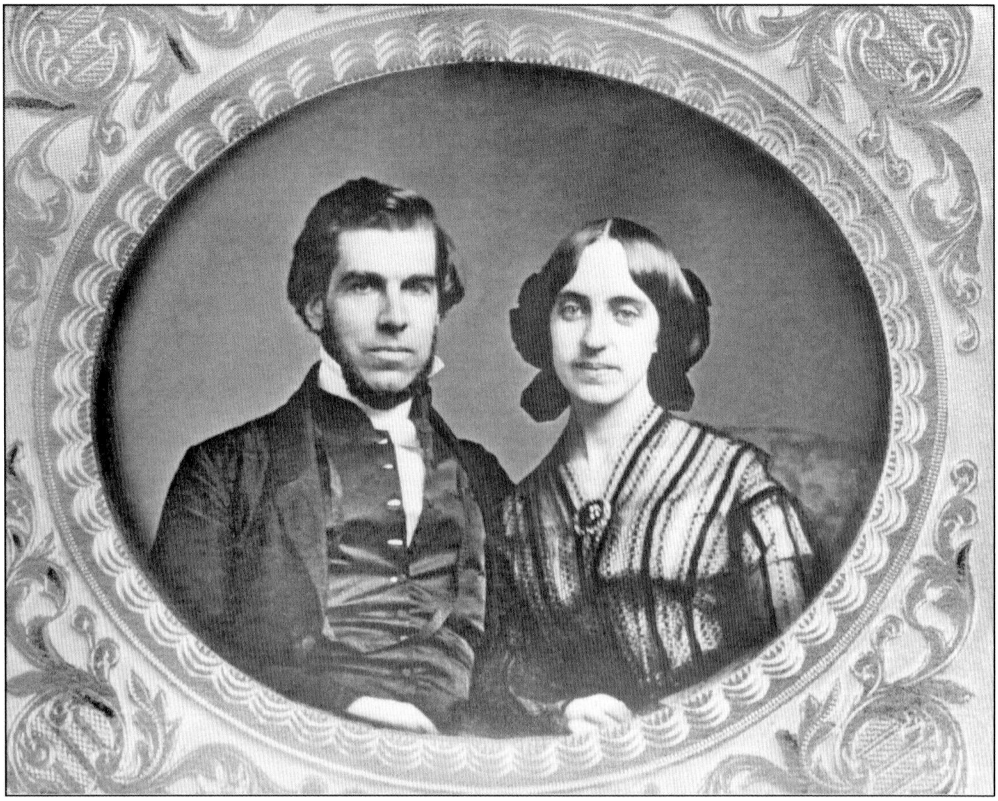

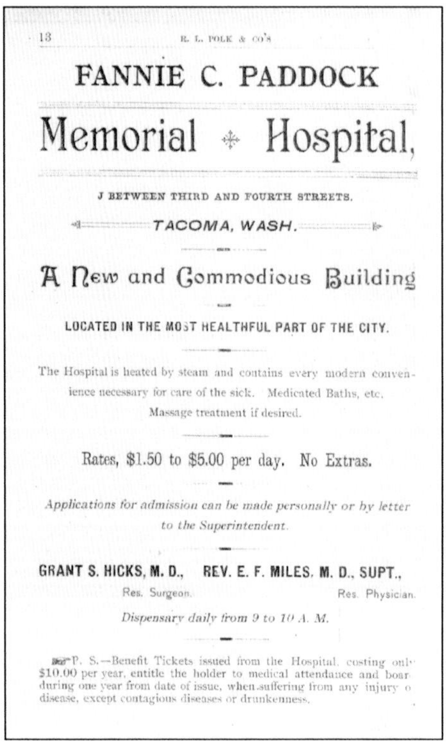

13 R. L. POLK & CO'S

FANNIE C. PADDOCK

Memorial ✥ Hospital,

J BETWEEN THIRD AND FOURTH STREETS.

TACOMA, WASH.

A New and Commodious Building

LOCATED IN THE MOST HEALTHFUL PART OF THE CITY.

The Hospital is heated by steam and contains every modern convenience necessary for care of the sick. Medicated Baths, etc. Massage treatment if desired.

Rates, $1.50 to $5.00 per day. No Extras.

Applications for admission can be made personally or by letter to the Superintendent.

GRANT S. HICKS, M. D., Res. Surgeon. REV. E. F. MILES, M. D., SUPT., Res. Physician.

Dispensary daily from 9 to 10 A. M.

P. S.—Benefit Tickets issued from the Hospital, costing only $10.00 per year, entitle the holder to medical attendance and board during one year from date of issue, when suffering from any injury or disease, except contagious diseases or drunkenness.

John Adams Paddock and Fannie Chester Paddock posed for the photograph above around 1860. Hailing from Brooklyn, New York, they headed west in March 1881 to take up John's post as the first Protestant Episcopal missionary bishop of Washington Territory. Fannie, who ardently wished to open a hospital, began soliciting donations in New York before embarking on the couple's five-week rail journey to San Francisco. On the steamer passage in April from San Francisco to the Northwest, Fannie developed pneumonia and died. Bishop Paddock kept his wife's dream alive, establishing the hospital first on Starr Street in Old Town and dedicating it in her memory in April 1882, one year to the day of her death. In 1889, the Fannie C. Paddock Memorial Hospital relocated to the Wright Park neighborhood, having outgrown its original building. (Above courtesy MHS.)

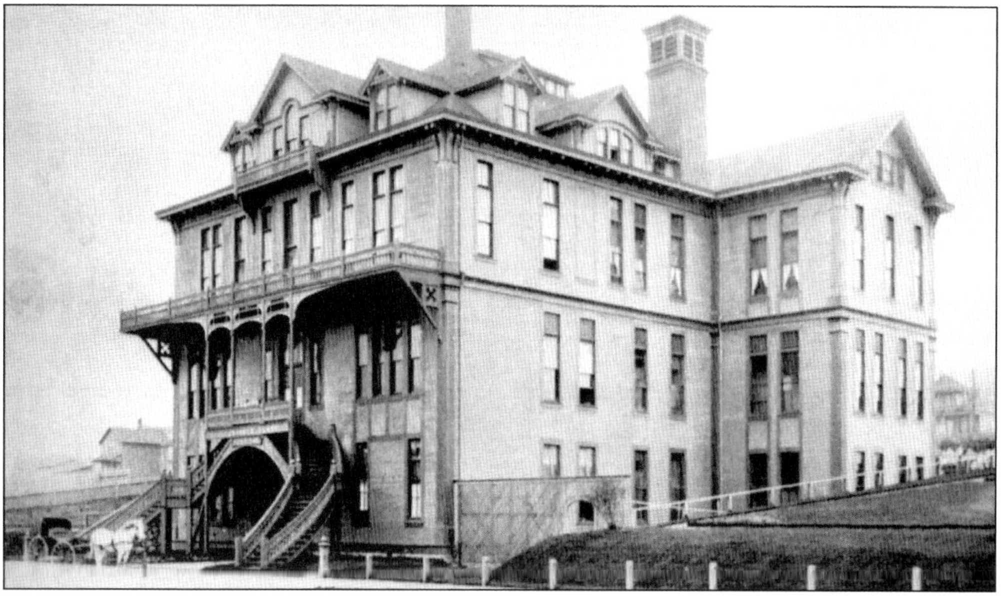

The new home of the Fannie C. Paddock Memorial Hospital faced South J Street between South Third and South Fourth Streets; once again, Charles Wright encouraged the donation of the property by the Tacoma Land Company. The hospital's main entrance, shown from both sides, looked down the hill one block onto Wright Park. As advertised in the 1890 city directory, the "new and commodious building (above)," completed in November 1889 at a cost of $35,000, housed 100 patients in its four stories. Though the main entrance fronted South J Street, early accounts of the hospital record that most people used the rear South K Street door to reach the wards on the upper floors more directly. By 1890, Tacoma boasted a population of some 36,000 residents; the biggest public health problem was typhoid. The postcard below depicts the hospital in 1904. (Both courtesy MHS.)

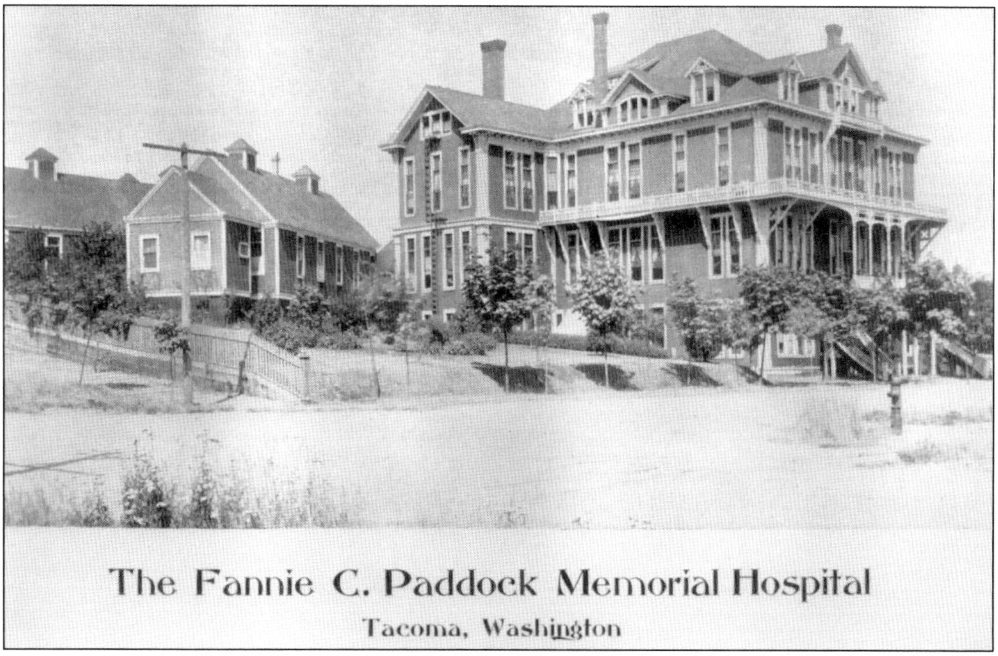

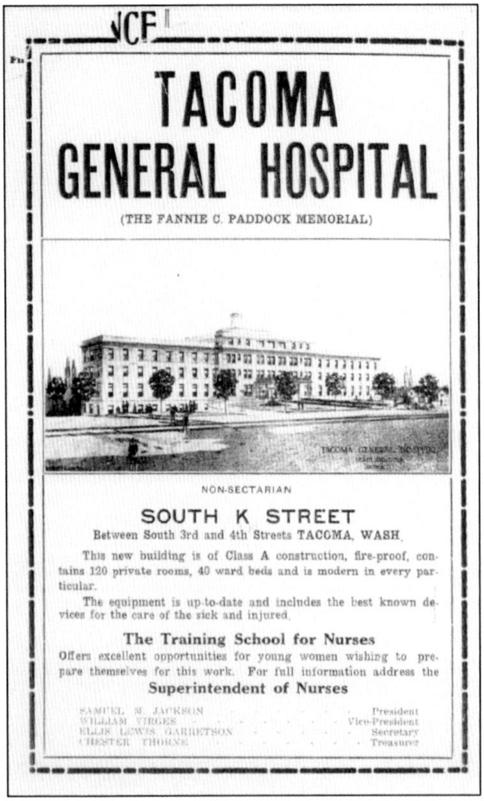

The Fannie C. Paddock Memorial Hospital became Tacoma General Hospital in 1915, and this brick and concrete building replaced its wood-framed predecessor at the same location. The formal entrance to the new building now faced South K Street, facilitated by the streetcar line whose tracks had been laid on the thoroughfare in 1895.

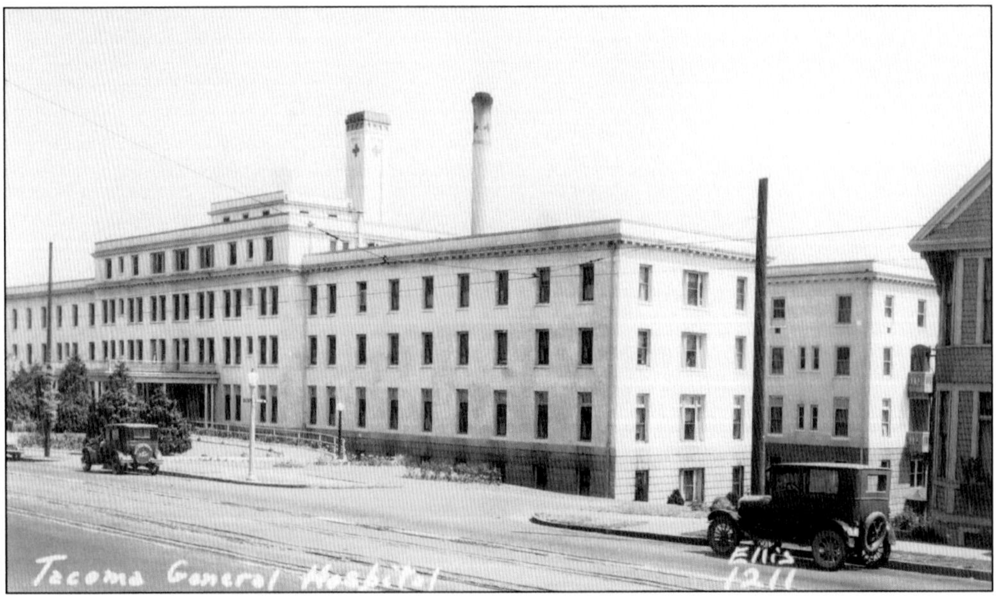

This 1920s view of Tacoma General Hospital depicts the edifice from the South K Street entrance side, at the intersection with South Fourth Street. This building was used in its entirety until the early 1980s; portions of the building still exist, offering office and classroom space. The intersection is now covered by today's main entrance doors to Tacoma General Hospital and Mary Bridge Children's Hospital. (Courtesy TS.)

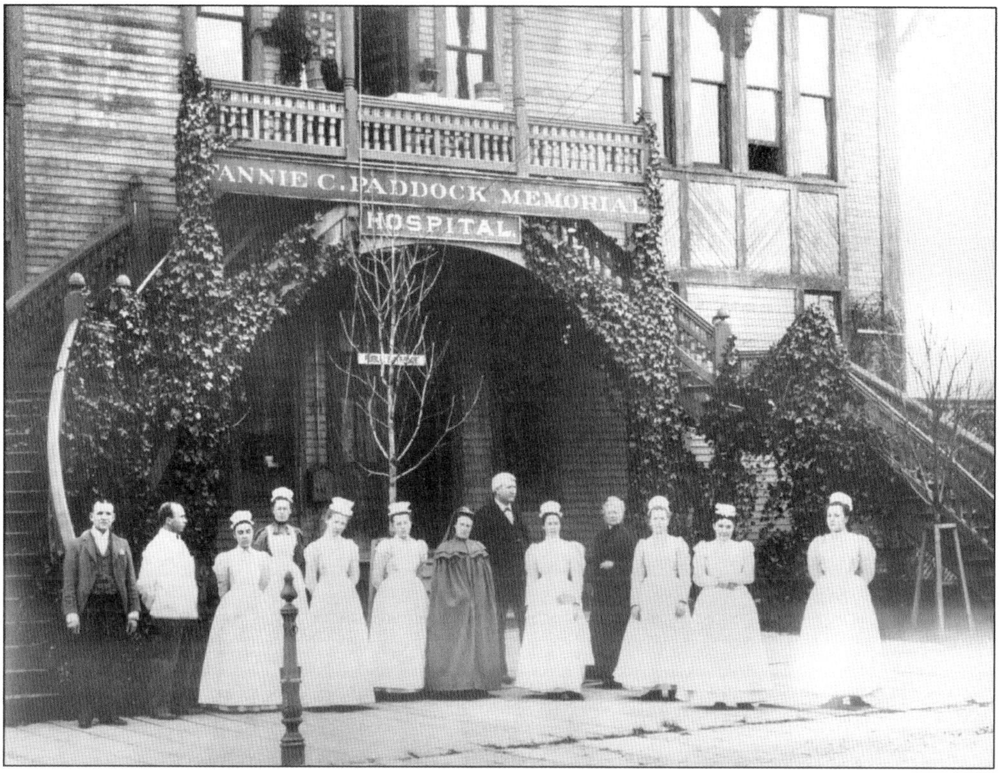

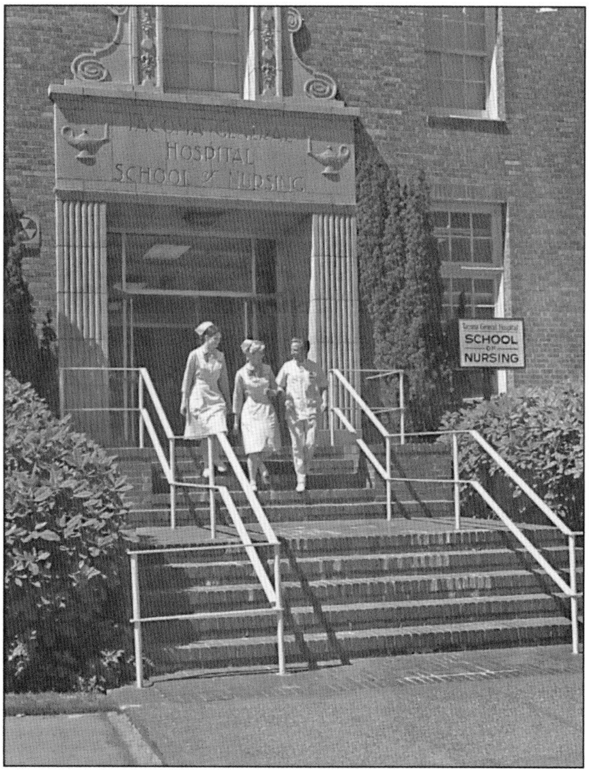

The Fannie C. Paddock Memorial Hospital School of Nursing began in the mid-1890s and evolved into the Tacoma General Hospital School of Nursing, which graduated its last class in 1980. Above, graduates of the first class pose outside the sweeping double-stairway entrance on South J Street. Fannie C. Paddock Memorial Hospital superintendent Dr. Charles McCutcheon stands at the middle of this grouping of graduate nurses. Second from the left is George Smith, who had been a patient in the very first Old Town location of the institution. Smith was the first formally trained male nurse in the new state of Washington. In the late-1960s image at right, unidentified nurses leave Jackson Hall, home of the School of Nursing since the late 1940s. (Both courtesy MHS.)

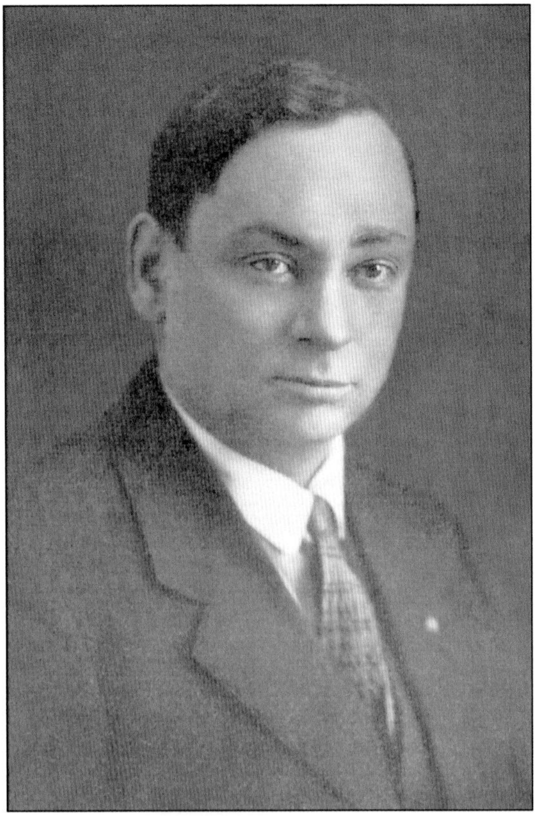

Dr. Albert W. Bridge (1879–1947) was a local physician who left money to the Tacoma Orthopedic Association for the creation of a local children's hospital. Gertrude Baker had established the association in 1921 for pediatric care purposes; Dr. Bridge's bequest made the hospital a reality. His donation stipulated that the hospital bear the name of his mother, Mary, who had worked so hard to help him become a doctor. (Courtesy MHS.)

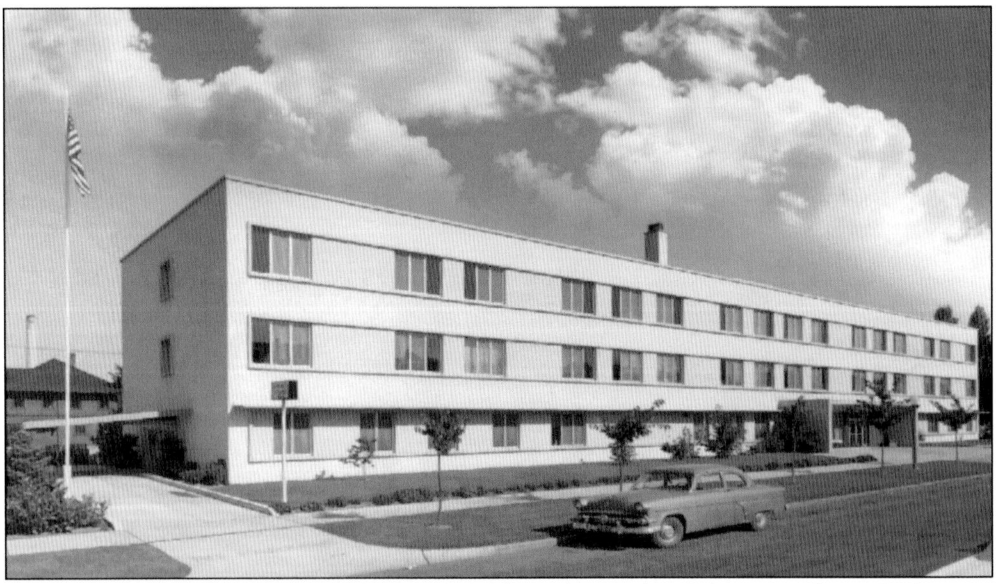

Construction began on the 40-bed general children's hospital in February 1954, and television host Ed Sullivan laid the cornerstone in May of that year. Mary Bridge Children's Hospital opened at South Third and South L Streets in 1955, geographically expanding the health-care district adjacent to Wright Park, as well as the scope of medical services concentrated in the immediate neighborhood. (Courtesy MHS.)

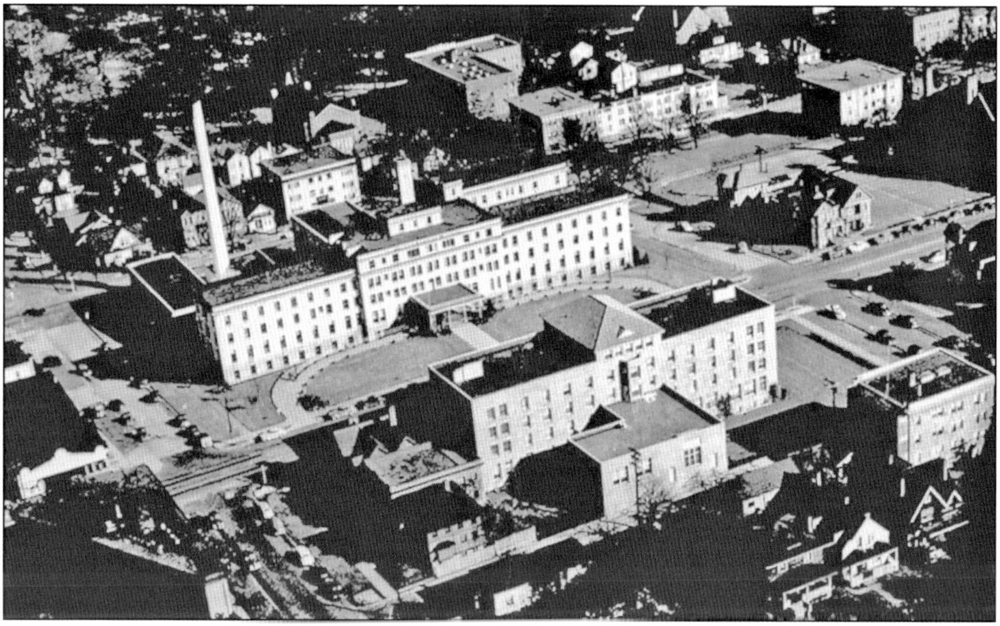

Aerial images document the evolving presence of the MultiCare Health System campus adjacent to Wright Park, visible in the upper portion of these views. At the time of the 1947 image above, the Tacoma General Hospital School of Nursing had just moved into Jackson Hall, directly across from the hospital building. The 2005 photograph below documents the expansion over the previous 60 years. In 1979, Tacoma General Hospital merged with Mary Bridge Children's Hospital to form a new health-care corporation that eventually became MultiCare. The core sections of the Tacoma General and Mary Bridge buildings are still visible, even with the considerable expansion of both by 2005. Fannie Chester Paddock would be astounded at both the significance and scope of her realized hopes for a hospital, and its vitality in the greater Wright Park neighborhood. (Both courtesy MHS.)

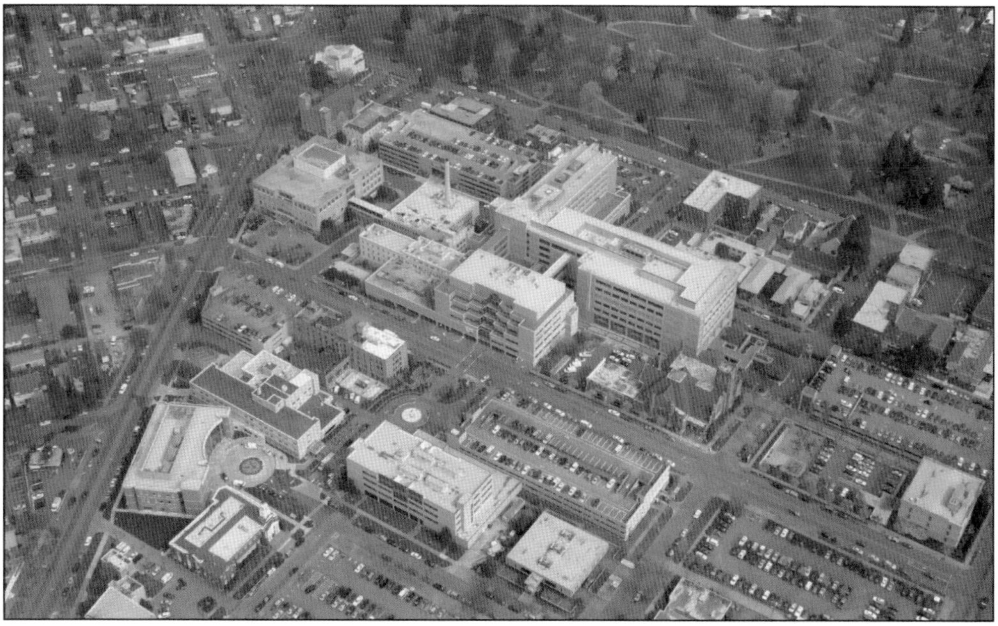

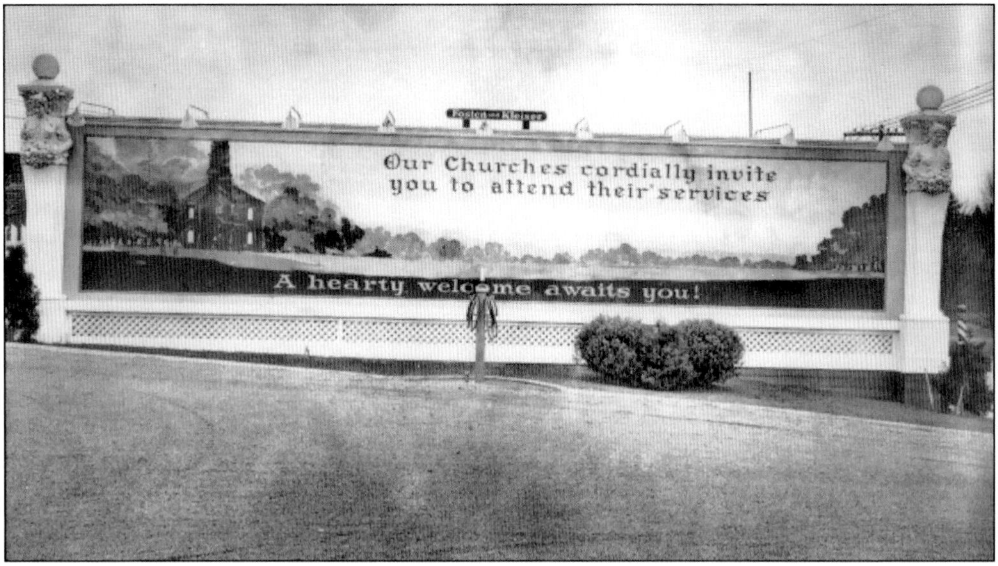

Religious institutions resided in Tacoma since Old Town's origins in the late 1860s, when many houses of worship were simple frame structures. As congregations grew and prospered with the fortunes of Tacoma's boom times, several moved from their previous humble locales and established impressive architectural edifices near Wright Park. An ecumenical billboard on Division Avenue welcomed churchgoers to the neighborhood in the 1920s. (Courtesy TPL.)

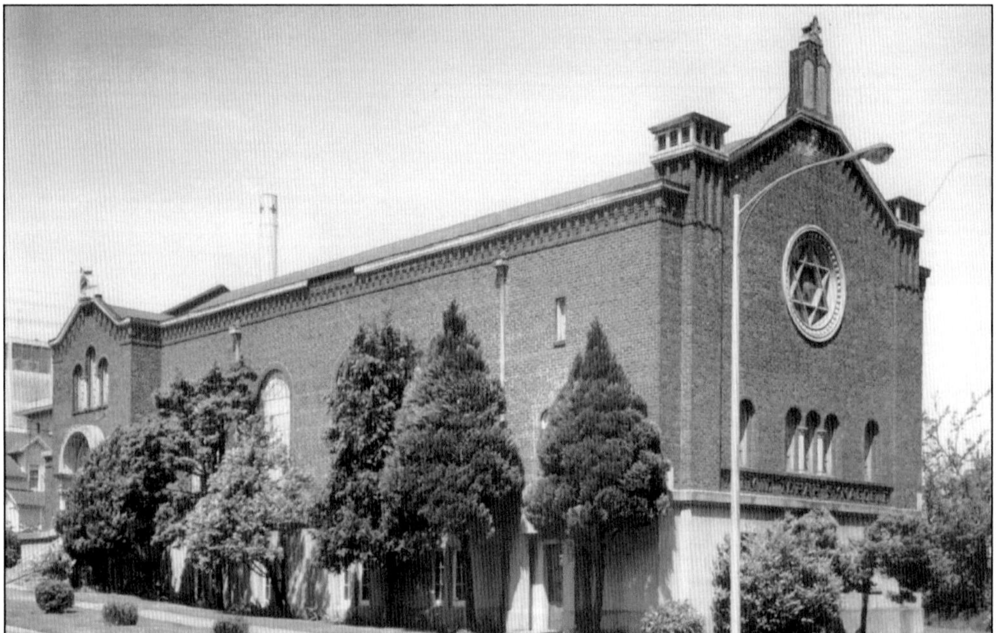

In 1925, one of Tacoma's early Jewish communities built the Orthodox synagogue Temple Talmud Torah at the corner of South Fourth and South I Streets, directly across from Wright Park. The structure is visible in the 1947 aerial view on the previous page, taken the year it was renamed Sinai Temple. Behind and up the hill from the synagogue is the stack from the steam power plant of Tacoma General Hospital. (Courtesy TPL.)

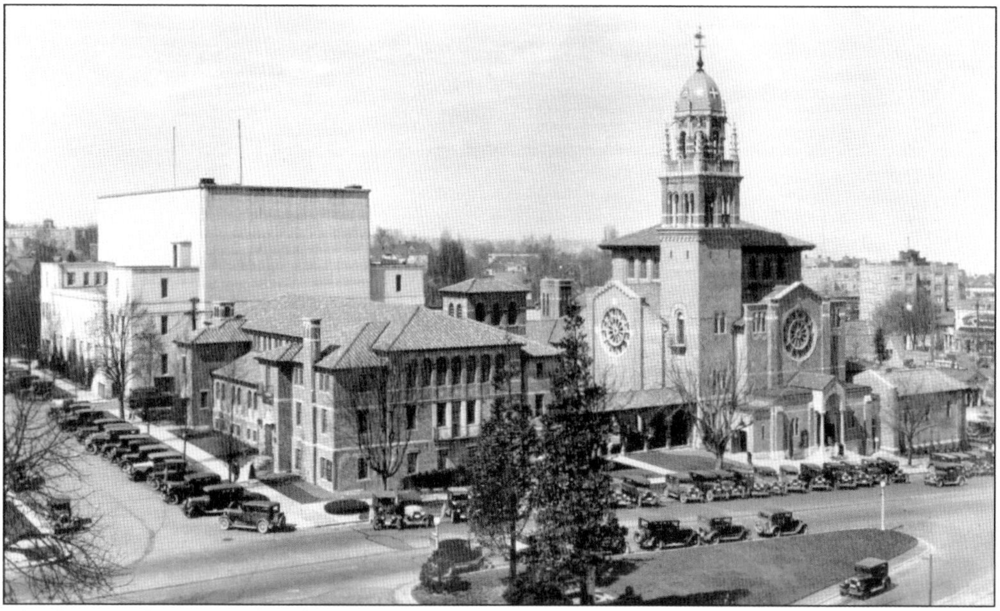

The First Presbyterian Church congregation moved to the Wright Park environs from its original downtown location, where the County-City Building currently stands, and built this impressive complex in 1925. While the church does not face Wright Park itself, it is the neighborhood's biggest ecclesiastical presence. The large white structure is the back side of the present Tacoma Bible Presbyterian Church. (Courtesy TS.)

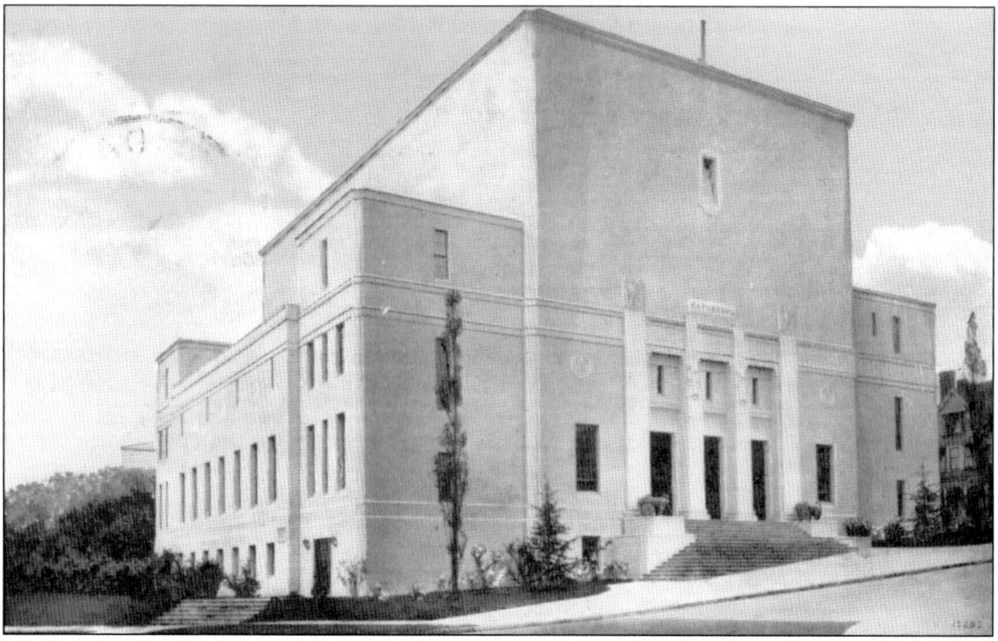

This postcard view depicts the front side of the same structure, from the corner it shared with Wright Park, about 1923. At that time, it was the newly built Scottish Rite Masonic Temple, which was styled in "the ancient architecture of King Solomon," according to its dedicatory program. In 1937, the building changed hands when it was purchased by part of the First Presbyterian Church congregation that had split from the main congregation two years earlier. (Courtesy TS.)

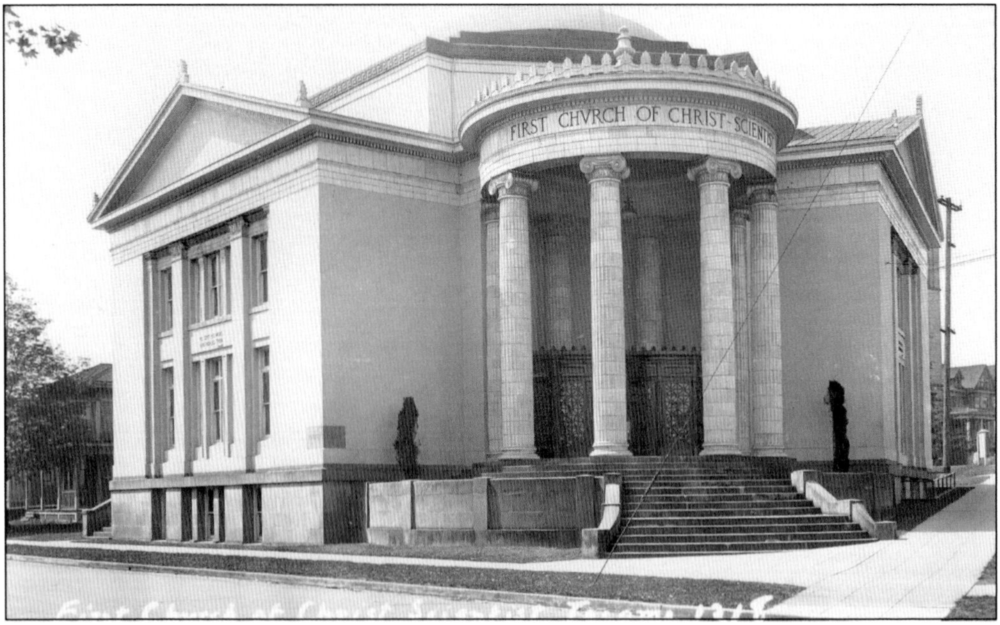

Built in the Greek Ionic style on the prominent corner of Division Avenue and South I Street in 1911, the First Church of Christ Scientist was one of many Tacoma churches designed by the prolific local architect Frederick Heath. Tacoma owes many of its iconic buildings to Heath's talents, perhaps most notably the transformation of an ill-fated railroad hotel into Stadium High School in 1906. (Courtesy TS.)

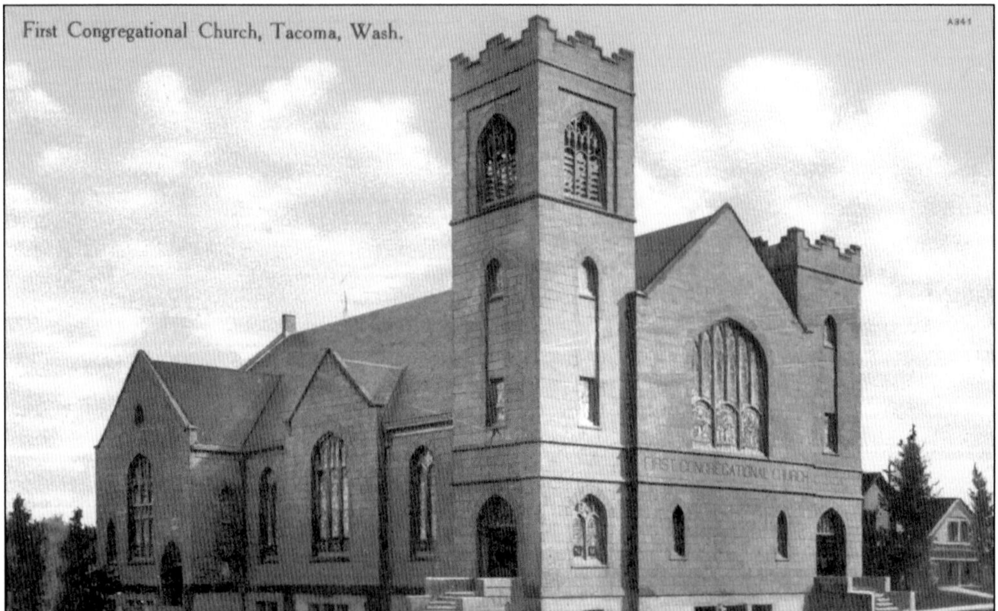

The First Congregational Church has a long history in Tacoma, dating back to tent meetings of a small group of worshippers in Old Town in 1873. This view of the church, situated on the corner of Division Avenue and South J Street, dates from soon after its dedication in 1909 but before construction of the adjacent school building. (Courtesy TS.)

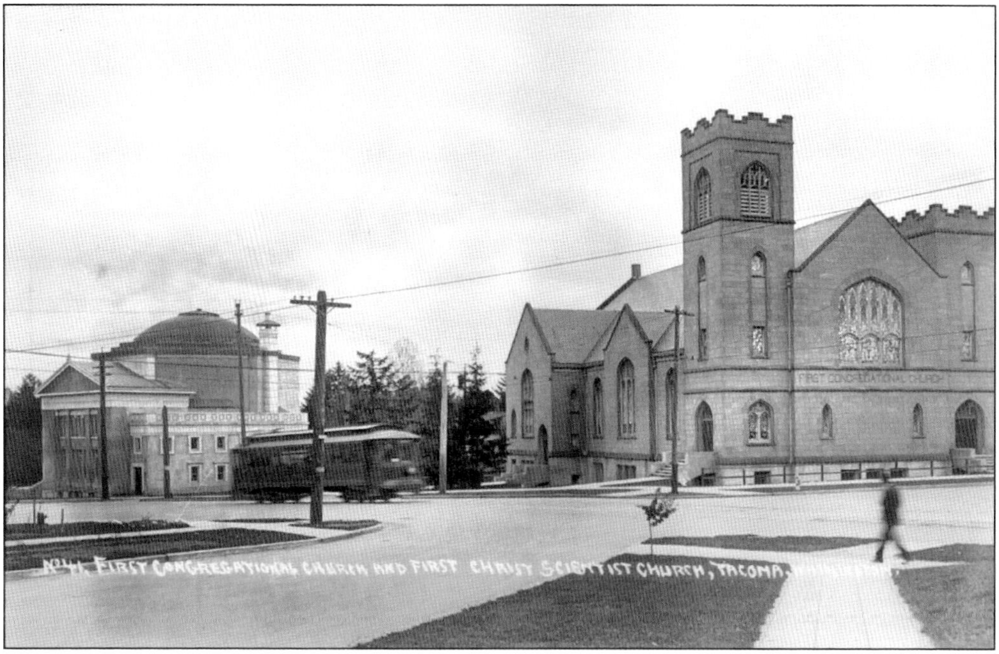

This interesting postcard illustrates the dual presence of the First Church of Christ Scientist and the First Congregational Church in the Wright Park neighborhood about 1915; the trees in between the buildings are located across South I Street in the park. A streetcar and a pedestrian are captured in motion—they are both long past, but the churches remain. (Courtesy TS.)

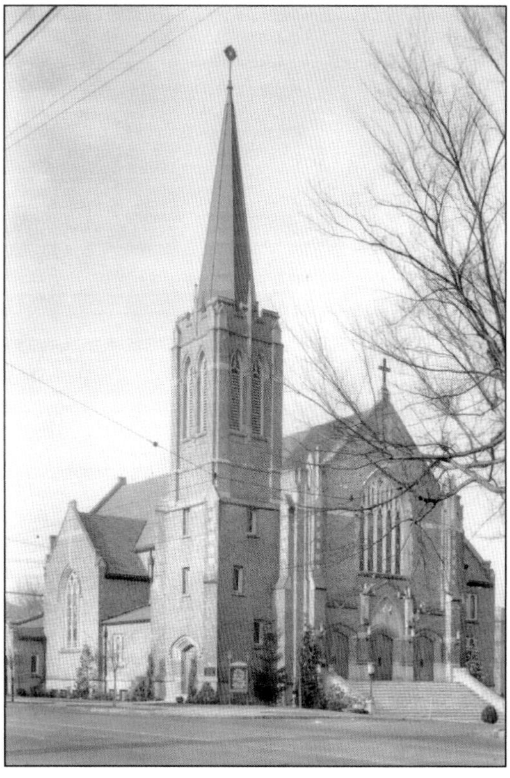

Another ecclesiastical edifice from Tacoma architect Frederick Heath, the First Evangelical Lutheran Church, was built at the other end of Wright Park, on the corner of South I Street and Sixth Avenue. The congregation traces its origins to 1882, when a small community of immigrants formed the Swedish Evangelical Lutheran Church of Tacoma. The church, pictured about 1932, was under construction from 1925 to 1929. (Courtesy TPL.)

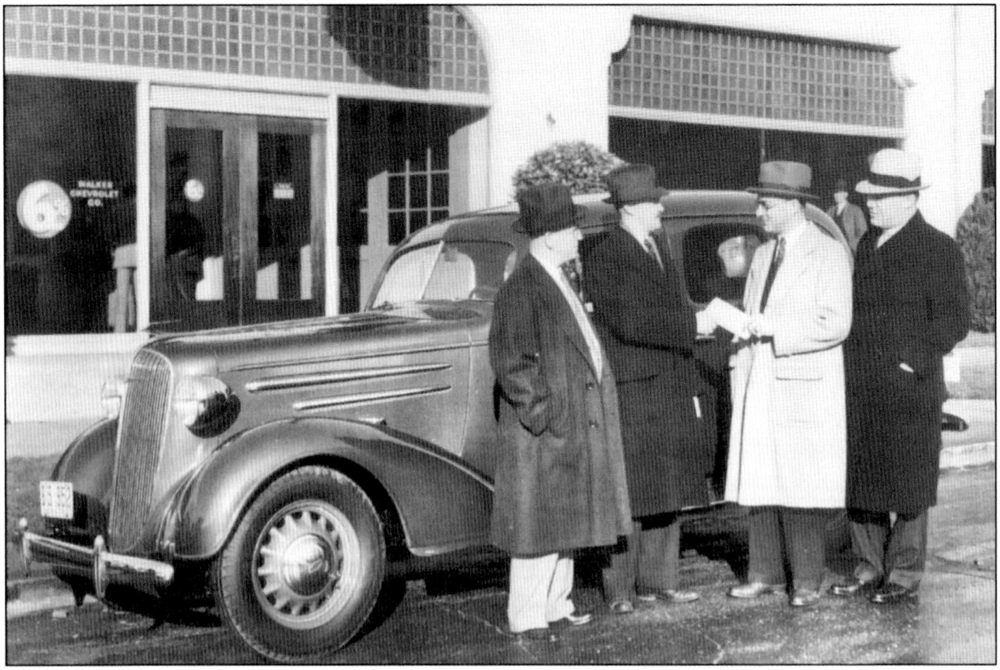

Hospitals and houses of worship were not the only neighbors of Wright Park. The Division Avenue and Sixth Avenue ends of the acreage comprise only a few short blocks, but these two ends of the park have hosted most of the adjacent commercial enterprises. Along Division Avenue, commercial space developed early in the 1890s with small markets and grocers. Two of the longest-lived types of business fronting Wright Park are shown here. The Walker Chevrolet Company, seen above, opened in 1933 at the structure built in 1925 for the Allen Motor Company on the large triangular lot where the Annie Wright Seminary originally stood. Lee's Shell Oil filling station, pictured below in 1950, stood on the corner of North Yakima and Division Avenues. A Shell service station has operated on this corner for almost 80 years. (Both courtesy TPL.)

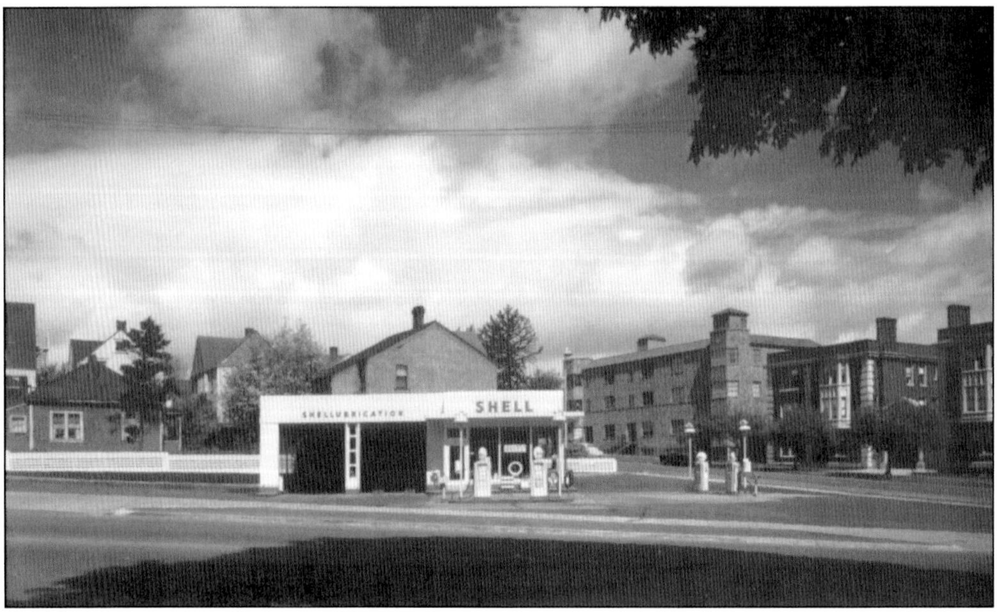

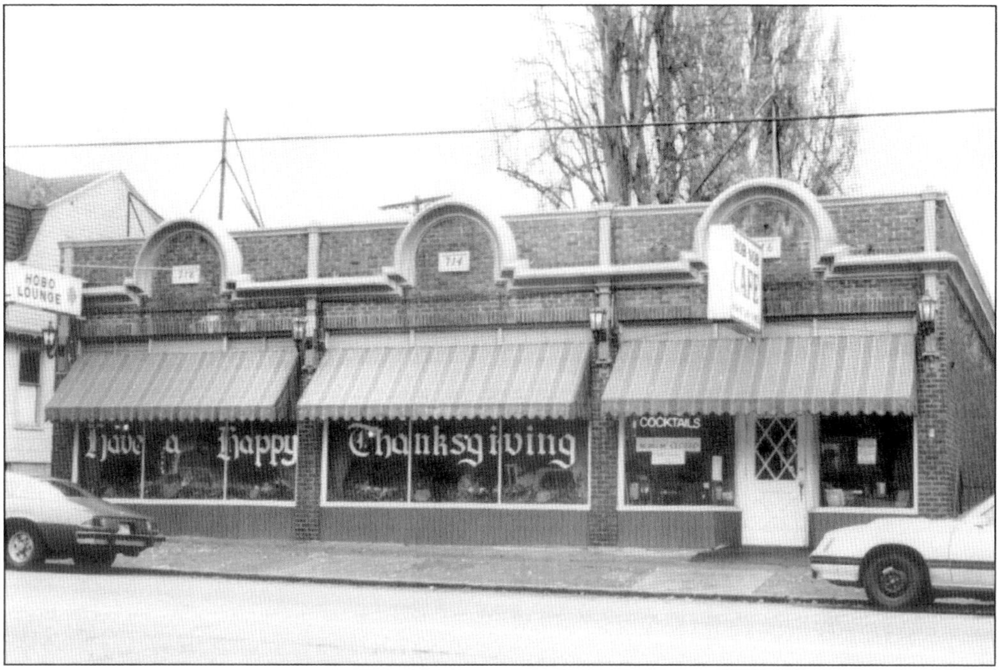

Along the Sixth Avenue end of Wright Park, development in the years surrounding 1900 was largely residential; Division Avenue tended to be the more mercantile location at this time. Dating from the 1920s, these photographs show Sixth Avenue landmarks of note, specifically in the 700 block. William Virges—president of the Pacific Brewing and Malting Company, the National Coconut Butter Company, and the National Soap Company and owner of downtown drugstores on Pacific Avenue and Broadway—built a small brick commercial building (above) and an architecturally matching residential block called the Virges Apartments (below) in 1925. Since before World War II, the small commercial space has been home to the Hob Nob Café, a neighborhood institution appreciative of its ties to the history of Wright Park. (Both courtesy TPL.)

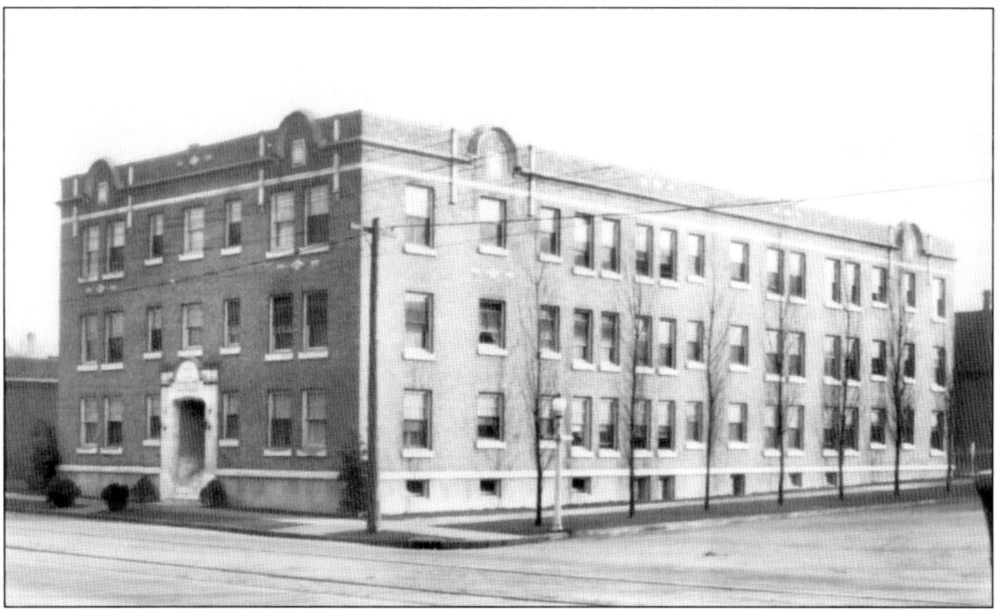

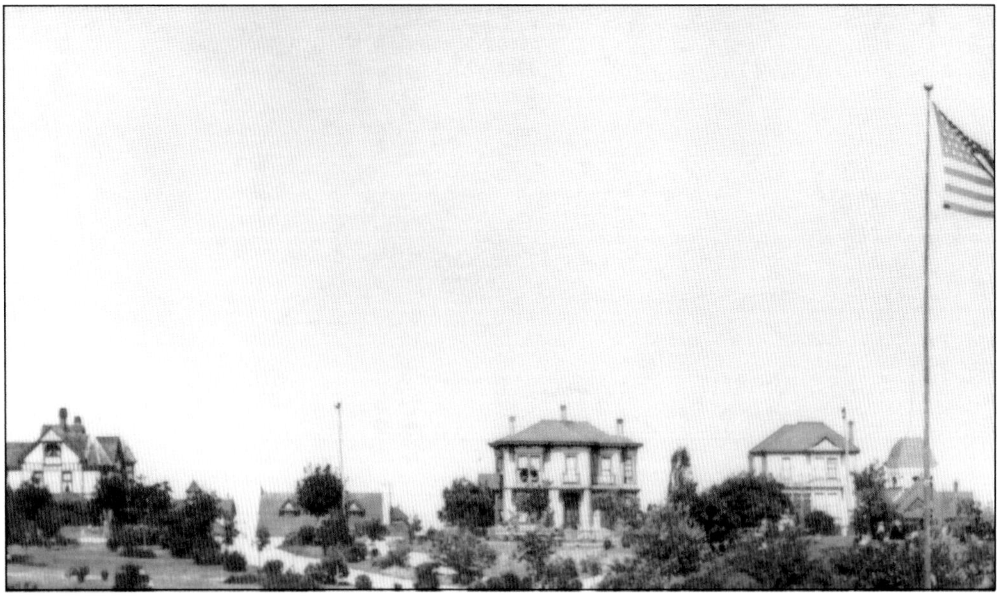

This enlargement of the top photograph on page 26 provides a close-up view of some of the homes built on South G Street and overlooking Wright Park in the period from 1888 to 1906, particularly those in the 200 block, closest to the flagpole. Most of these grand residences have been long demolished, having made way for newer apartment dwellings and in some cases, sadly, parking lots. (Courtesy WSHS.)

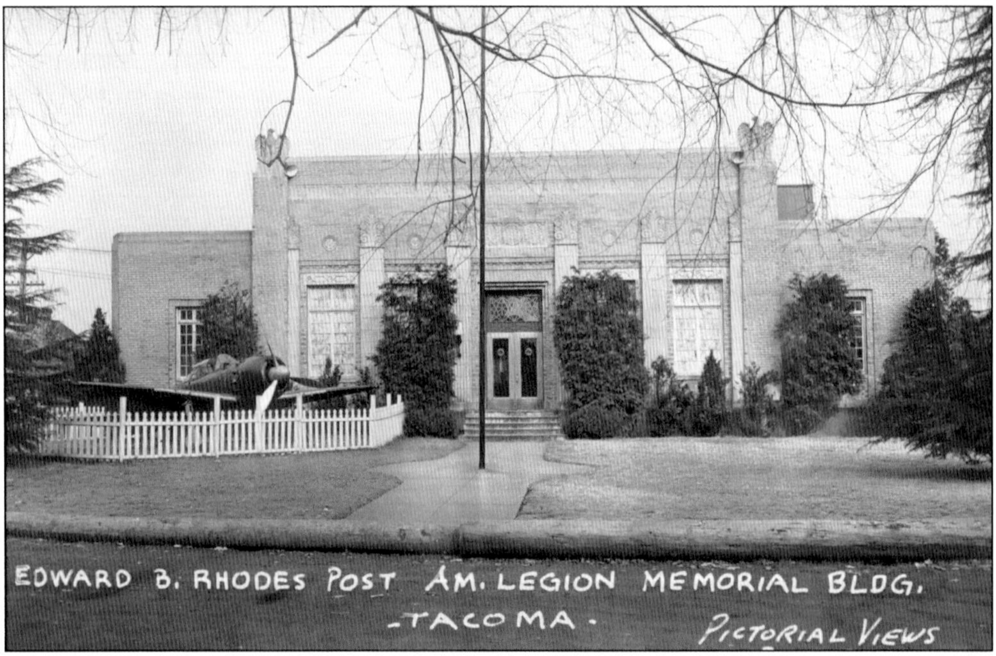

One such demolished property, at 407 South G Street, was the 1888 home of George Browne, the park commissioner who helped secure the original trees for planting in Wright Park, a de facto extension of his front yard. Replacing it in 1931, above, was the stately Edward B. Rhodes American Legion Memorial Building, named for a native son of Tacoma's Rhodes Brothers department store renown who perished while fighting in France in 1918. (Courtesy TS.)

Three

Statues, Monuments, and a Tree Stump

Even as Tacoma was rushing to meet the original landscaping conditions of the Wright Park donation, Clinton P. Ferry and S. A. Wheelwright sent a letter to the board overseeing park matters on August 4, 1890, suggesting that the design for the new park include statuary to improve its overall look. While traveling in Europe, Ferry developed an appreciation for art's educational and inspirational values. He was convinced that Tacoma needed to emulate European traditions of public art. Ferry did more than make recommendations. The following year, 1891, the *Tacoma Daily Ledger* reported that nine pieces of statuary purchased by Ferry had arrived. Later reports note that some of the statues were damaged en route, including copies of Antonio Canova's dancing maidens. Fortunately, local workmen were able to repair the maidens; however, others must not have been repairable, as records note only six statues being installed in Wright Park at this time.

Ferry's statues were the first decorative elements in Wright Park. In the ensuing years, other statues, monuments, and plaques were placed in the park to honor significant historical events, prominent individuals, unique natural features, or simply to add aesthetic value. Many of those features still stand while others have fallen victim to the ravages of time, poor construction, or vandalism. Others, such as a planned statue of Charles Wright, were never undertaken. Nor was park superintendent Ebenezer Roberts's planned Court of Honor ever realized. Once the conservatory was completed, Roberts hoped to move the two maidens from Division Avenue and place them on either side of the entrance to the conservatory. They were to be joined by statues of prominent Americans and a sundial.

Over time, the statues have become iconic features in Tacoma's landscape. Since the park's beginning, people have posed next to the monuments, and artists have rendered beautiful images of Wright Park's statuary.

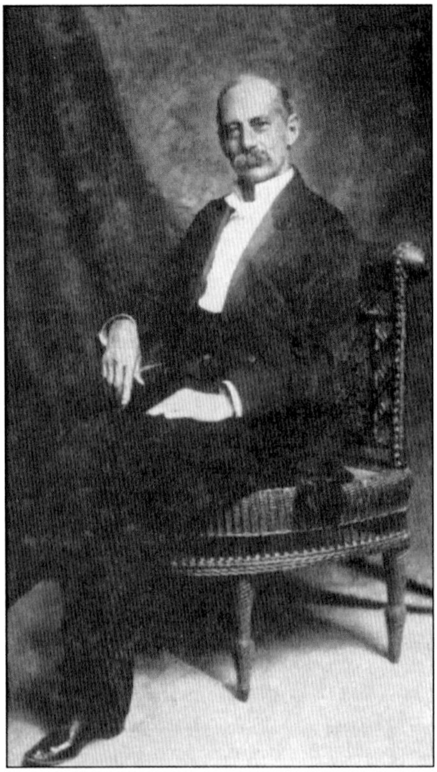

Early Tacoma entrepreneur Clinton P. Ferry (1833–1909) traveled to Paris with his new, young wife, Cynthia, in 1889 as the U.S. commissioner to the Paris Exposition. While in Europe, the couple purchased copies of several well-known works of art. When it was time to return to Tacoma, Cynthia chose to stay behind, and Ferry donated several of the pieces to the city for placement in Wright Park.

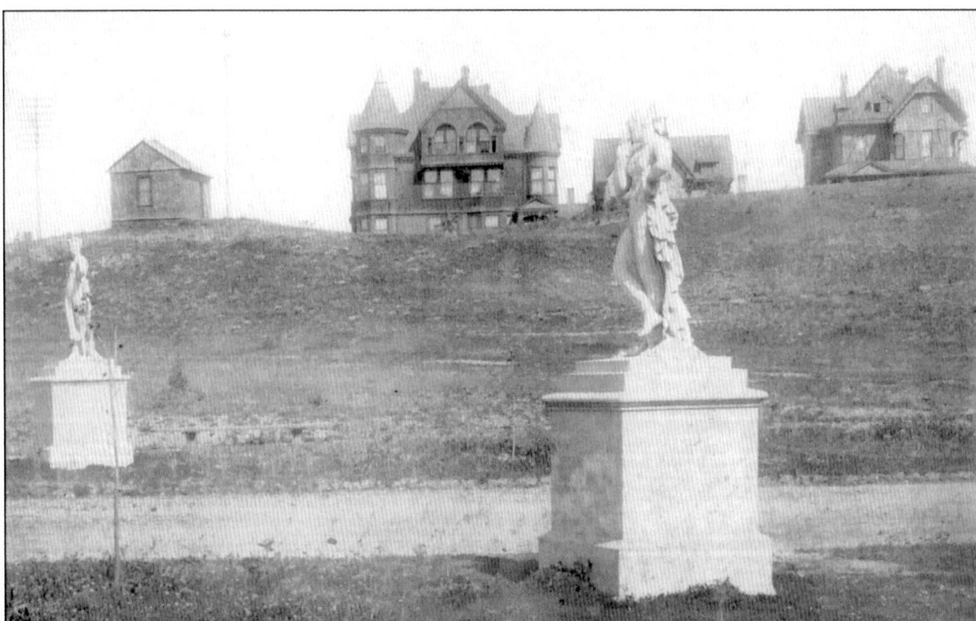

Before landscaping began, the six statues donated by Ferry were the only landmarks in Wright Park. Copies of two dancing girls by Antonio Canova were in place at the Division Avenue entrance to the park by 1892. Before long, they received the nicknames of "Annie" and "Fannie"—one for the daughter of Charles Wright, and the other for the nearby hospital's namesake. (Courtesy TPL.)

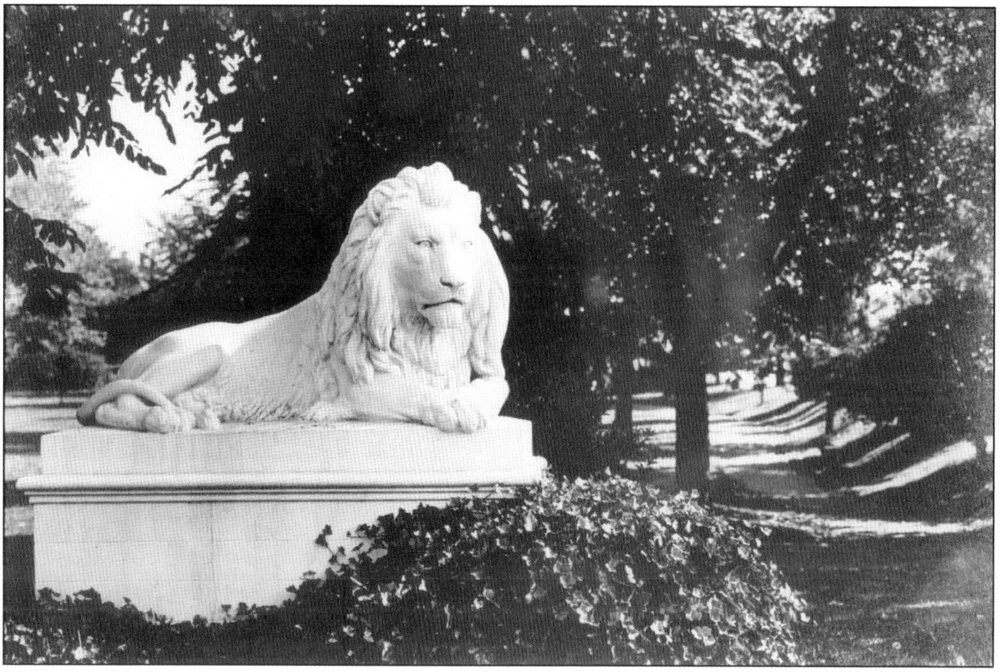

This stern-looking lion is one of two that guard the Sixth Avenue entrance to Wright Park. Early references to the lions called them copies of the famous Brussels Lions. As with the other statues donated by Clinton Ferry, the lions are made of a sandstone concrete composite and created from molds of original European artwork. (Courtesy UW.)

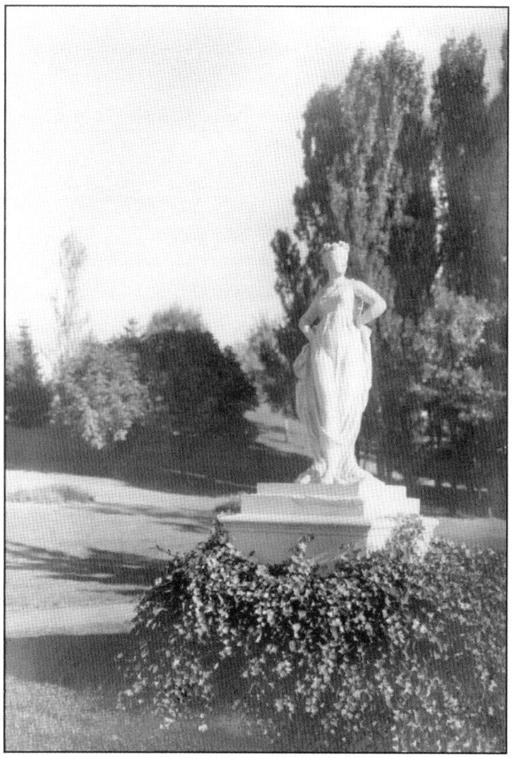

One of the two maidens who welcome visitors at the Division Avenue entrance to Wright Park is a copy of *Dancing Girl with Hands on Her Hips* by Antonio Canova. Even though the maidens are most often referred to as Annie and Fannie, apparently they have gone by other names. A 1933 newspaper article called them Pansy and Violet when a student prank resulted in Pansy wearing someone's pants. (Courtesy WSHS.)

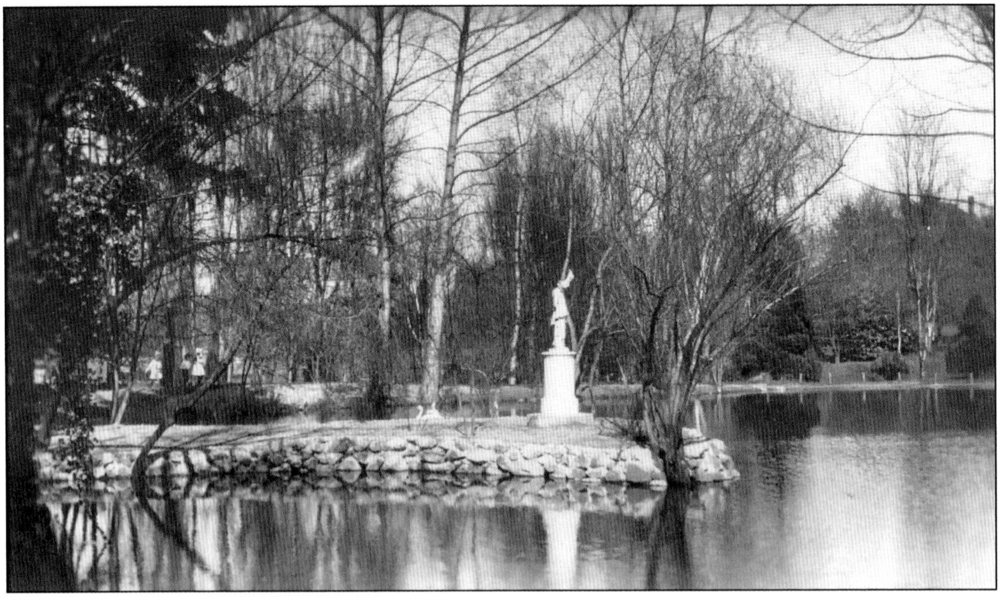

In early photographs of the Wright Park lake, this small maiden stands upon a peninsula jutting out into the pond. She holds a fish aloft in her outstretched right arm. One early photograph in the collection of the Washington State History Museum has a handwritten notation calling her the *Fisherman's Daughter.* (Courtesy WSHS.)

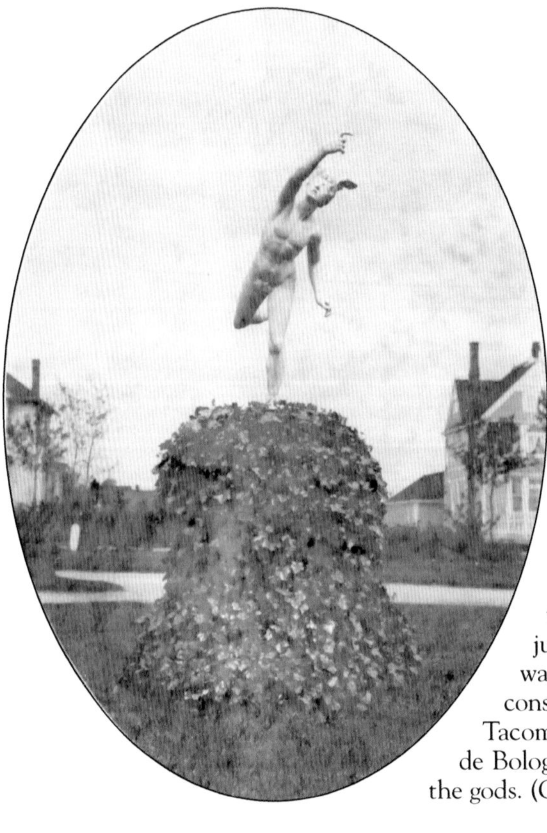

Of the six original Ferry statues, *Winged Mercury* is the only one not in existence today. Initially placed on the knoll near the junction of G and Fourth Streets, the statue was likely removed when construction on the conservatory began in 1908. Its fate is not known. Tacoma's statue was a copy of a work by Giovanni de Bologna. Mercury was the Greek messenger for the gods. (Courtesy WSHS.)

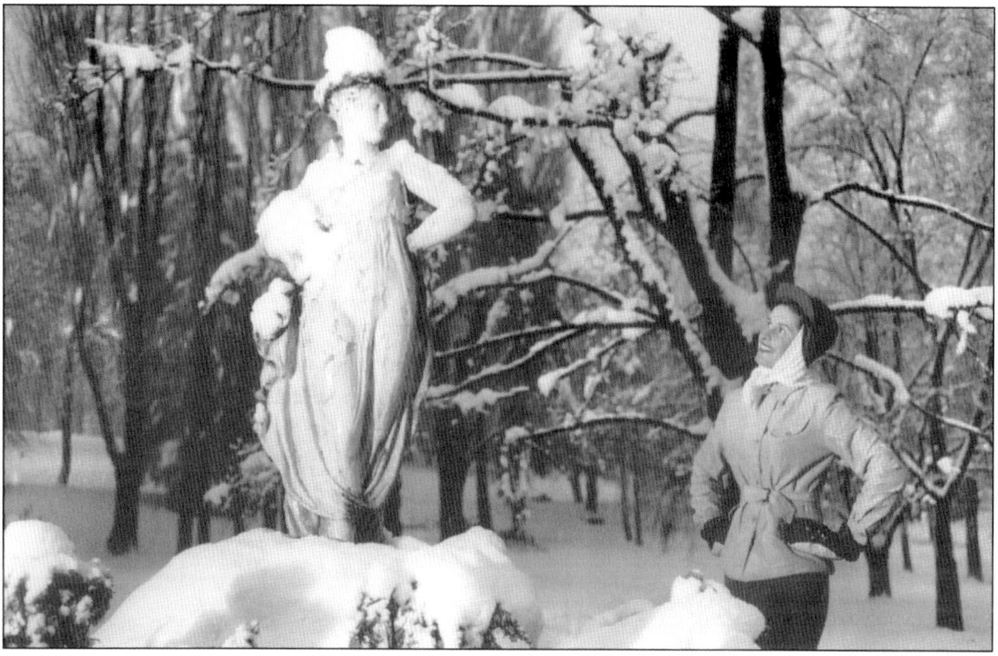

Both Annie and Fannie have long been favorites of photographers. Here Barbara Horjes imitates the saucy hands-on-hips pose during an unusual snowstorm in 1946. Snow totaled over 18 inches after a three-day storm hit Tacoma in November 1946. Besides playing in the snow and sledding down the hills, many people spent hours skating on the Wright Park pond. (Courtesy TPL.)

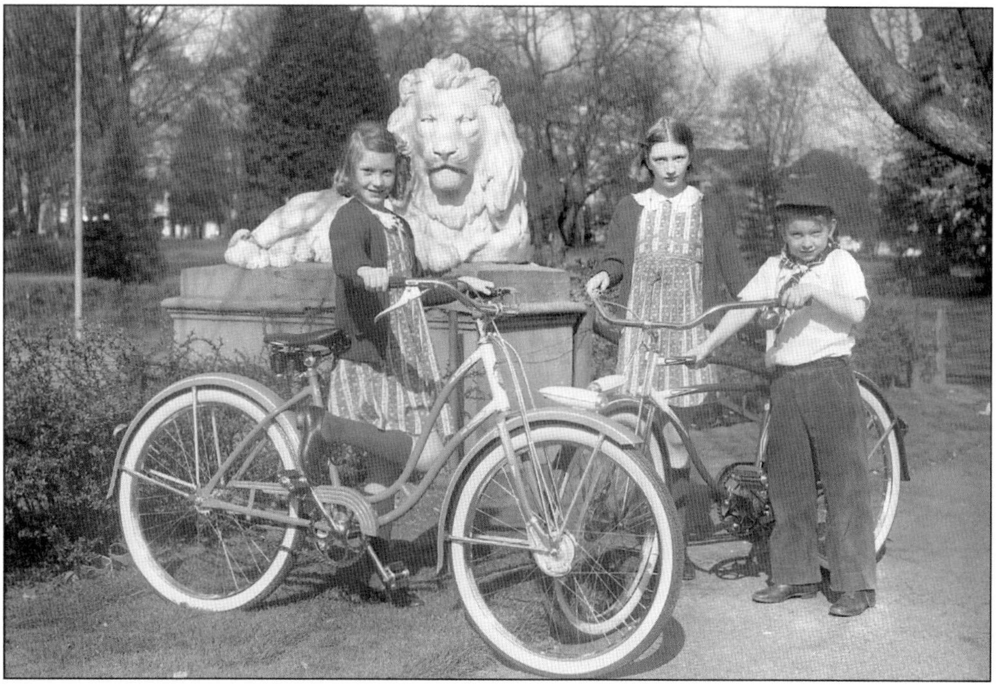

The Sixth Avenue lions also show up in many promotional photographs over the years. Bettegene Terry (left), Mary Cathern Terry (center), and Chuck Grisell pose on April 8, 1940, with bikes to be given away as top prizes in the *Tacoma Times*/Borden's Elsie cartoon contest. (Courtesy TPL.)

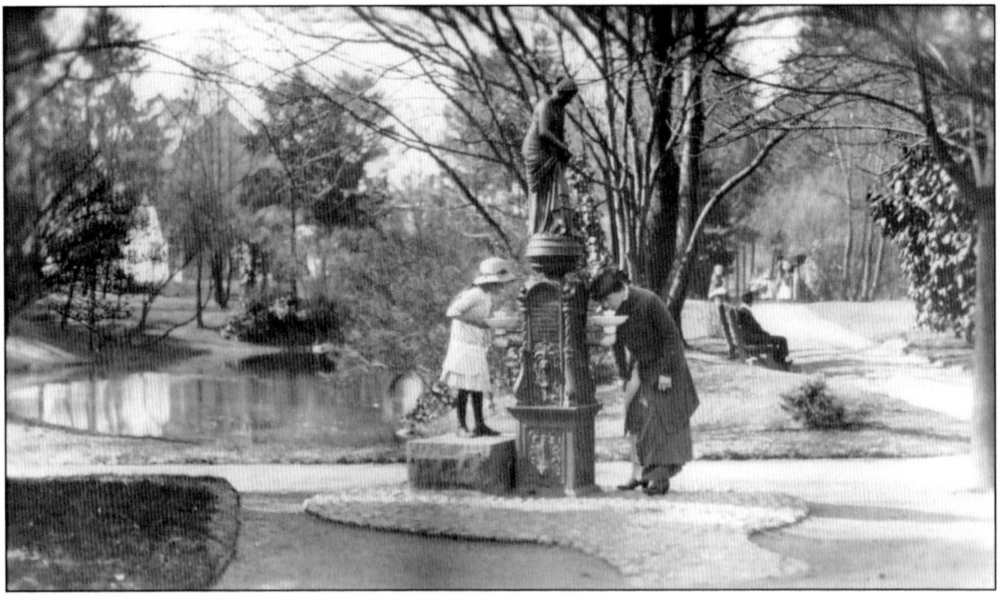

In 1899, the schoolchildren of Tacoma, the Sons and Daughters of the American Revolution, and the park commissioners raised money to erect a memorial fountain honoring pioneer Narcissa Whitman. The bronzed iron drinking fountain was manufactured in New York at a cost of $400. Above, a young girl takes advantage of a large stepping stone to reach one of the fountains. The maiden portrayed in the statue holds a water jug on her hip. The peaceful winter scene below does not portend the statue's future. In the early 1970s, vandals destroyed the statue. The fountain was dismantled and placed in storage to await restoration. (Above courtesy WSHS; below courtesy TPL.)

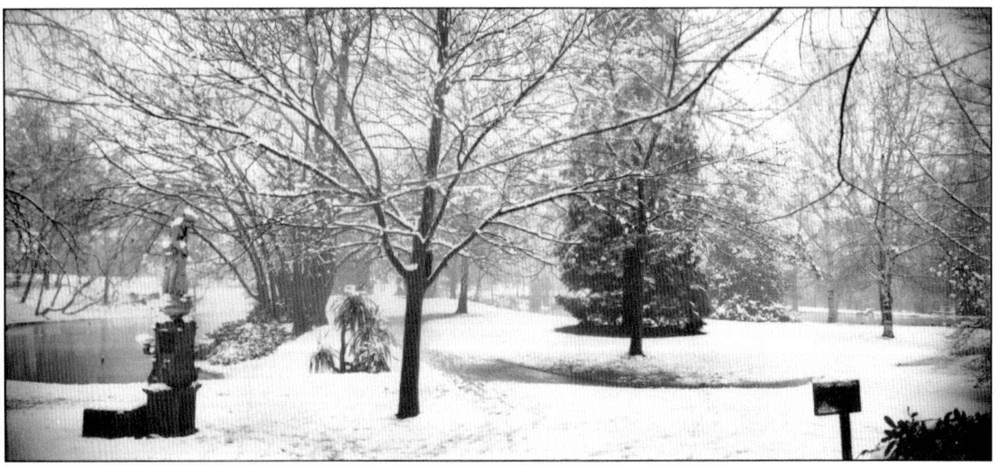

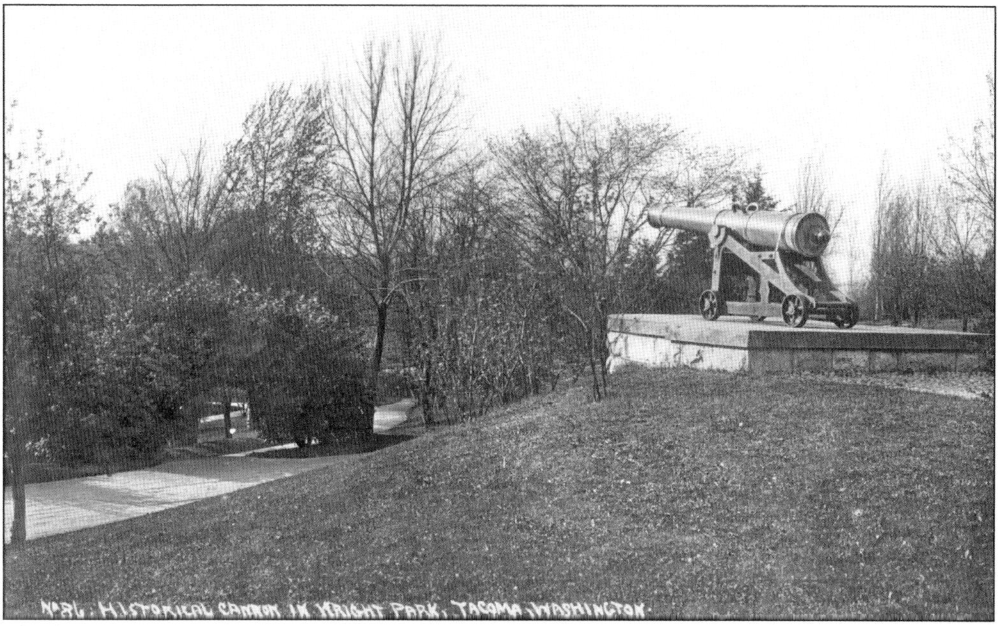

This bronze cannon was captured at Morro Castle in Havana, Cuba, during the Spanish American War. As a prize of that conflict, Sen. Addison Foster secured it for the city of Tacoma. The cannon's dedication was part of a three-day Fourth of July celebration in 1900. Originally placed near the bluff where the conservatory now stands, it was relocated closer to Sixth Avenue after 1907. (Courtesy TS.)

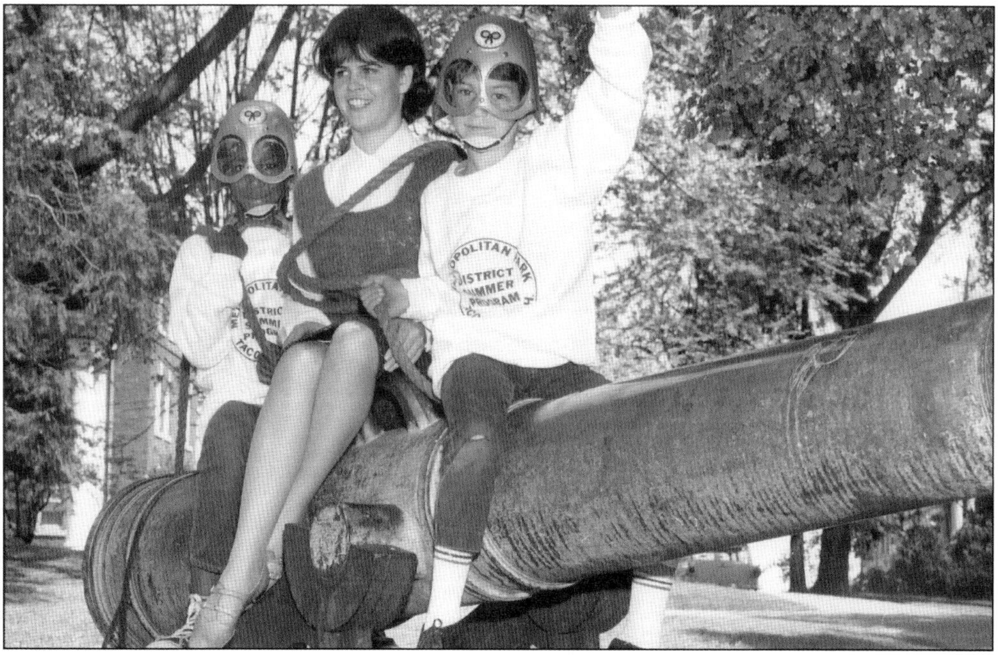

As their imaginations run wild, these young boys participating in a park district summer program may not be aware of the history behind Tacoma's Spanish cannon. The cannon is made of bronze and weighs 4,500 pounds. The engraving on the base ring reads, "No. 1,362 Sevilla, 23 de Julio de 1784."

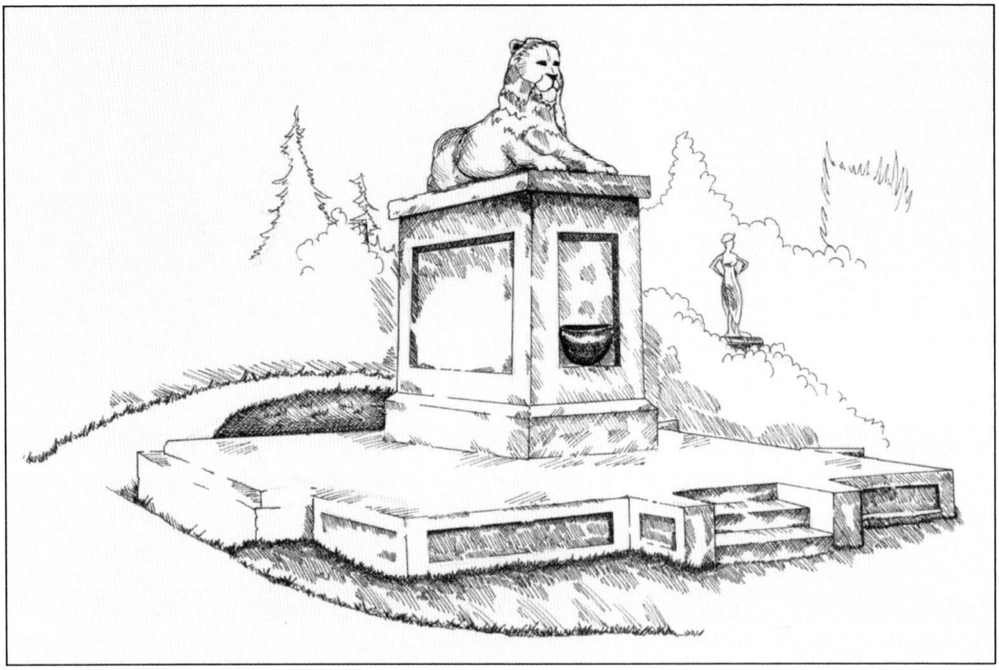

On May 23, 1908, the *Tacoma Daily News* reported that two sphinxes had been unveiled at the Division Avenue entrance to Wright Park, as depicted in the artist's rendering above. The statues were gifts from E. J. Bowes of the Narrows Land Company. Each sphinx was 5 feet high and 10 feet long, resting on a base 12 feet high on a concrete platform 22 feet square. In order to accommodate the new sculptures, the two maiden statues were moved farther back in the park, as shown below. Supt. Ebenezer Roberts planned to move the maidens to either side of the conservatory entrance once it was completed. That did not occur. Even though the sphinxes were to be made of a material harder than concrete, something went terribly wrong. They began to melt after the first rain, and by March 1909, their remains had been removed from the park. (Above courtesy Mike McGuire; below courtesy UW.)

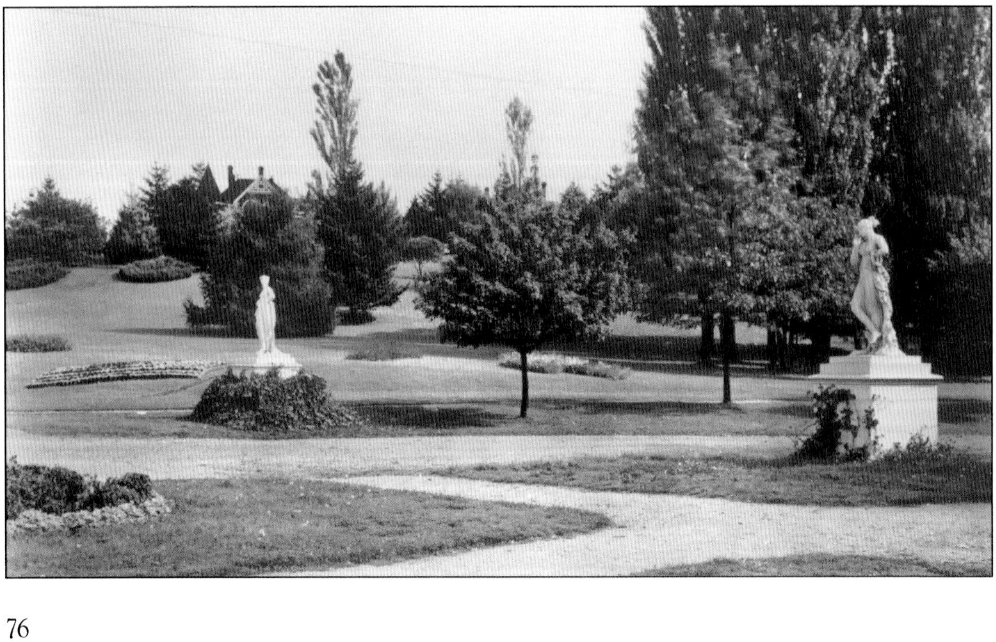

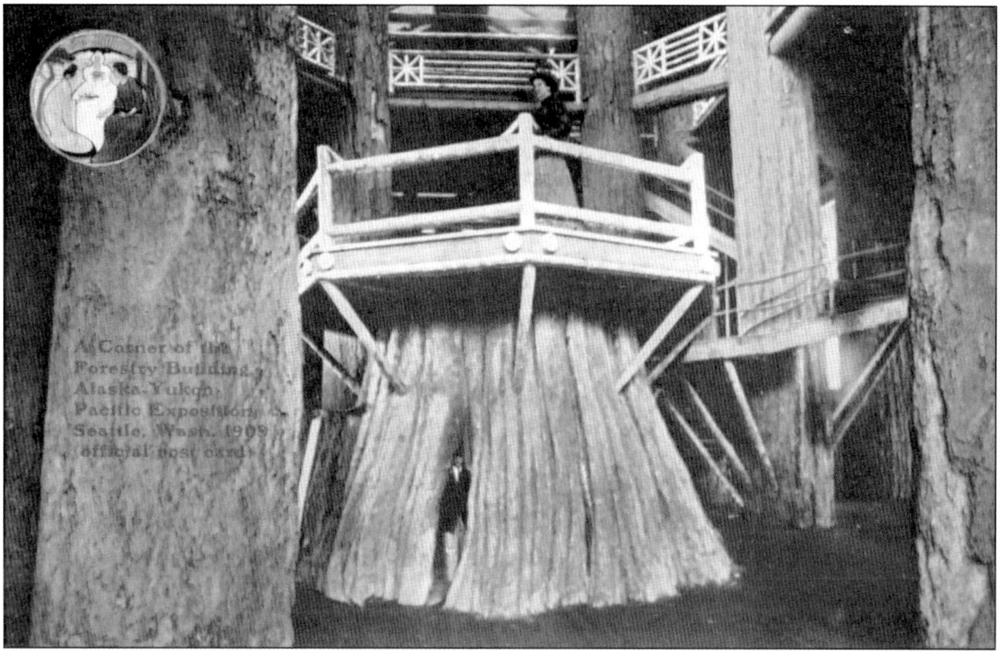

The Alaska Yukon Pacific Exposition was held in Seattle in 1909. One of the items on display in the Forestry Building was this large, hollow cedar stump with a deck built upon the top. At the conclusion of the exposition, the stump was relocated to Wright Park, where it served as a bandstand, a children's playhouse, and the central feature for many civic events until the 1930s. (Courtesy ES.)

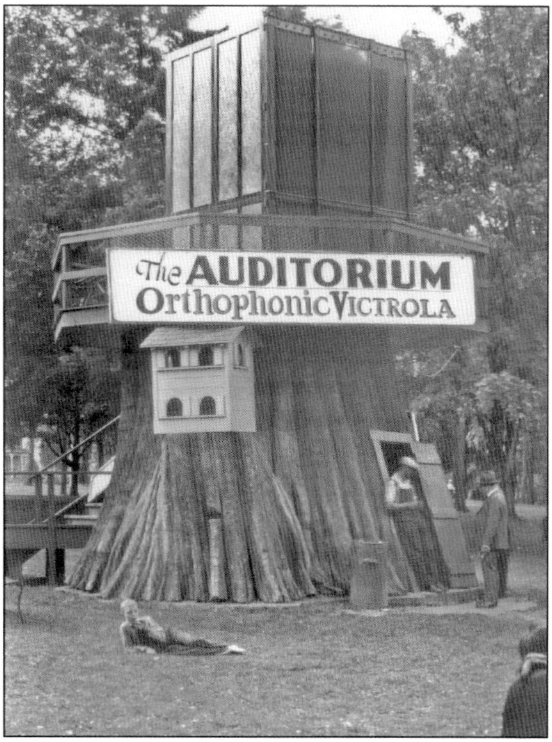

In 1925, the Victor Talking Machine Company introduced the Orthophonic Victrola, offering the latest in sound-reproducing technology. Though most models were designed for home use, the company also made this large Victrola for use in parks, at fairs, and anywhere large groups gathered to listen to music. (Courtesy TPL.)

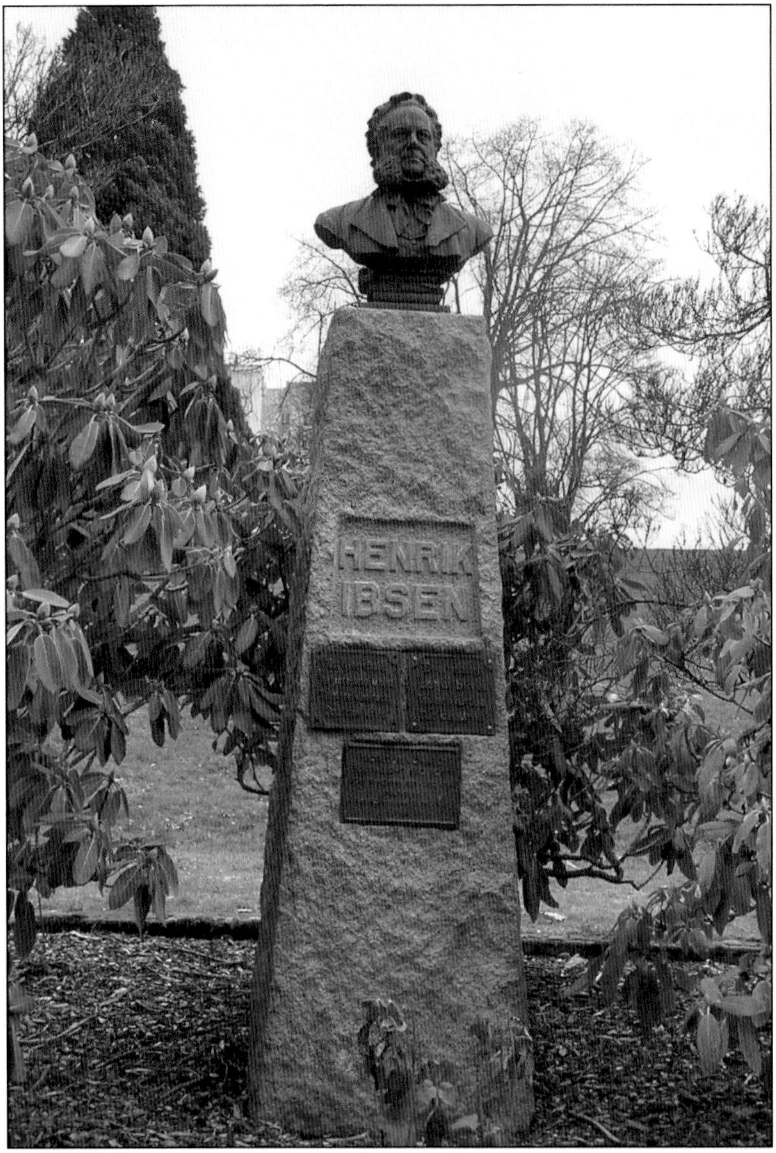

On May 17, 1913, Tacoma's large Norwegian community gathered to celebrate the 100th anniversary of Norway's independence. A parade led by Johnson's band of 30 pieces marched from Pacific Avenue to Wright Park, where the formal began at 3:00 p.m. near the Ibsen monument (above). The monument honors Henrik Ibsen, a Norwegian playwright and poet, and includes an Ibsen quotation in both English and Norwegian: "Our lives should be pure and white/ Tablets wherein God can write." (Courtesy Terri Walton.)

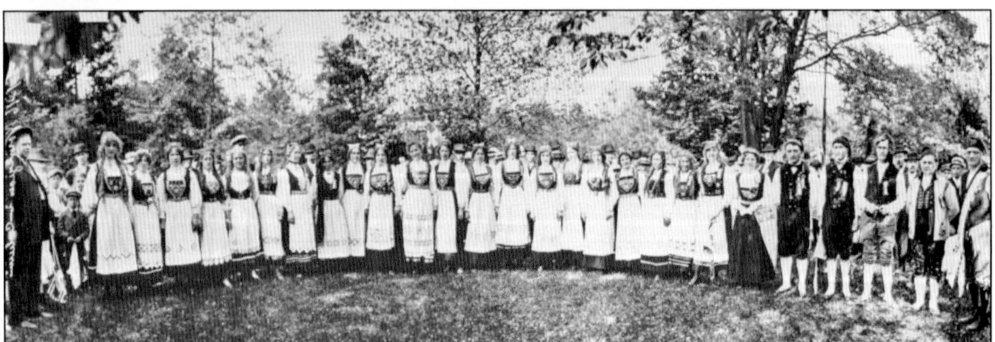

As part of the ceremony, many participants dressed in traditional clothing. (Courtesy TPL.)

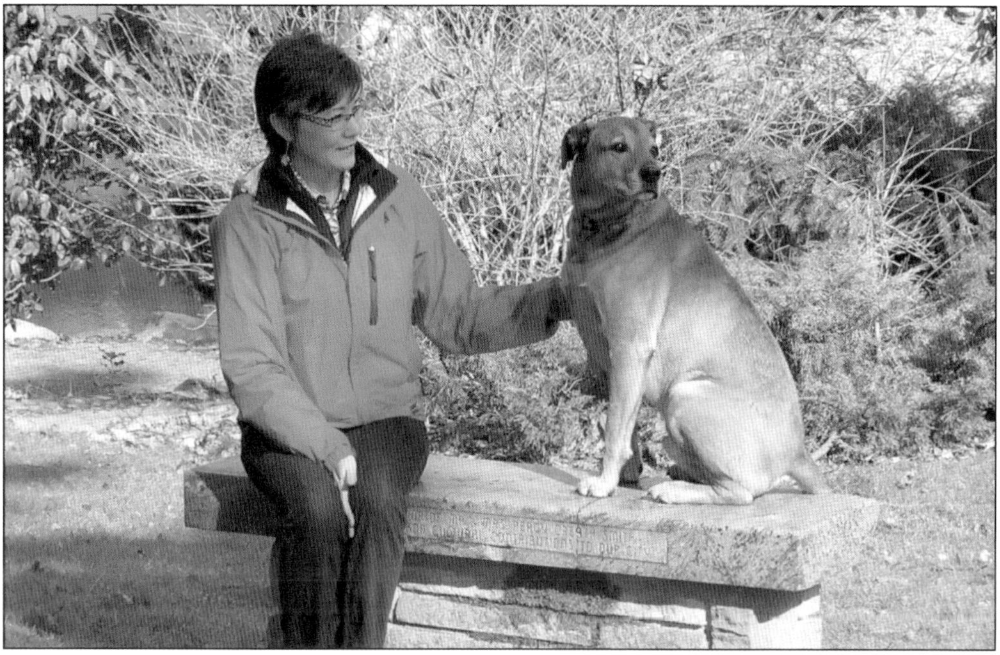

Lois Stark and her dog George enjoy a brief rest during their visit to Wright Park. This bench was placed in the park by the Tacoma Garden Club in 1936 to honor Mr. and Mrs. Percy Creath Smith for their civic and cultural contributions to Tacoma. Mrs. Smith participated in many Wright Park gardening activities and in promoting civic involvement among young women. (Courtesy Terri Walton.)

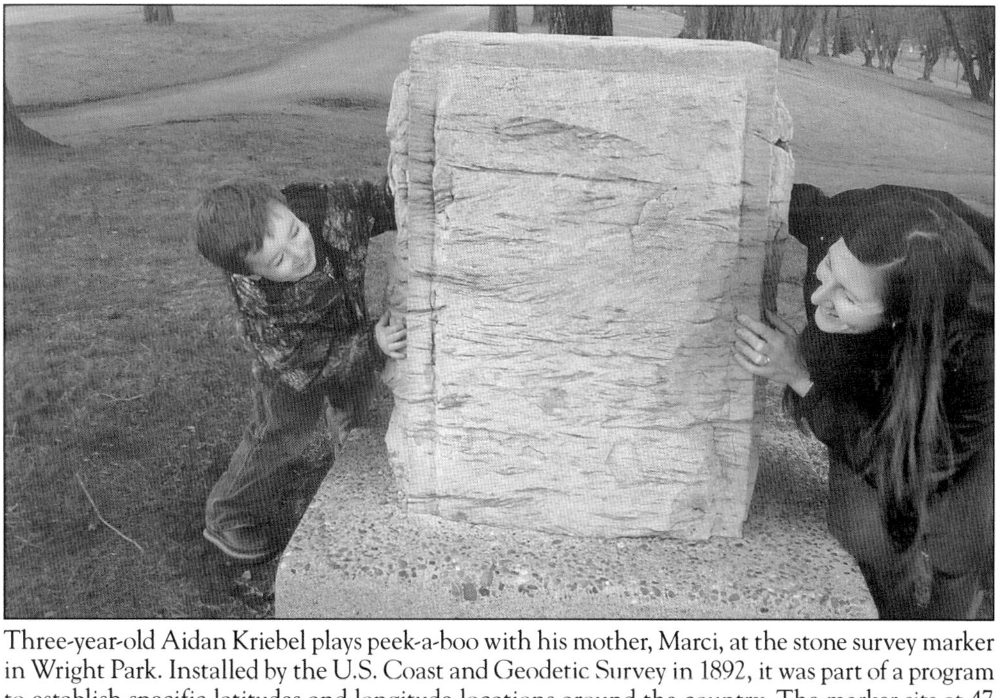

Three-year-old Aidan Kriebel plays peek-a-boo with his mother, Marci, at the stone survey marker in Wright Park. Installed by the U.S. Coast and Geodetic Survey in 1892, it was part of a program to establish specific latitudes and longitude locations around the country. The marker sits at 47 degrees 15 minutes latitude, or halfway to the North Pole. (Courtesy Terri Walton.)

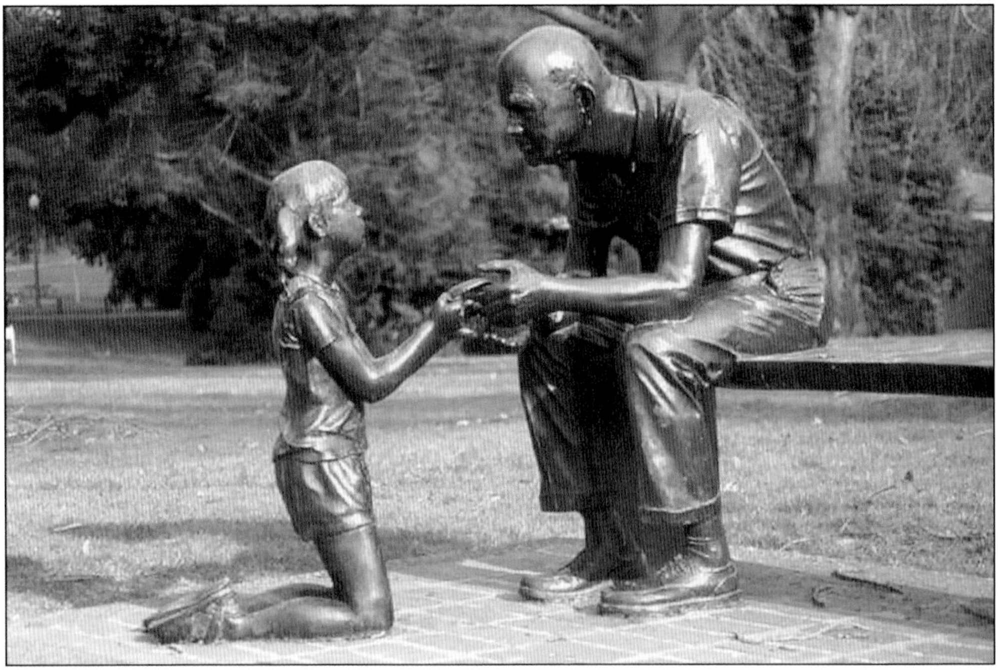

The two most recent additions to the Wright Park landscape are the bronze statues by local artist Larry Anderson. Both were funded through the City of Tacoma and the Comprehensive Employment and Training Act. *The Leaf* (above) was dedicated in 1976. Anderson's daughter Marti posed for the sculpture of the little girl, and Merle Legg modeled for the figure of the elderly man. As planned in the design, visitors can sit on the bench to share the experience and become part of the artwork. *Trilogy* (below) was dedicated in 1978. Anderson chose three children running hand in hand to capture a typical carefree childhood moment. The models for this piece were Anderson's daughter Kristen (left), Steve Minor (center), and Tony Hughes.

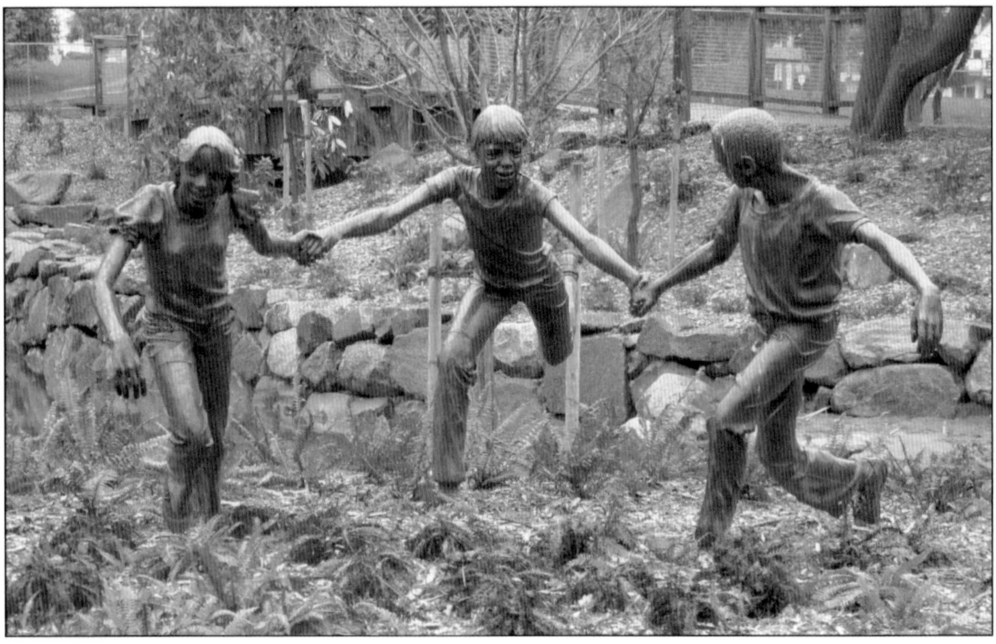

Five

Arboreal Splendor

When the Tacoma Land Company donated the 27 acres that would become Wright Park, one of the stipulations was the planting of at least 300 ornamental shade trees within four years. From the very beginning, Wright Park was destined to be a haven of horticultural delight, an arboretum with a varied collection of woody plants for display and study.

Early men of influence in Tacoma society, including Isaac Chilberg, A. V. Fawcett, Allen C. Mason, and R. F. Radebough, wanted to see the park take shape as quickly as possible. They recruited William Montjoie Forde, an Englishman knowledgeable in landscaping and botany, to come to Tacoma to help plan the park. Charles Wright paid him to identify all the flowers and plants growing naturally on the 27 acres. Ford made little wooden tags and wrote upon them with India ink, specifying each sample's botanical and common name. He also worked with George Browne, future park board chairman, and helped order trees and shrubs native to every state and some European countries. When the city council appointed a board to oversee the growing park system in 1890, Forde hoped to be appointed superintendent; instead the board hired Edward O. Schwagerl to design the park and Ebenezer Roberts to serve as superintendent and implement the design. One of the board's earliest requests was that the manure gathered in the city be deposited in Wright Park instead of the bay to help enrich the soil.

Once Schwagerl had laid out the design for the park, it was up to Ebenezer Roberts to oversee the planting of hundreds of trees, shrubs, and flowers to bring the plan to life. Roberts, who had studied at Kew Gardens, provided park board president George Browne a letter of introduction to the famous London gardens, along with a list of needed plants for the park. Newspapers reported that Browne returned with train cars filled with plants. Since that time, the varieties of trees in Wright Park have continued to grow. There are currently 635 individual trees representing 136 species; 29 are state champions.

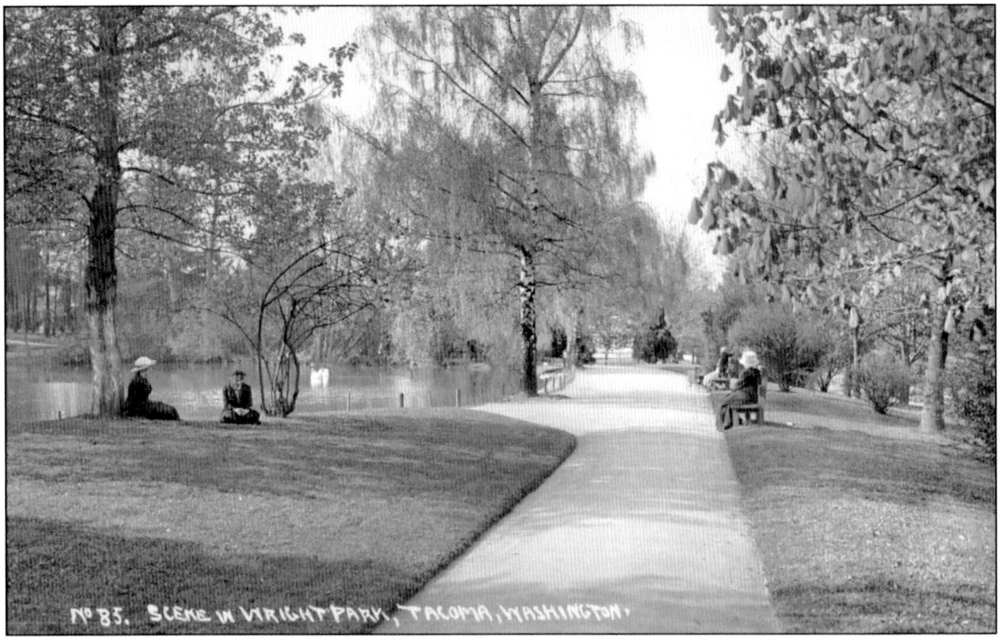

Schwagerl's plan for the landscaping of Wright Park called for 9 to 10 large trees per acre with rows of alternating red oak and horse chestnut along the main drive of Yakima Avenue. The pedestrian pathways were planted with varieties of maple, birch, poplar, elm, locust, cypress, ash, and laurel, among others. (Courtesy ES.)

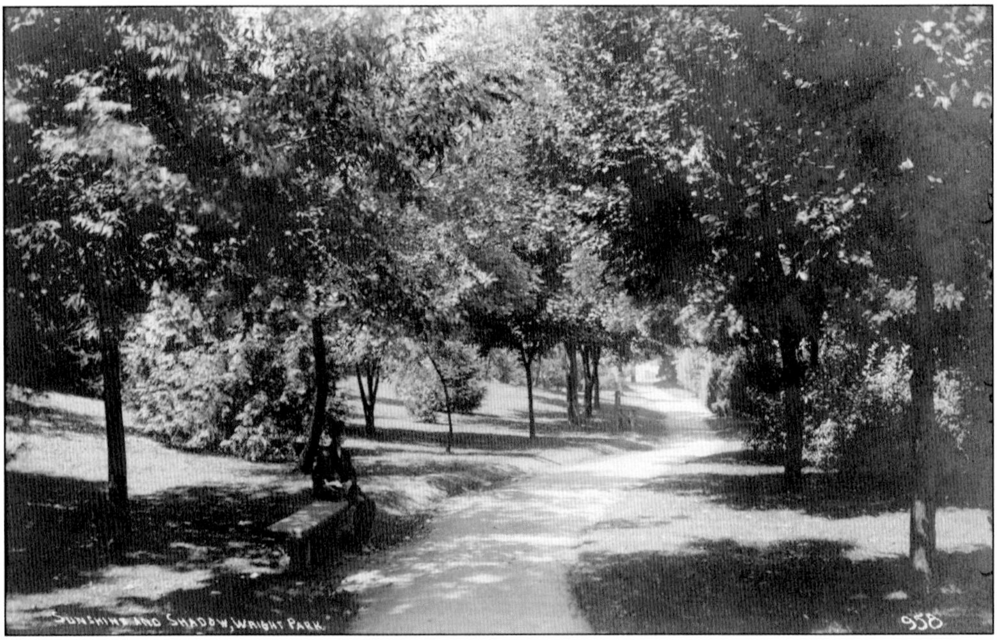

A constant theme of early writers describing the beauty of Wright Park was the play of shadows and sunlight upon the landscape. The great diversity of plant life contributed to these changing impressions. Benches placed along the pathways provided seating for those wanting to relax and escape the noise of the city and the heat of a warm summer day. (Courtesy ES.)

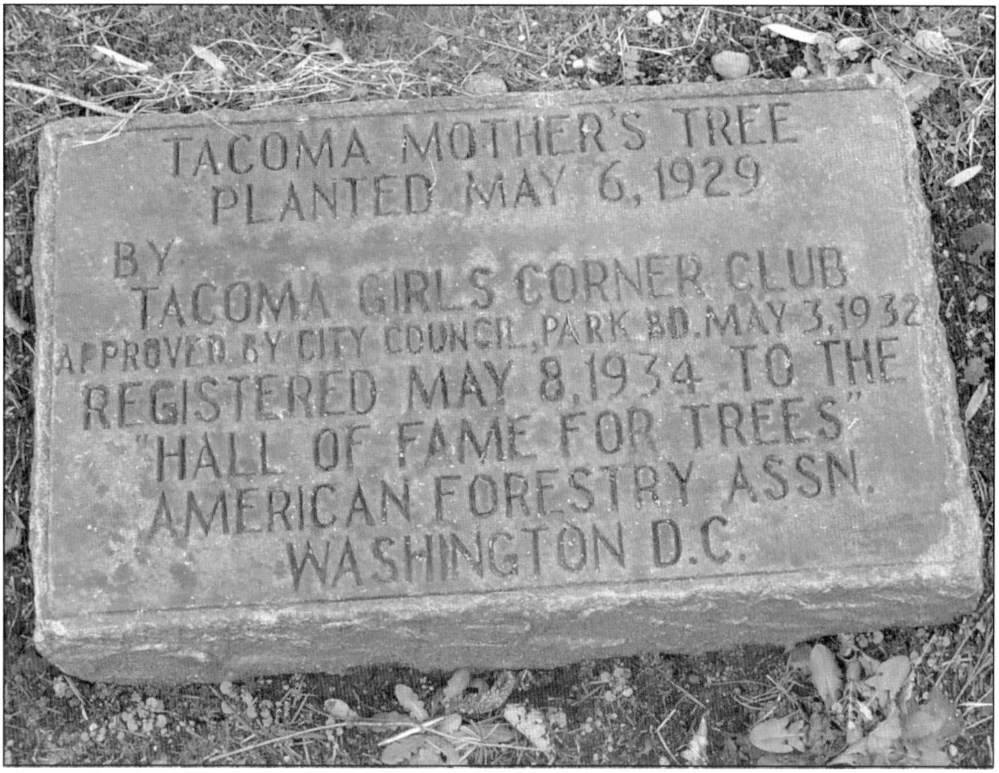

Tacoma Mother's Tree was officially recognized with a stone marker (above) on Mothers Day in 1934. The Girls' Corner Club had planted the white birch (right) in Wright Park on May 6, 1929, to honor all the mothers of the city. Two years later, Mayor M. G. Tennet officially designated it Tacoma Mother's Tree. The occasion for the plaque was the registration of the tree in the Hall of Fame for Trees of the American Forestry Association in Washington, D.C. The Girls' Corner Club was established by Mrs. Percy Creath Smith to encourage young women to become involved in activities for the betterment of the city. (Courtesy Terri Walton.)

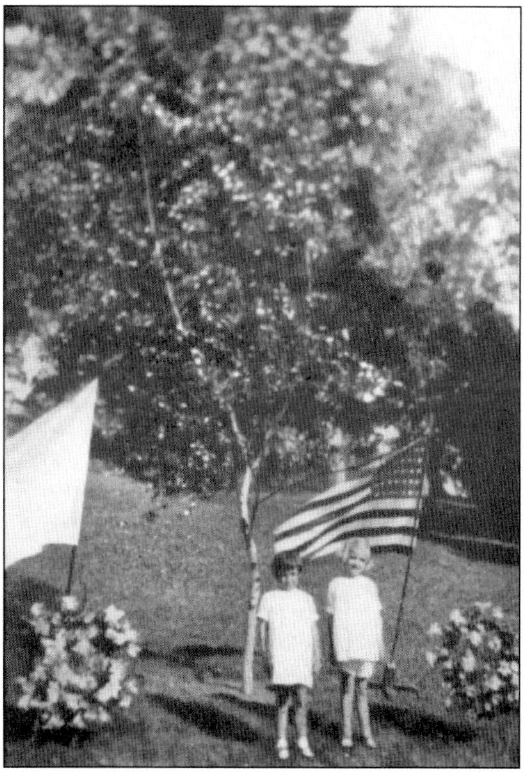

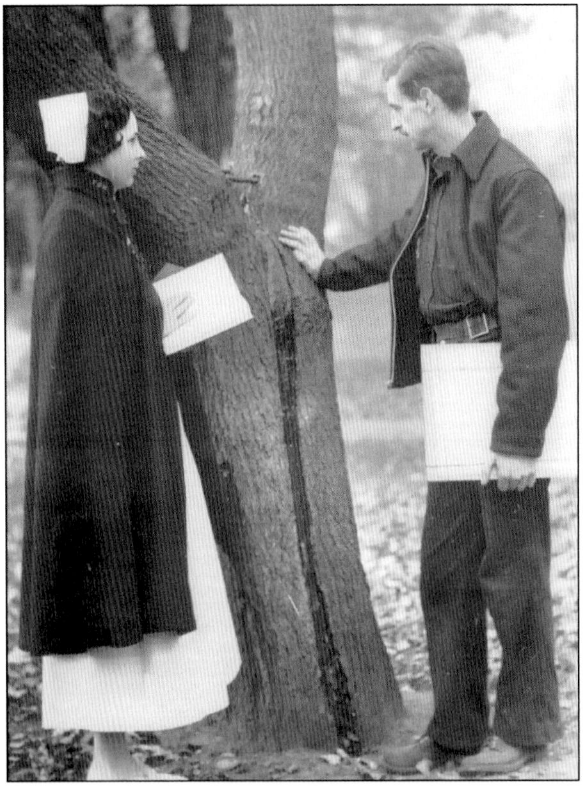

Gilbert McLean, a tree surgeon, and Doris Cook, a nurse at Tacoma General Hospital, examine a wind-damaged tree in Wright Park. The tree has been sealed and braced with an iron rod in an attempt to prolong its life. The Metropolitan Park District hired McLean after a disastrous windstorm hit Tacoma on October 21, 1934, and destroyed 34 trees in Wright Park. (Courtesy TPL.)

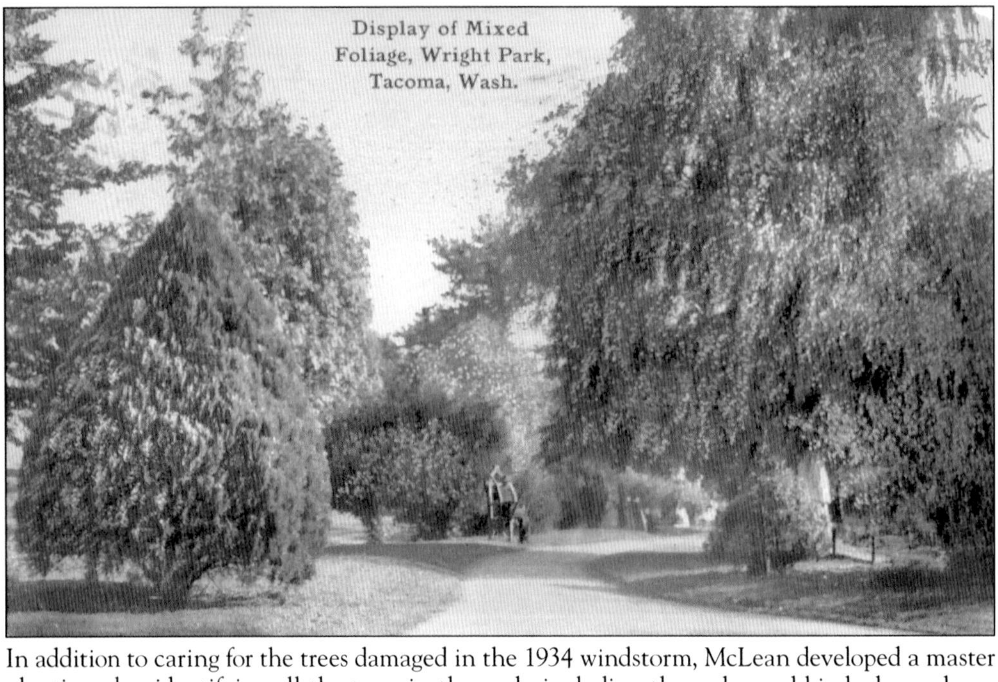

In addition to caring for the trees damaged in the 1934 windstorm, McLean developed a master planting plan identifying all the trees in the park, including the cedar and birch shown here. A rustic bench sits at the intersection of two paths for visitors to stop and enjoy the view. (Courtesy ES.)

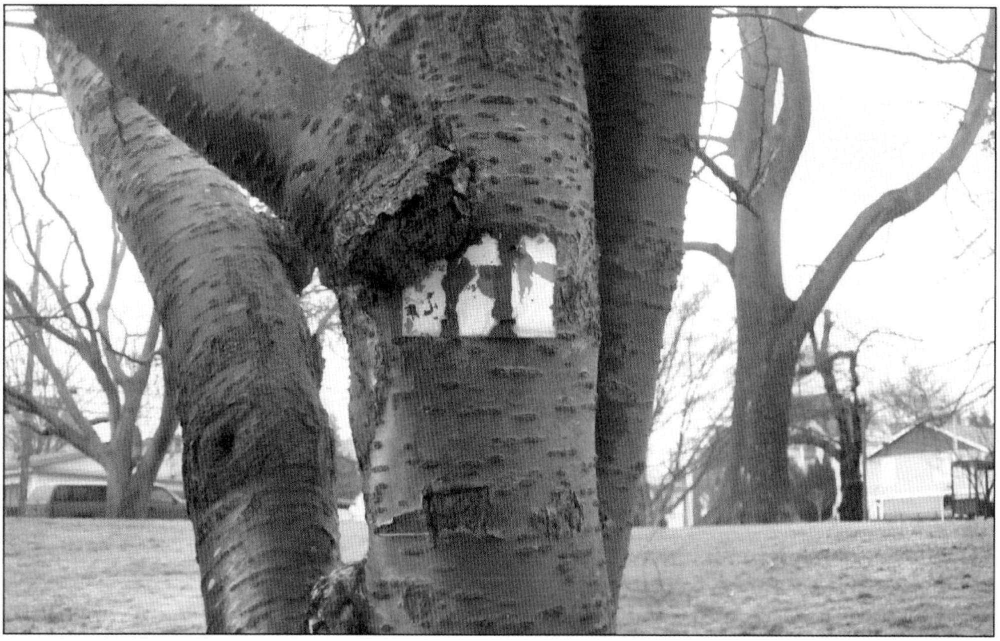

By 1935, most of the original wooden tree labels installed by William Forde had disappeared, so McLean initiated a program to install new galvanized iron labels. A newspaper article about the project proclaimed, "The labels will do much to attract attention to the beauties of Wright Park and to the educational advantages it offers for nature students. Unlabeled, the trees have been just trees to those passing through the park. Labeled, each tree takes on a new interest and personality. Even the most casual pedestrian pauses to admire when a label informs him he is gazing at an ailanthus, or Chinese Tree of Heaven." Above, one of McLean's tree labels has grown into the bark of a Japanese cherry. The next generation of plastic labels, an example of which can be seen below, are easier to read and require less maintenance.

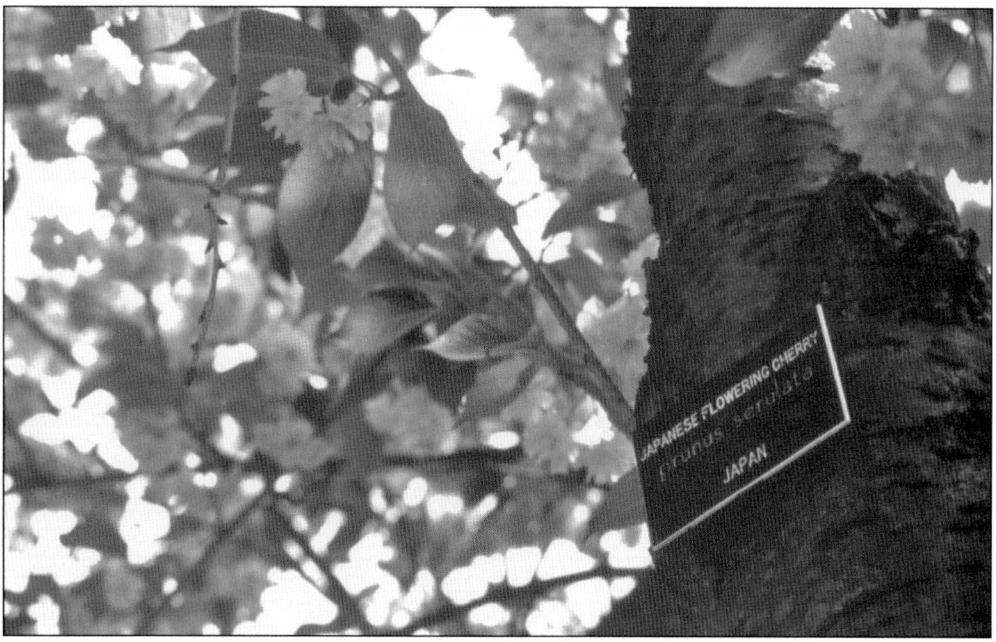

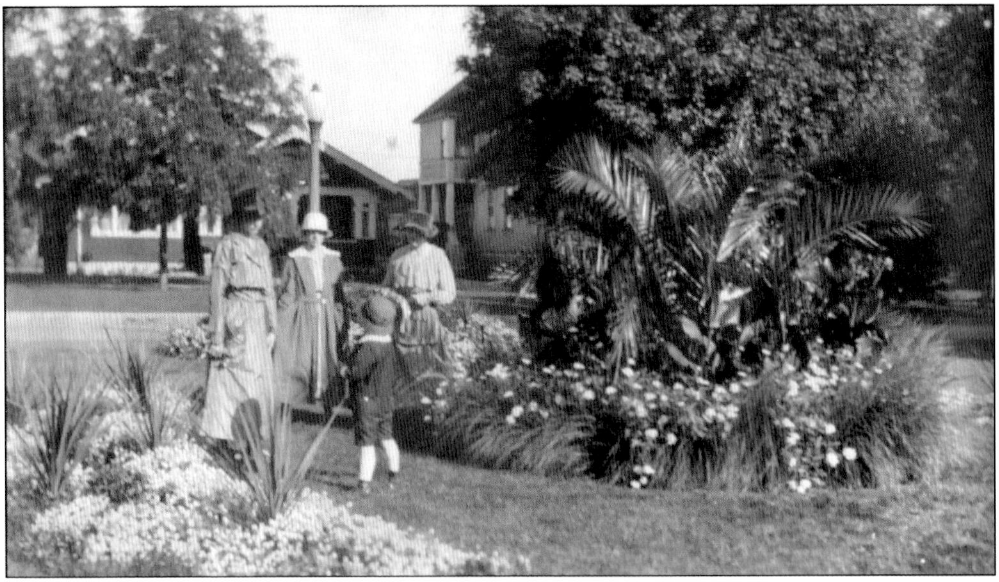

Before the tree canopy covered the majority of the acreage, as it does today, numerous lovely floral plantings were found throughout the park. Here a group of women and a young boy enjoy a sunny day along the I Street side of the park at the start of the 20th century. (Courtesy WSHS.)

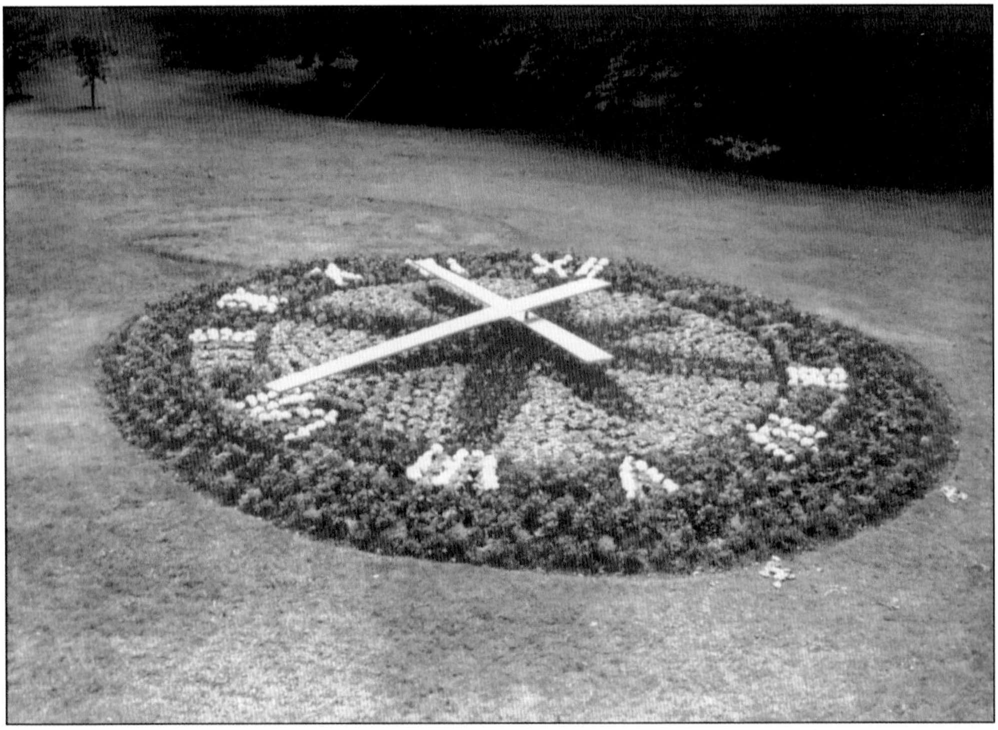

The Tacoma Garden Club presented this beautiful floral clock to the park board on June 24, 1941. Inspired by a similar model in Ostend, Belgium, the electric clock was placed on a slope near the intersection of Division and Yakima Avenues for all to see. The 26-foot circle face was designed to change with the seasons. The Hunt and Moffett Company created the clock's mechanical workings, including the aluminum hands. (Courtesy TPL.)

In the early 1900s, park commissioners planted a white birch tree along the shore of the Wright Park pond in honor of Charles B. Wright. Over time, birch trees such as the one at left were also planted near the pond. No records remain identifying the tree grown specifically for Wright. (Courtesy TPL.)

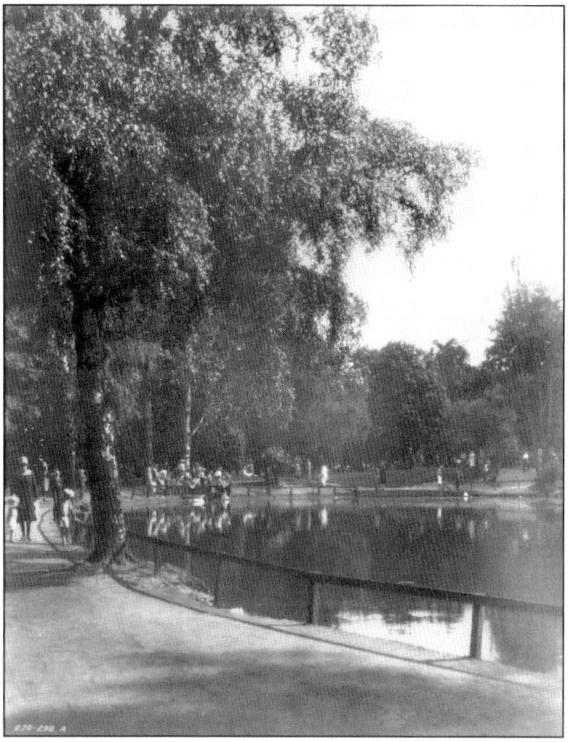

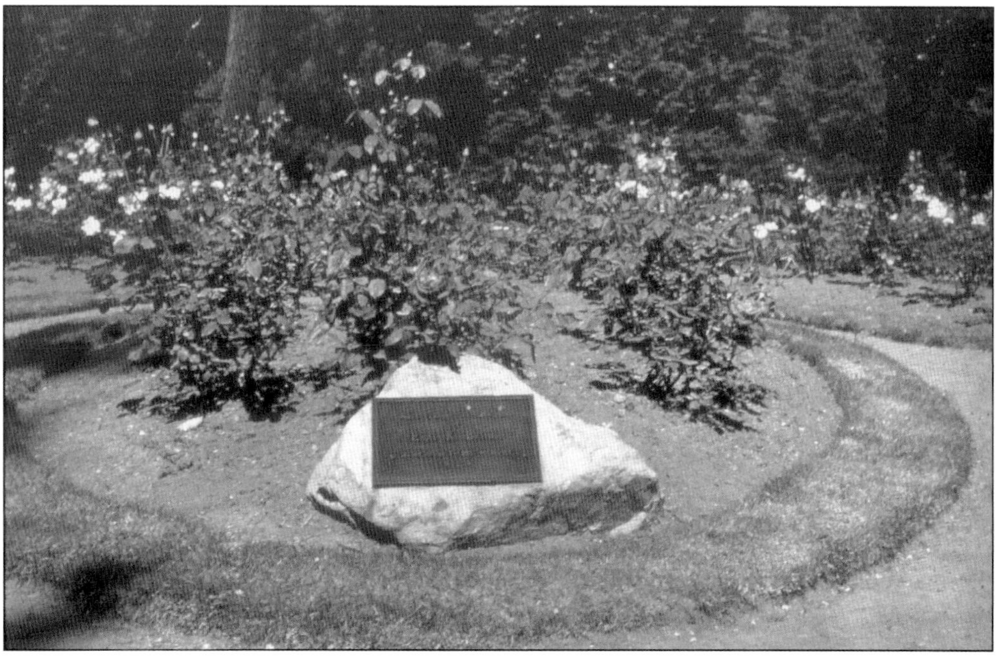

In January 1936, some 100 rose bushes from the Tacoma Rose Society were donated to Wright Park in memory of Earl K. Bishop. Bishop was a longtime Tacoma mail carrier and ardent rose lover. A plaque designed by his brother Ralph marked the garden. Planted near the I Street side of the park, the garden fell victim to the shade of the ever-expanding tree canopy and was removed in 2007.

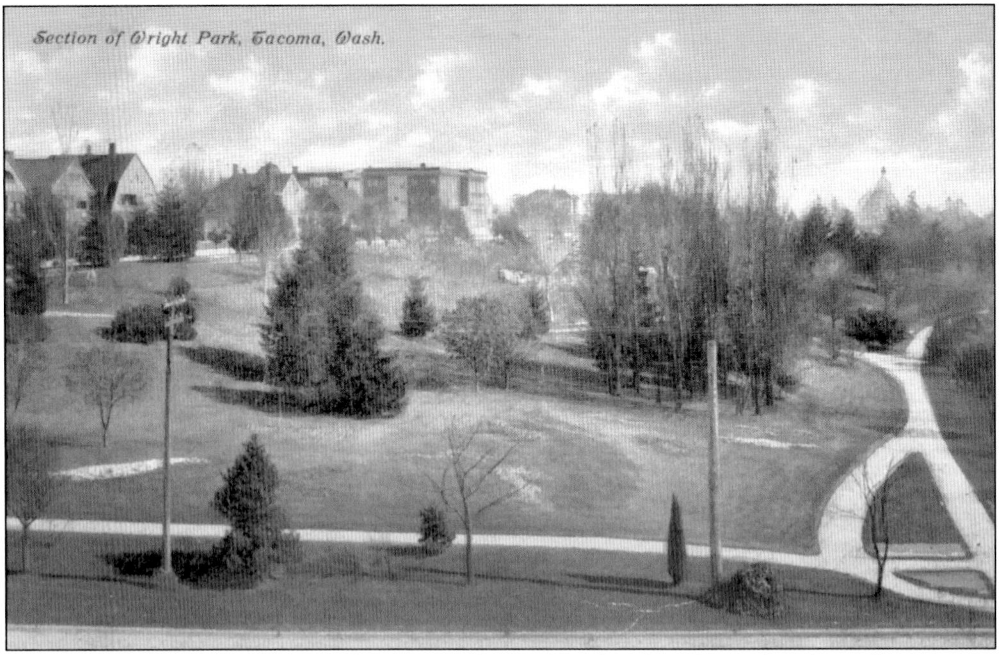

This early view illustrates the wide variety of trees found within the park. Along the G Street hill are Lombardy poplars, flowering plums, and ash trees. Farther down the hill, paper birch, holly, black locust, Japanese maple, Wych elm, and a grouping of Lombardy poplars once thrived, filling a large portion of the park. (Courtesy ES.)

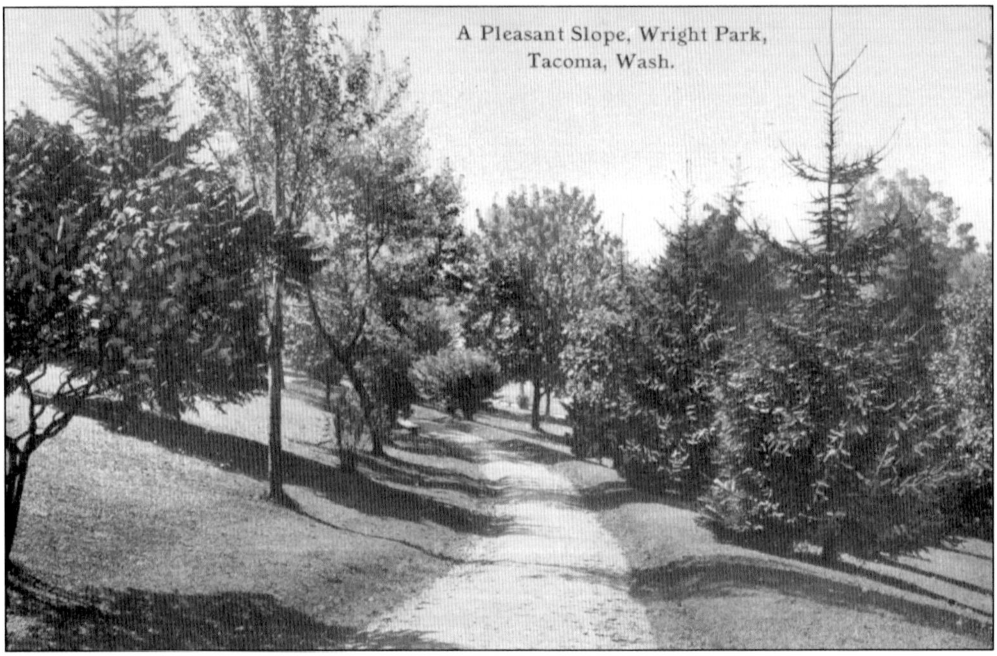

A visitor strolling along this pleasant slope in the northeast section enjoys the beauty of Norway spruce, Douglas fir, and ash trees. In the early years, some of these larger trees were planted too close together in an attempt to fill out the park. In the 1930s and 1950s, some of the trees were thinned to make room for the maturing trees.

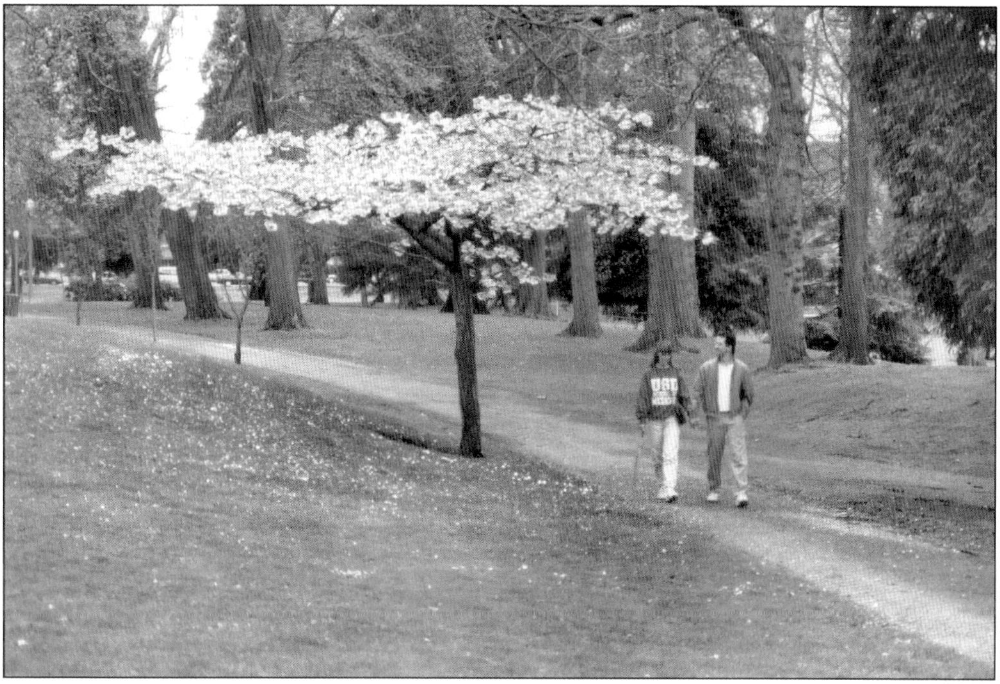

Twelve Japanese flowering cherry trees were donated to the park district in 1936 by Japanese employees of the St. Paul and Tacoma Lumber Company. Several were planted near the Sixth Avenue entrance and the rest near the conservatory. Only one of the original cherry trees survives today.

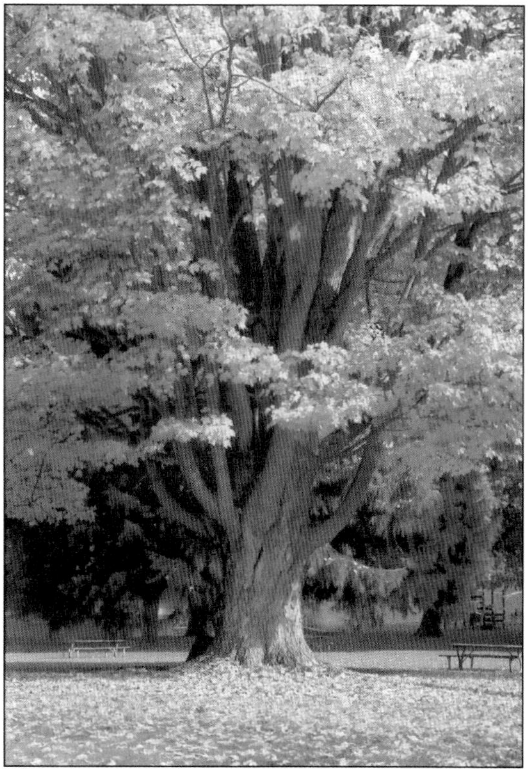

This huge sugar maple, with a crown spread of 83 feet, is just one of Wright Park's 29 champion trees. Champion trees are the largest of their variety in the state. Wright Park is also home to the widest planted tree in Washington: a red oak that measures over 15 feet around its trunk, one of the original trees planted at the end of the 19th century. (Courtesy Connie Hardy.)

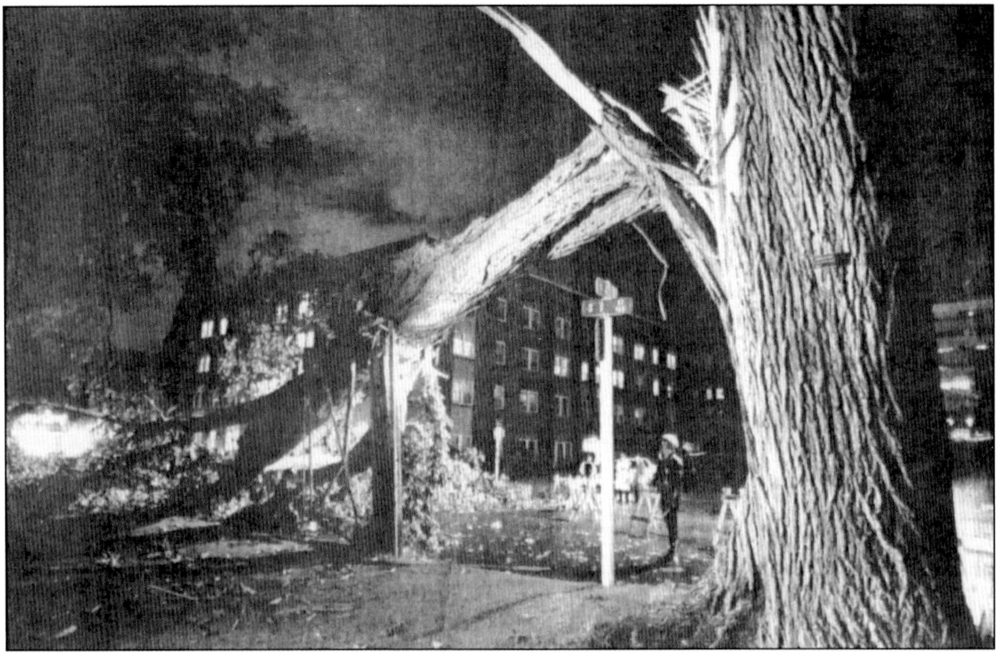

On June 24, 1983, this dramatic photograph was taken when the trunk of a huge American elm tree split near the corner of South Fourth and I Streets. At one time there were more than 75 elm trees in Wright Park. Since 1996, Dutch Elm Disease has claimed the majority of elms in the park. Only eight of them remain alive and well today. (Courtesy Tacoma *News Tribune*.)

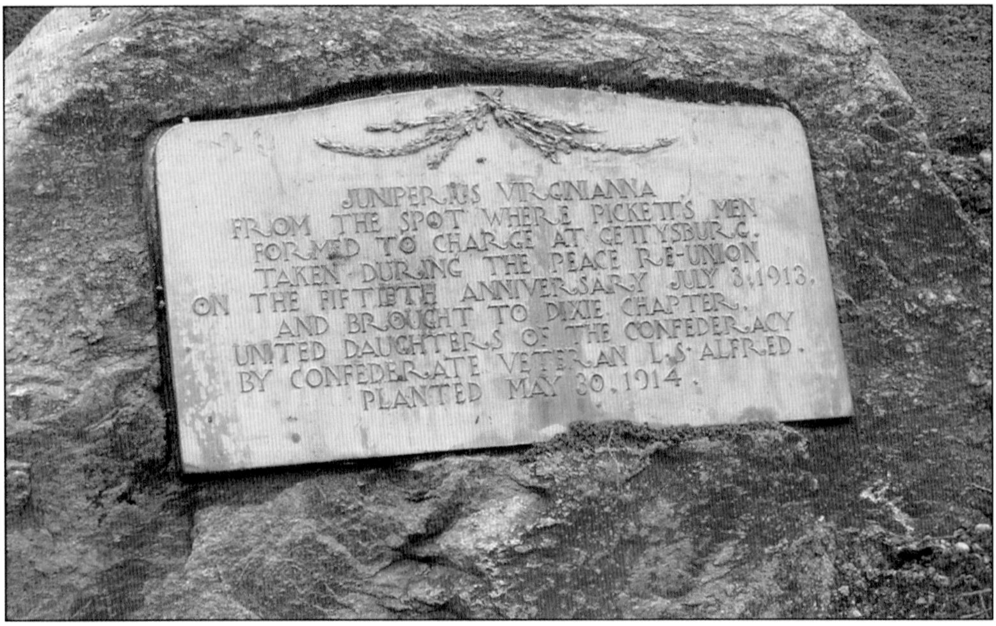

Storms, disease, and age have all taken their toll on the trees of Wright Park. Other trees, such as the Virginia juniper brought to the park by L. S. Alfred from the 1913 Peace Reunion at Gettysburg, Pennsylvania, were not situated in the most beneficial section for their needs and therefore did not thrive. The juniper was blown down in the infamous 1962 Columbus Day storm. (Courtesy Terri Walton.)

Jim Barborinas is not inflicting pain on the trunk of this tree. Instead he is inspecting it for rot during the 1989 Tree Maintenance and Replanting Plan. It is essential that Wright Park have a comprehensive plan for maintaining its collection of trees in the best way possible and for adjusting to future needs as older trees die or other damage occurs.

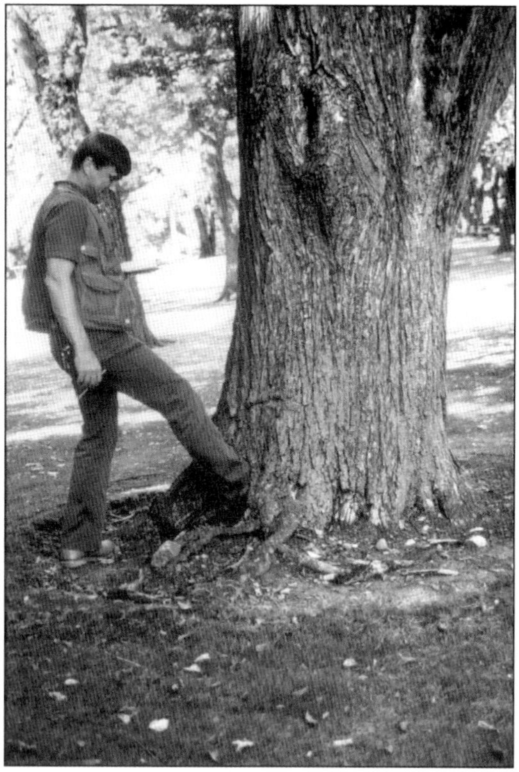

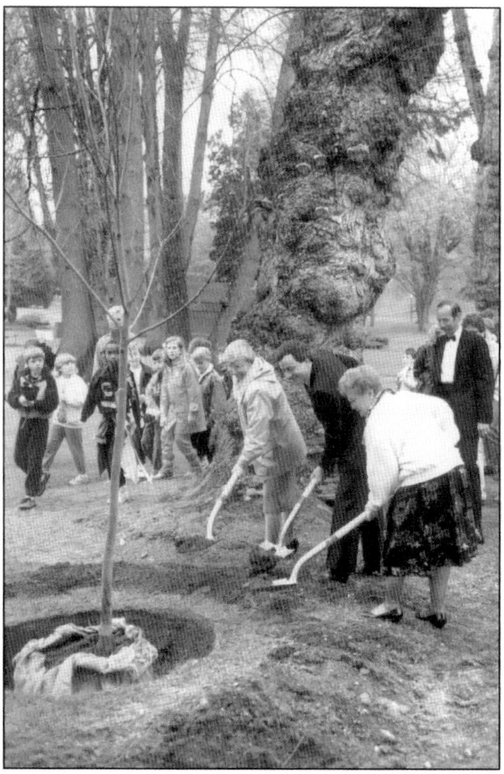

Karen Vialle (left), Tacoma mayor; Tim Thompson (center), administrative assistant to Congressman Norm Dicks; and park board commissioner Cathy Egan all dig in to plant a new tree as part of the 1990 Arbor Day celebration. New trees are constantly being added to the park to increase variety and to prepare for the time when the older ones reach the end of their normal life cycle.

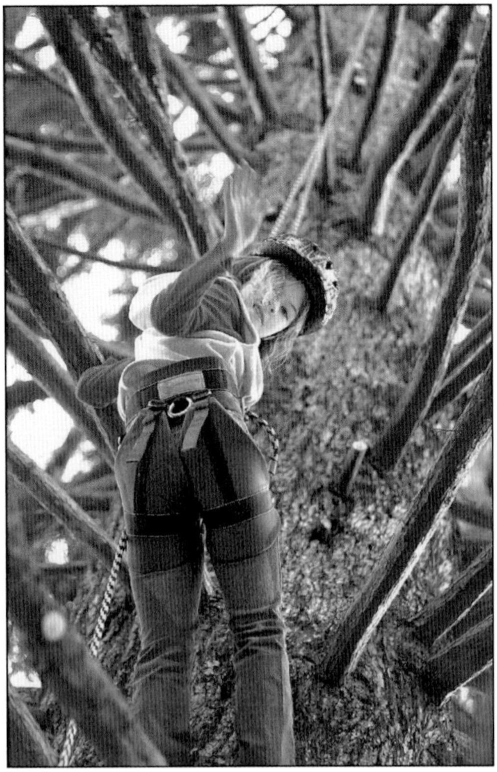

The first Fall Tree Festival, held in 2004, allowed families to celebrate the glory of trees. People like the young girl on the left were given the opportunity to safely rise up into the upper branches of a giant sequoia. As shown below, volunteers used stout ropes to secure the climbers to ensure that their visit to the tree canopy was both exciting and safe. The young girl commented, on her return to solid ground, that she wished she had brought a book because the peace and quiet of the treetop was wonderful.

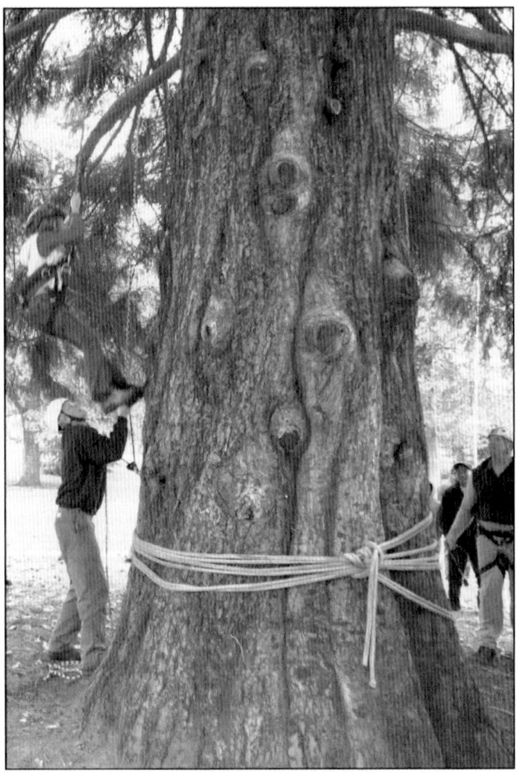

Six

Festivals, Concerts, and the Easter Bunny

With Wright Park's proximity to downtown and several Tacoma neighborhoods, 27 acres of gently rolling landscape, and beautiful scenic vistas, it is the perfect location for a wide variety of community events. As early as 1896, the Rose Carnival drew nearly 15,000 people, and when Pres. Theodore Roosevelt visited Tacoma in 1903, the city decided to use Wright Park as the setting for his speech to the community. For decades, elaborate May Day celebrations were held within its borders. The first festivals were sponsored by the neighboring Annie Wright Seminary and later ones by all the elementary schools in the city.

Civic holidays, such as Memorial Day, the Fourth of July, and Flag Day, were the focus of some of the largest gatherings, but summer evening concerts were also popular. One of the first amenities built for the park was a large bandstand located below the G Street bluff, adjacent to Bird Lake and overlooking a large open area in the center of the park. Wright Park can easily accommodate thousands of people attending any single event. Over 50,000 people attend today's popular summertime Ethnic Fest.

With its miles of wandering pathways, cozy tree-shaded nooks, and open spaces, Wright Park has proven to be the perfect spot for smaller gatherings and intimate occasions. These special events and accomplishments have often been documented with photographs taken in the park.

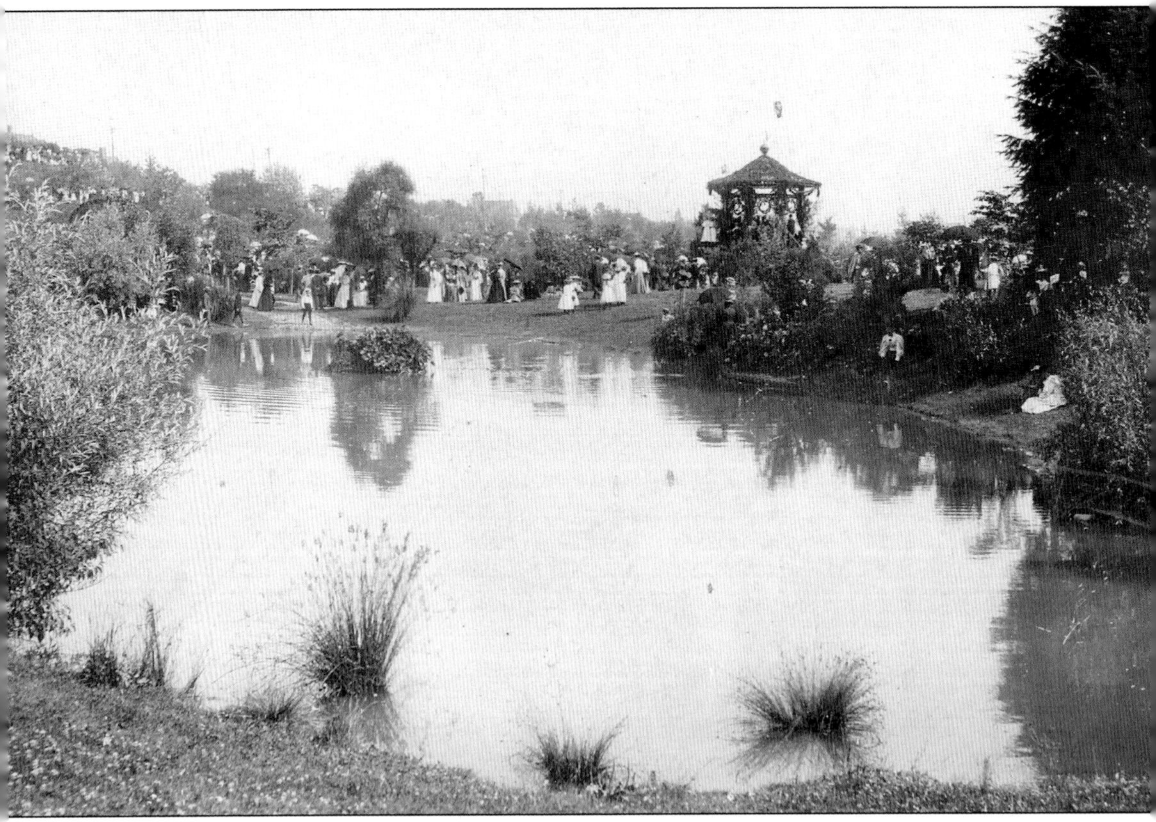

The minutes of the June 18, 1896, meeting of the board of park commissioners recorded that the Rose Carnival was granted permission to hold its summer festivities in Wright Park. In this view, looking across Bird Lake in the direction of Sixth Avenue, the flower- and garland-bedecked bandstand is thronged by celebrants in summer finery on July 2, 1896. On this day, Gov. John H. McGraw crowned Elizabeth Dunster Foster the Queen of Roses during Tacoma's first Rose Carnival. She was presented a silver key to the city by Mayor Angelo V. Fawcett. Some 15,000 viewed the coronation exercises. By 1905, the Rose Carnival had grown to a three-day event with band concerts, children's parades, and a carnival ball. (Courtesy TPL.)

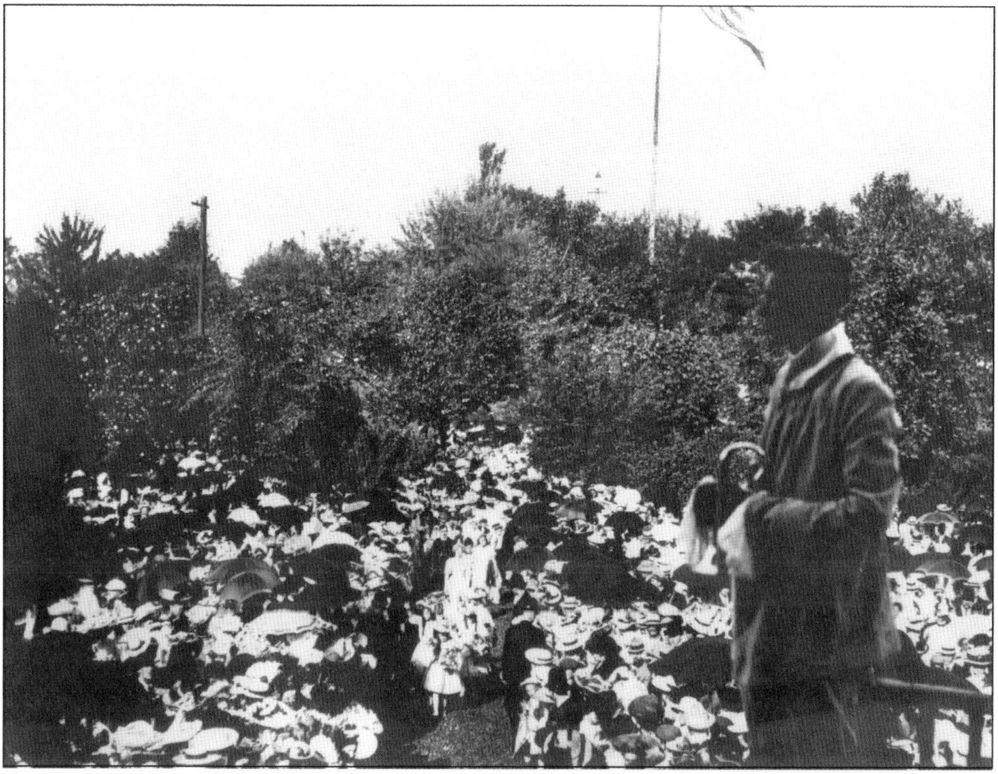

On May 22, 1903, Pres. Theodore Roosevelt made a stop in Tacoma on his western tour. The largest event of the day was a speech in Wright Park with nearly 30,000 in attendance. Employees moved the bandstand from the center of the park to the I Street entrance and decorated it with flowers, vines, and grasses. As part of the welcoming ceremony above, young girls such as Trillium Roberts, the daughter of Supt. Ebenezer Roberts, brought flowers to the president. In the photograph at right, Fred Edwards (left) and Ebenezer Roberts pose with the unique horn chair given to the president that day. The antlers were shed from an elk named Roosevelt that Roberts had raised in Point Defiance Park. Edwards, a taxidermist, made the chair. In honor of this visit, an oak tree was planted near where the conservatory stands today. (Courtesy Jean Insel Robeson.)

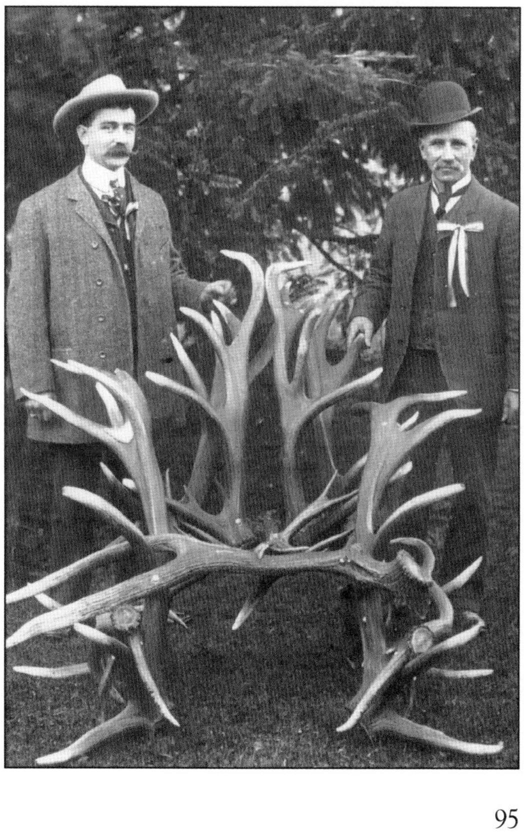

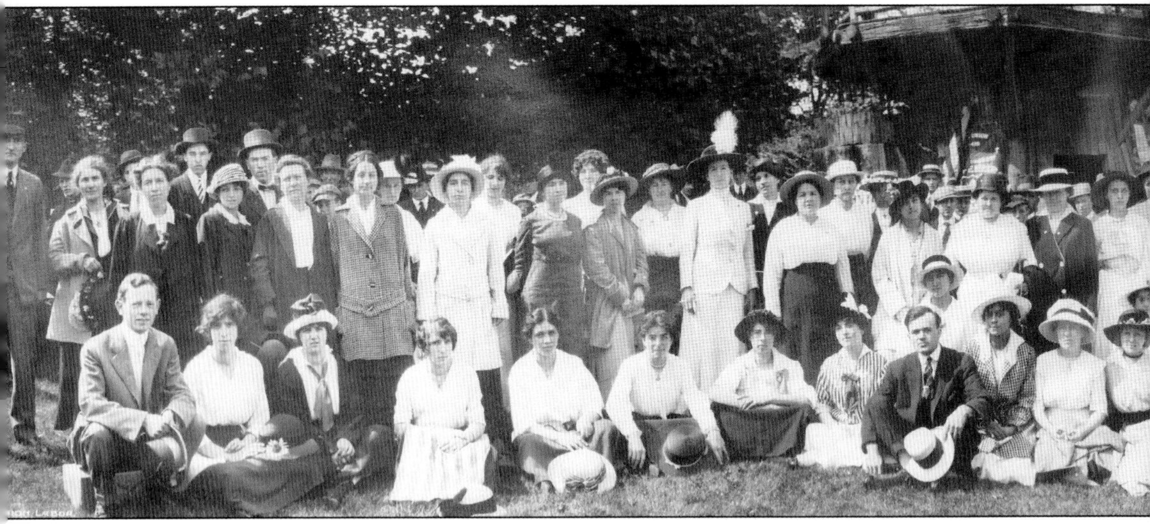

Members of the United Garment Workers of America, Local Number 201, pose in a World War I–era photograph. Visible in the background is the large cedar stump bandstand that came to Wright Park following the Alaska Yukon Pacific Exposition in 1909. Local 201 was chartered on January 24, 1903. Although women had belonged to unions and been active in ladies auxiliaries for many years, Local 201 was the first union in Tacoma composed predominately of women. In 1916,

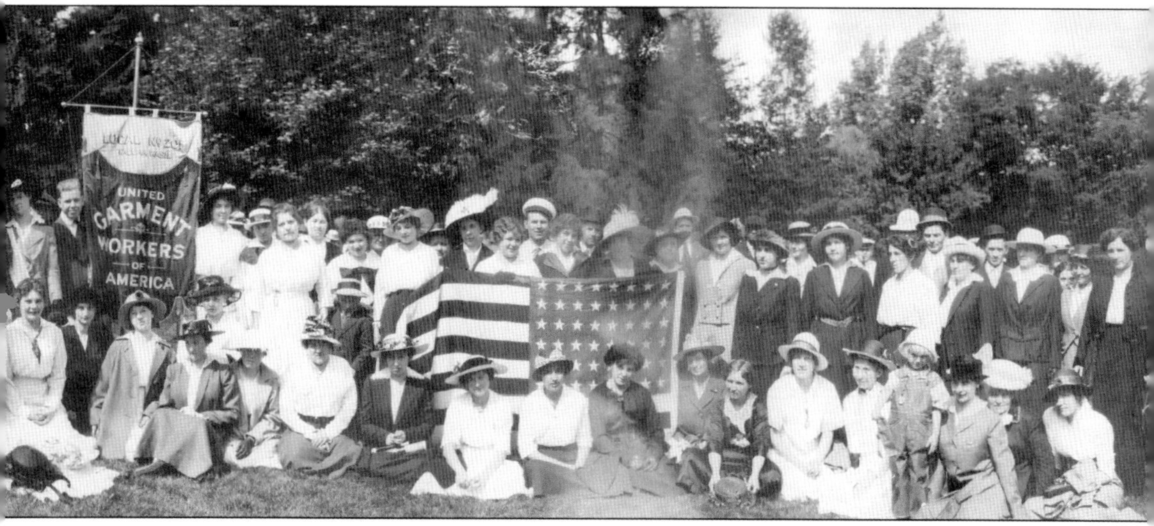

it numbered 95 women and 7 men. This outing in Wright Park was just one of many social activities sponsored by the union. Winter events included cross-country hiking and gymnastics and dramatics at the YWCA. During the summer, trips to the mountains, lakes, and islands were planned. (Courtesy ES.)

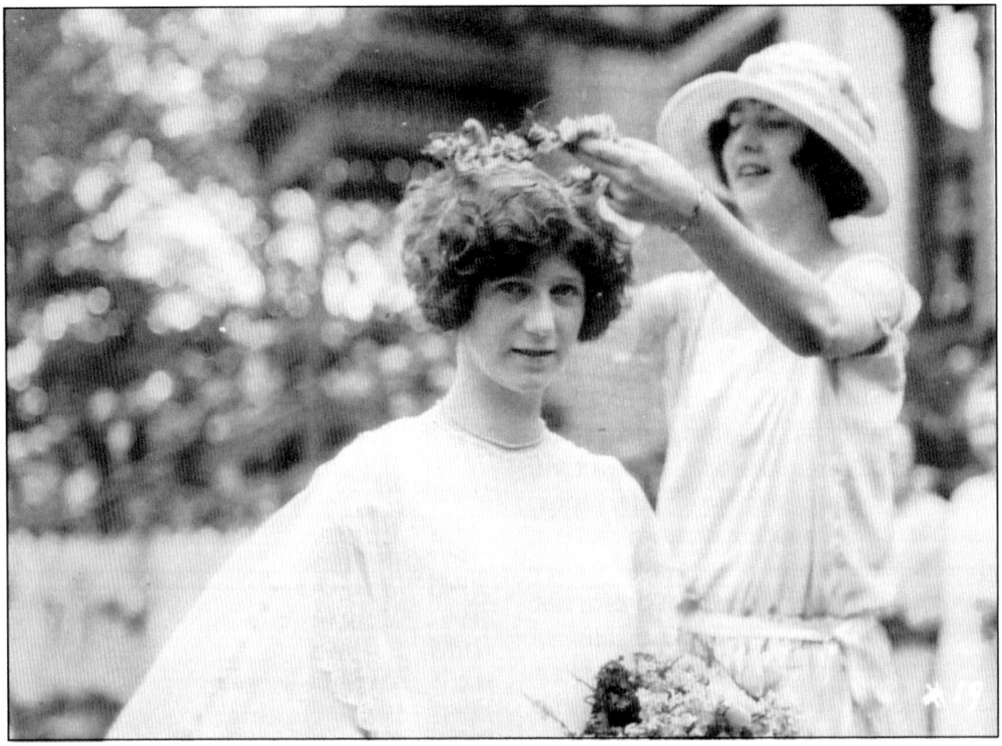

Elaborate May Day festivals were popular in Wright Park from the first Annie Wright Seminary celebration in 1911 through the 1920s and 1930s, when other schools held similar activities. With the school's proximity to the park, the lush, open grounds made the perfect setting. Days of music, dance, and sports climaxed with the crowing of the queen. Above, 1922 May Queen Babbie Gilpin accepts the flower wreath that serves as her crown. Gilpin was entertained by elves, nymphs, and fairies from the lower school. Below, a later May Queen sits in her royal chair as she is entertained by lavishly dressed dancers and others. (Above courtesy AWS.)

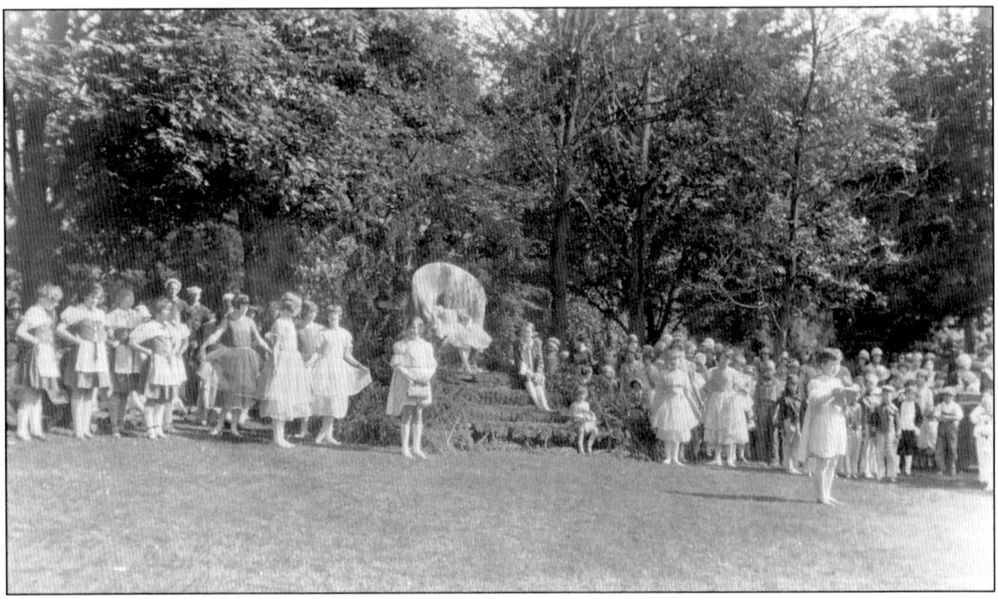

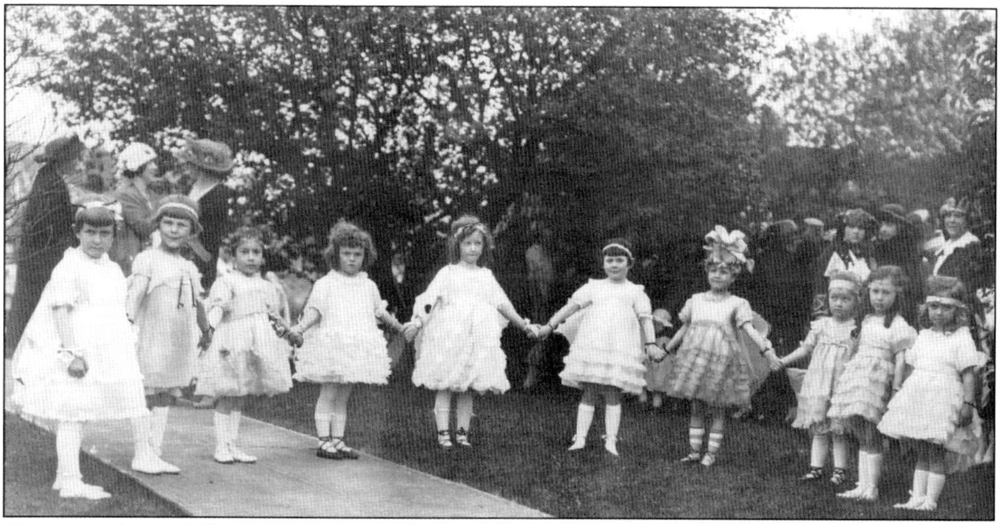

Here seven beautifully dressed young girls await their turn to participate in the May Day activities. As part of Annie Wright's May Day, the queen walked to her throne while her train was borne by two diminutive pages in white satin, followed by flower girls from the youngest classes. The girls of the school all dressed in white for the occasion. (Courtesy AWS.)

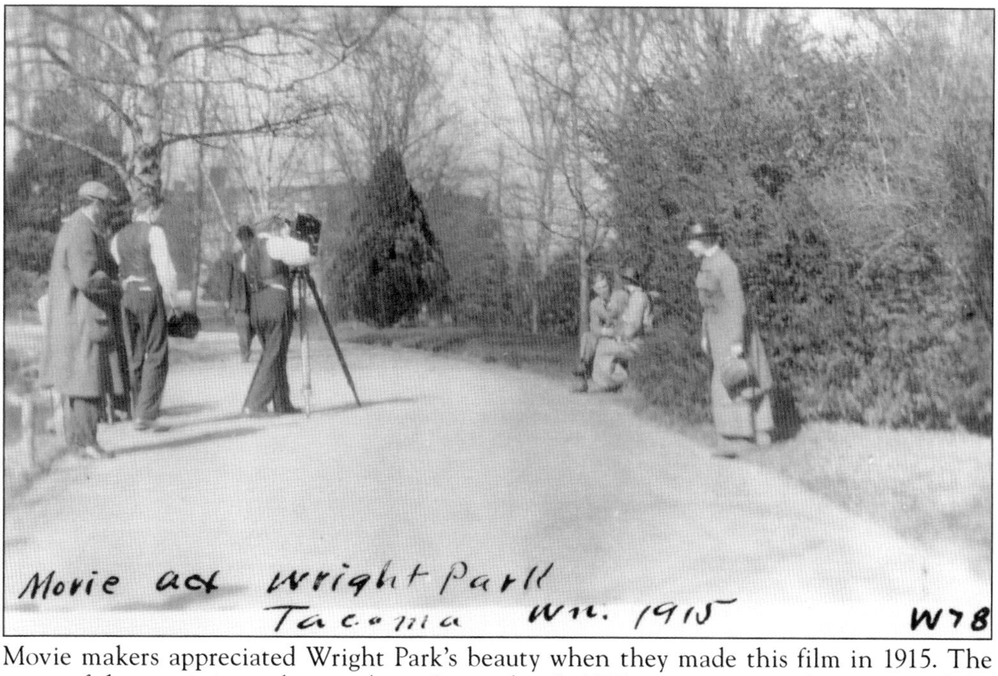

Movie makers appreciated Wright Park's beauty when they made this film in 1915. The name of the movie is not known, but a September 5, 1915, newspaper article announced the construction of a studio near Point Defiance Park by the Alliance Film Company. The first film they planned to create was a work by Tacoma resident Alice Palmer Henderson called *Only Ride, Box and Tango.* (Courtesy WSHS.)

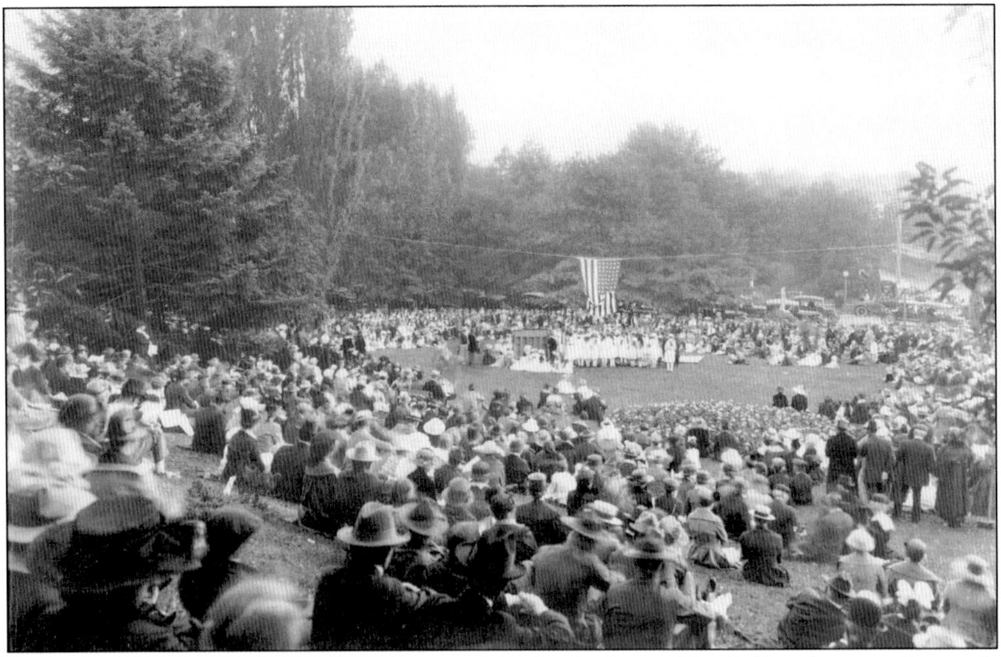

On August 5, 1919, nearly 2,000 people turned out for the first public children's sing at the north end of Wright Park. The program was arranged and directed by Zoe Pearl Park, who had rehearsed the children for three months. Edward Benedict's "Tacoma, We're Proud of You" was one of the more popular numbers performed that evening. (Courtesy TPL.)

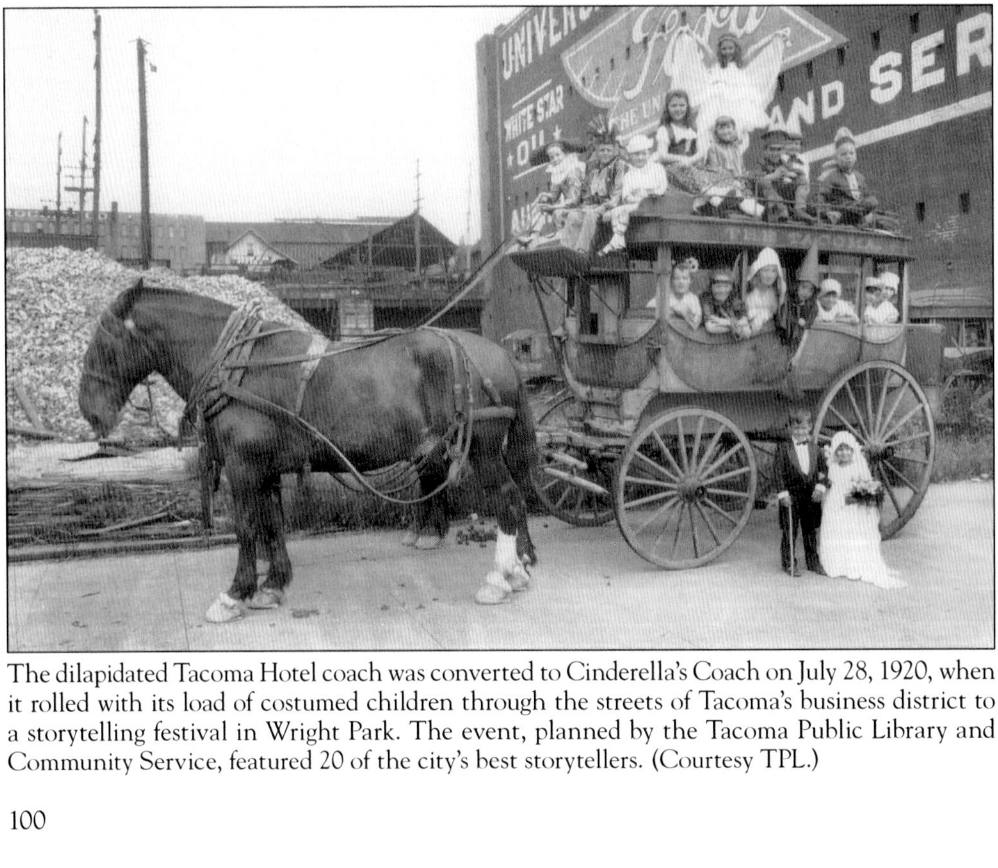

The dilapidated Tacoma Hotel coach was converted to Cinderella's Coach on July 28, 1920, when it rolled with its load of costumed children through the streets of Tacoma's business district to a storytelling festival in Wright Park. The event, planned by the Tacoma Public Library and Community Service, featured 20 of the city's best storytellers. (Courtesy TPL.)

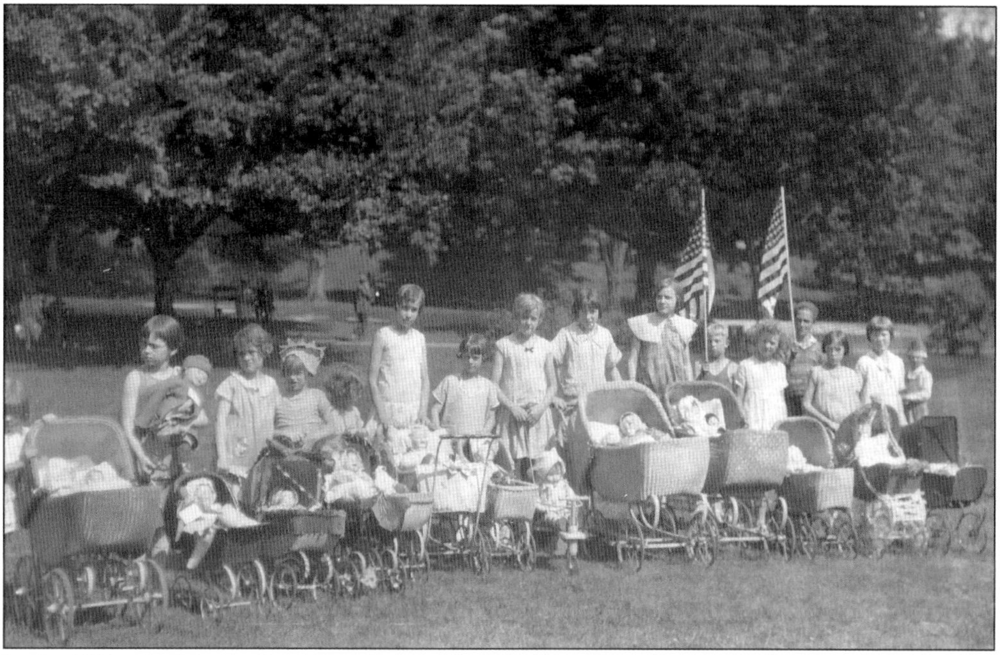

In the 1920s, the Metropolitan Park District began offering a wide variety of recreational programs for youth. Some of the activities in the early years were segregated by gender as was deemed appropriate for the time. Here young girls participate in a parade of dolls. A variety of sizes and styles of carriages are evident. Two young men have also joined in as flag bearers.

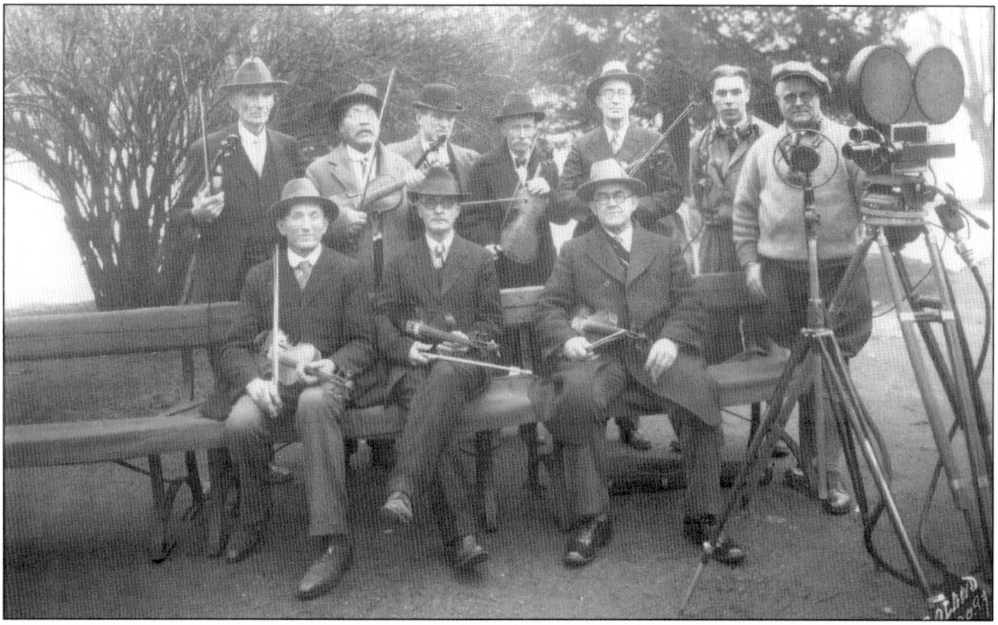

In February 1930, the RKO Pantages Theater and the *News Tribune* sponsored a five-day contest to choose the best old-time fiddler in Tacoma/Pierce County. All contestants would appear on a *Pathe News Weekly* sound newsreel to be shown throughout the country. Charles Kahana (believed to be standing second from left) of the Puyallup tribe won the first-place prize of $25. (Courtesy TPL.)

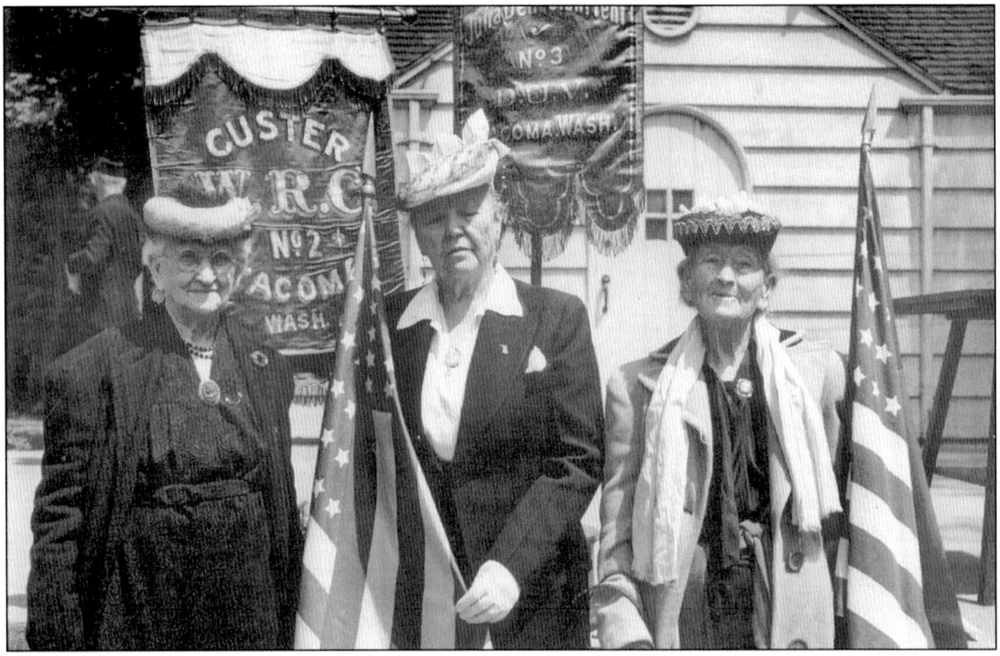

As widows of Civil War heroes, Millie Ball (left), 96; Eleanor Crossen (center), 84; and Lena Haskell, 87, participated in the Memorial Day exercises held at Wright Park on May 30, 1946. All Tacoma veteran organizations and their auxiliaries were invited to attend the first peacetime service in five years. (Courtesy TPL.)

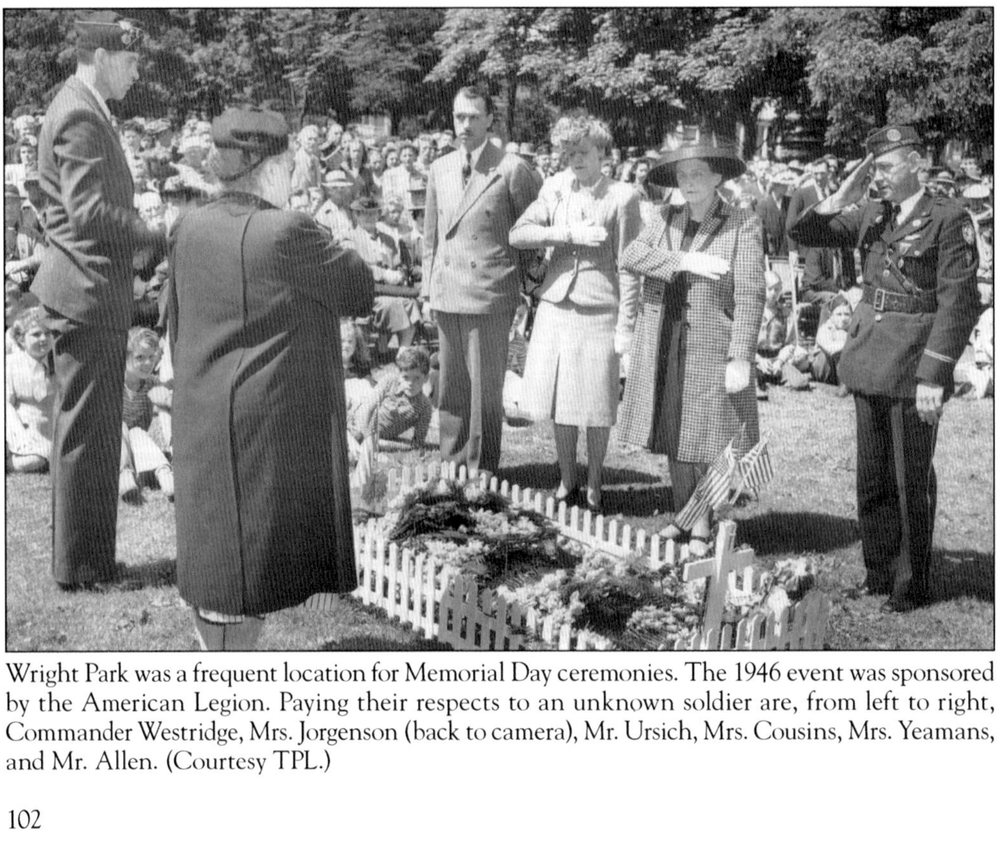

Wright Park was a frequent location for Memorial Day ceremonies. The 1946 event was sponsored by the American Legion. Paying their respects to an unknown soldier are, from left to right, Commander Westridge, Mrs. Jorgenson (back to camera), Mr. Ursich, Mrs. Cousins, Mrs. Yeamans, and Mr. Allen. (Courtesy TPL.)

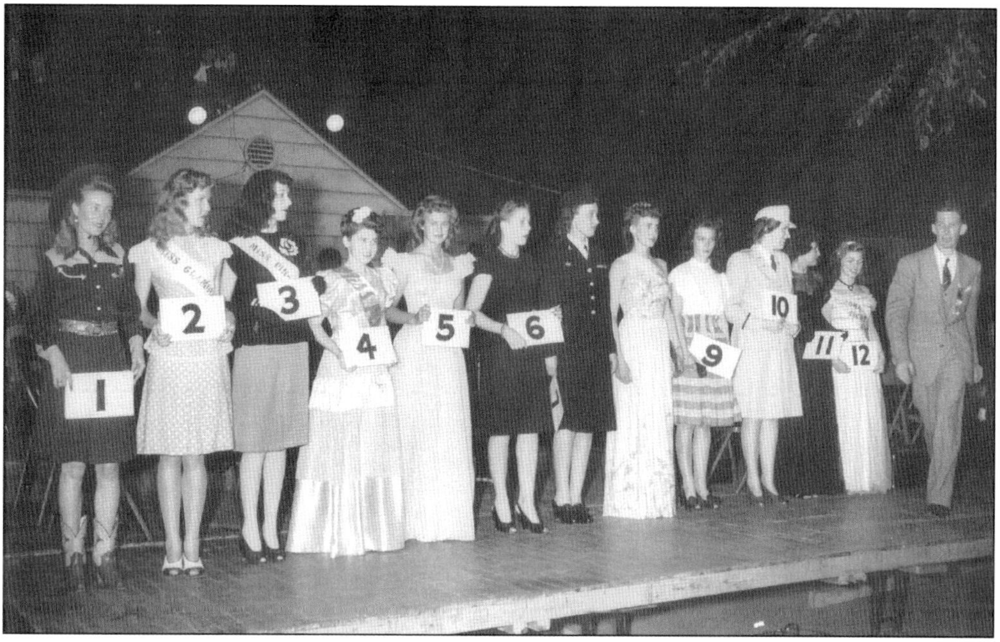

On June 25, 1946, a competition was held to determine who would be crowned Tacoma's Jubilee Queen. The 12 contestants (above) stand outside Wright Park's Shelter House awaiting the judges' decision. Winner Phyllis Hale (below), contestant No. 5, receives her crown from Maj. John H. Potter. The contest followed a concert by the Washington State Guard Band, led by Lt. J. R. Gress. The concert and crowning ceremony kicked off the 10-day Tacoma Jubilee, which included two parades, barnyard golf, volleyball, and marble tournaments, and a daily rodeo sponsored by Wild West Post No. 91 of the VFW. The Tacoma Jubilee of 1946 did not celebrate any particular event in city history. (Both courtesy TPL.)

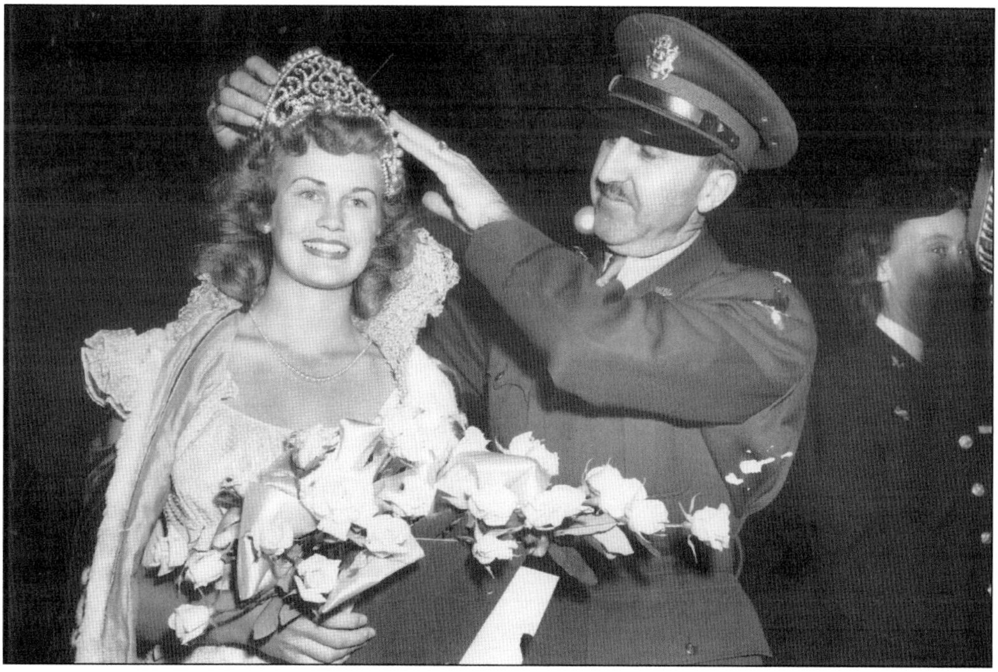

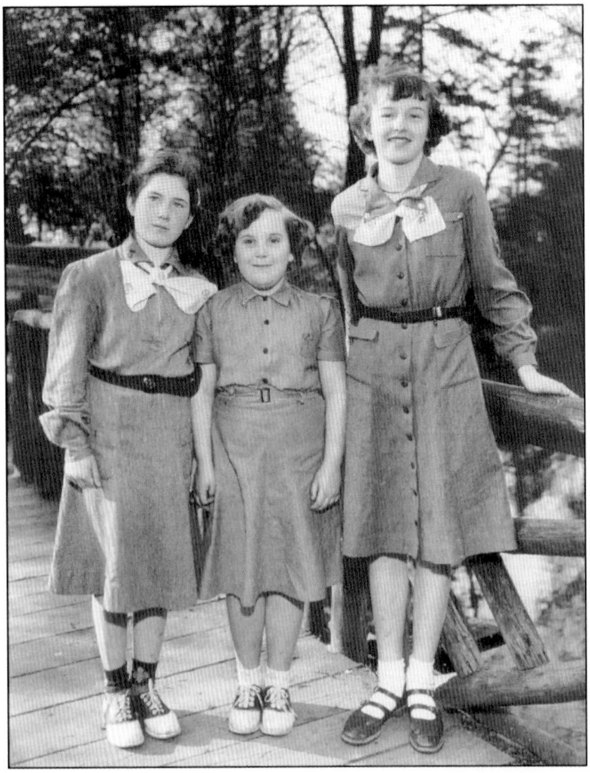

The 1952 Pierce County Girl Scout cookie sales champions pose on the rustic bridge across the Wright Park pond. The winners are Girl Scout Beverly Burton (left), third place; Brownie Jo Ann Walker (center), first place; and Girl Scout Sandra Sommer, second place. (Courtesy TPL.)

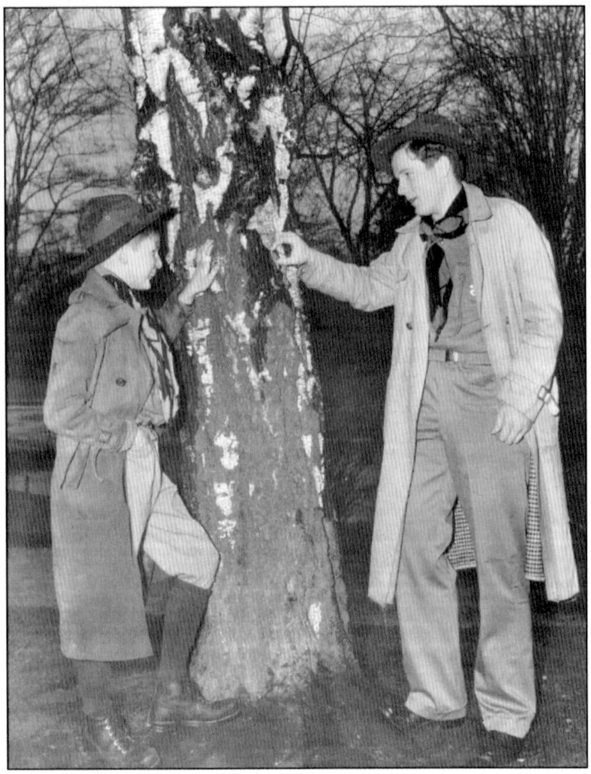

Donald Fowler (left) and John Hewitt of Troop 53 talk over a tree problem during National Boy Scout Week in 1939. More than 2,200 Tacoma-area Boy Scouts, Sea Scouts, and Cub Scouts, representing the 110 organized scouting units in Tacoma, gathered to celebrate the event. The repercussions from the 1934 windstorm were still evident on many of Wright Park's trees. (Courtesy TPL.)

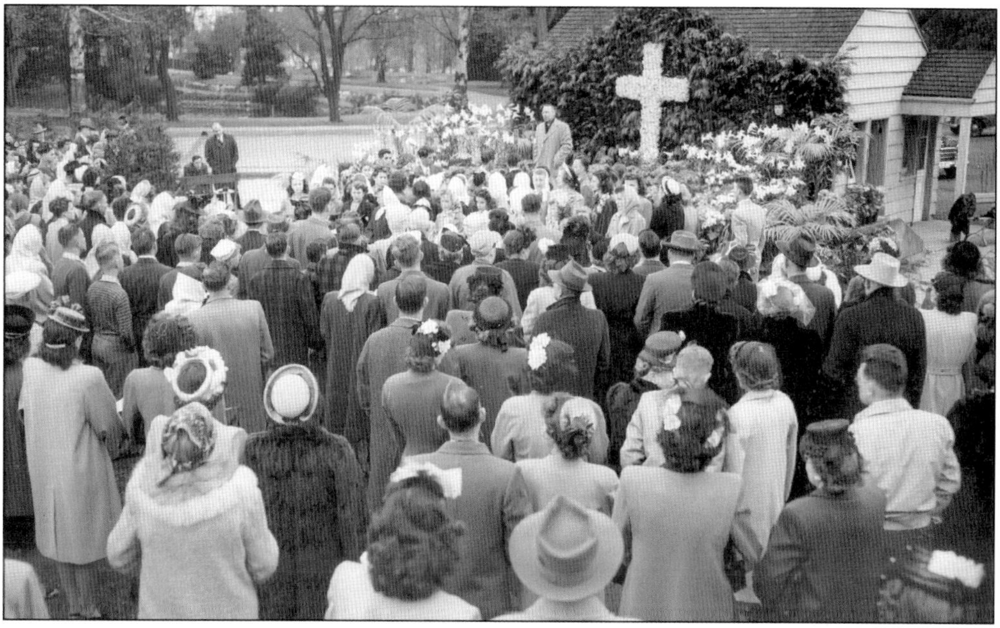

With so many churches surrounding Wright Park, Easter morning services in the park were extremely popular. Because park board members received numerous requests for this occasion each year, they encouraged churches to combine services. This April 6, 1947, Easter sunrise service was sponsored by the Youth Division of the Council of Churches. The park's early Shelter House can be seen to the right.

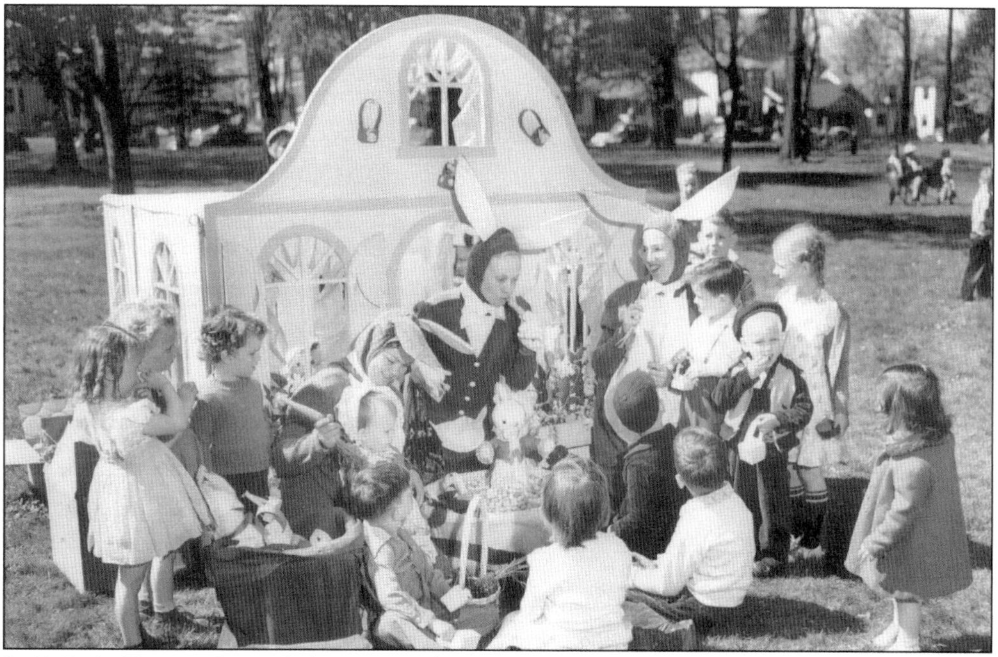

In 1949, the Tacoma Council of Parent-Teacher Associations sponsored an Easter egg hunt in Wright Park for preschool- and kindergarten-age children. Hazel Churchill, who served as chairperson, is one of the three women wearing bunny ears. A second "bunny" is Suzanne Marcy. The third is unidentified. (Courtesy TPL.)

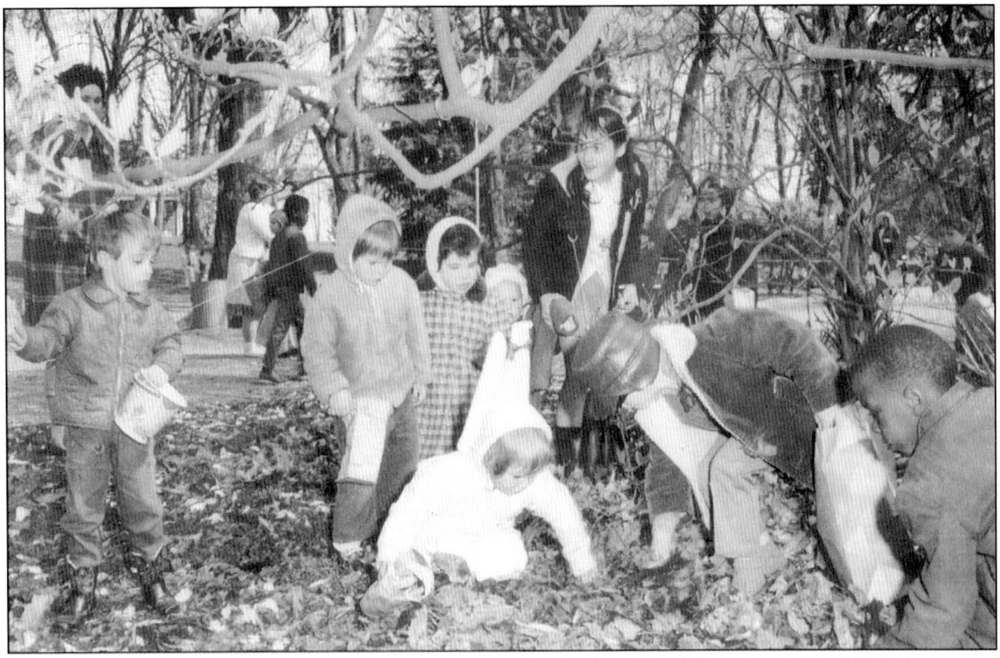

Easter egg hunts have been popular in Wright Park for decades. This April 12, 1968, hunt was sponsored by the Hilltop Multi-Service Center. Besides the colorfully dyed eggs, hidden within the park were special gold, brown, and silver eggs stuffed with gift certificates. Around 500 children were expected; when it became apparent that attendance would be higher, a "Help Your Tacoma Bunny" plea went out to the community. (Courtesy TPL.)

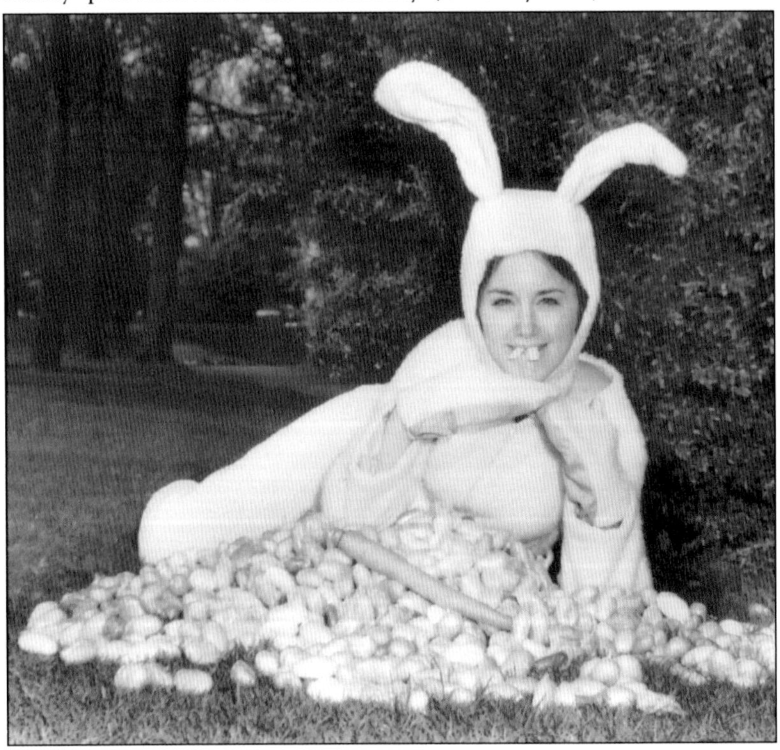

To promote the upcoming Easter egg hunt at Wright Park in 1973, Pacific Northwest Bell employee Candy Young poses with a large cache of eggs. Surely the children of Tacoma were anticipating the event after seeing Young in her bunny costume, complete with floppy ears and two enormous front teeth. (Courtesy TPL.)

In 2001, world-renowned glass artist and Tacoma native Dale Chihuly installed a unique and beautiful exhibit of his work behind the W. W. Seymour Botanical Conservatory. The graceful pieces of modern glass appear to be waving in a field of grass strewn with straw. The display makes for a wonderful contrast of old and new. In 2008, the centennial year of the conservatory's construction, local artists from various studios, including Chihuly's, will exhibit modern glasswork inside the century-old building.

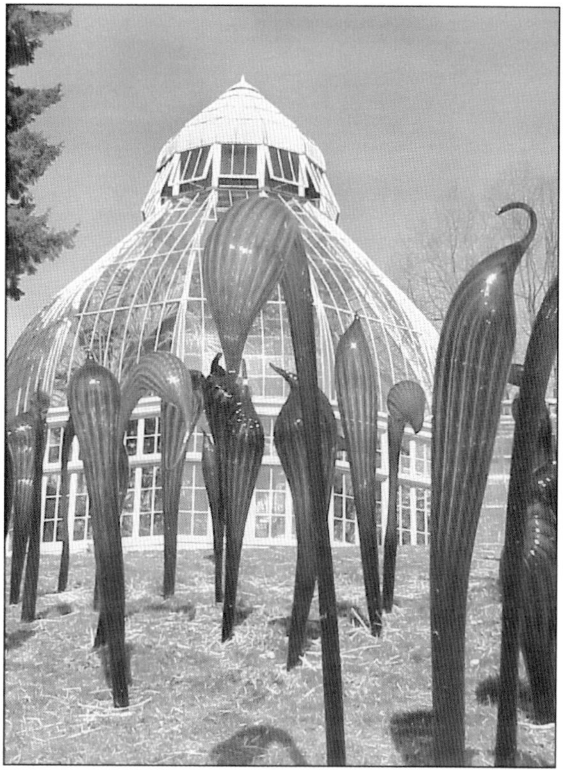

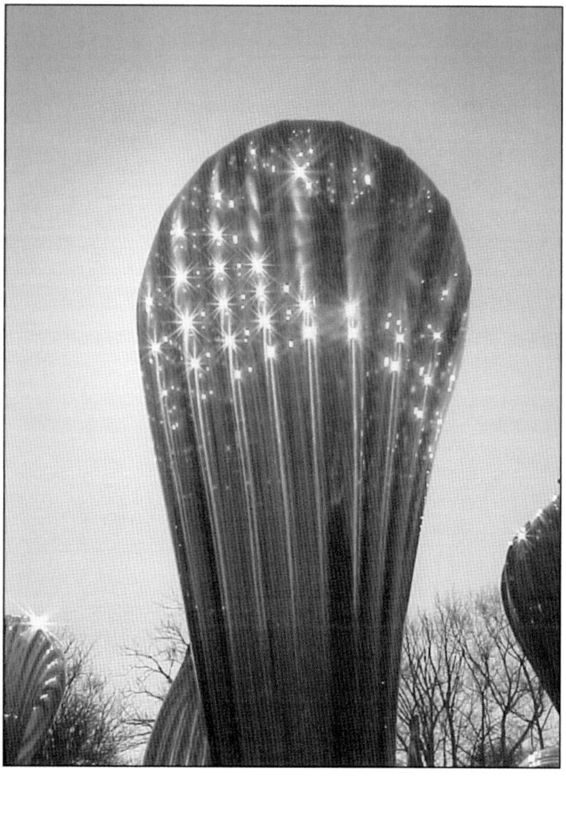

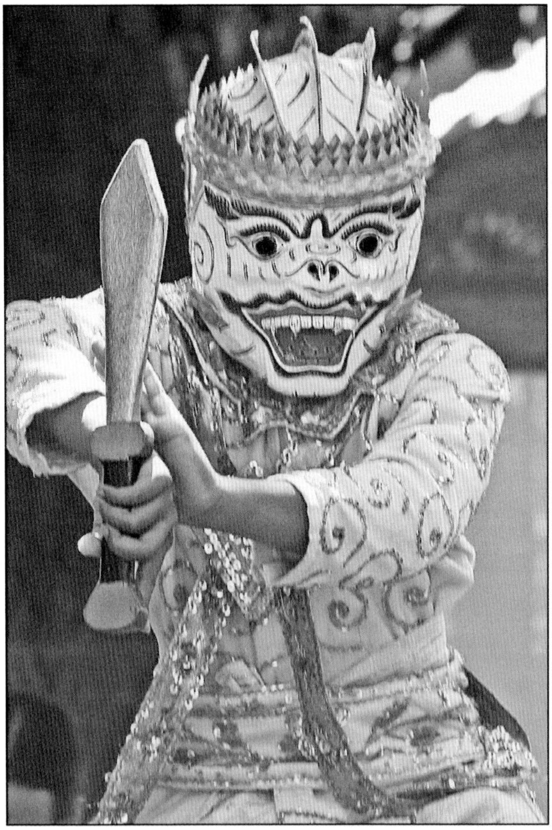

The first annual Ethnic Fest was held in 1986. This community festival celebrates the diversity of cultures in Pierce County. Traditionally occurring on the last weekend in July, the two-day event features entertainment, art, crafts, and food from cultures around the globe. Wright Park's canopy of trees provides just the right amount of shade to keep everyone cool as they enjoy the music, dancers, and other entertainment. In an effort to keep their native culture alive, members of Tiene Tama Samoa, below, teach traditional dance to their youth. At left, a young man wearing a fierce-looking mask and an intricately decorated costume performs with the Roosevelt Dancers, an organization devoted to teaching Cambodian dance and culture.

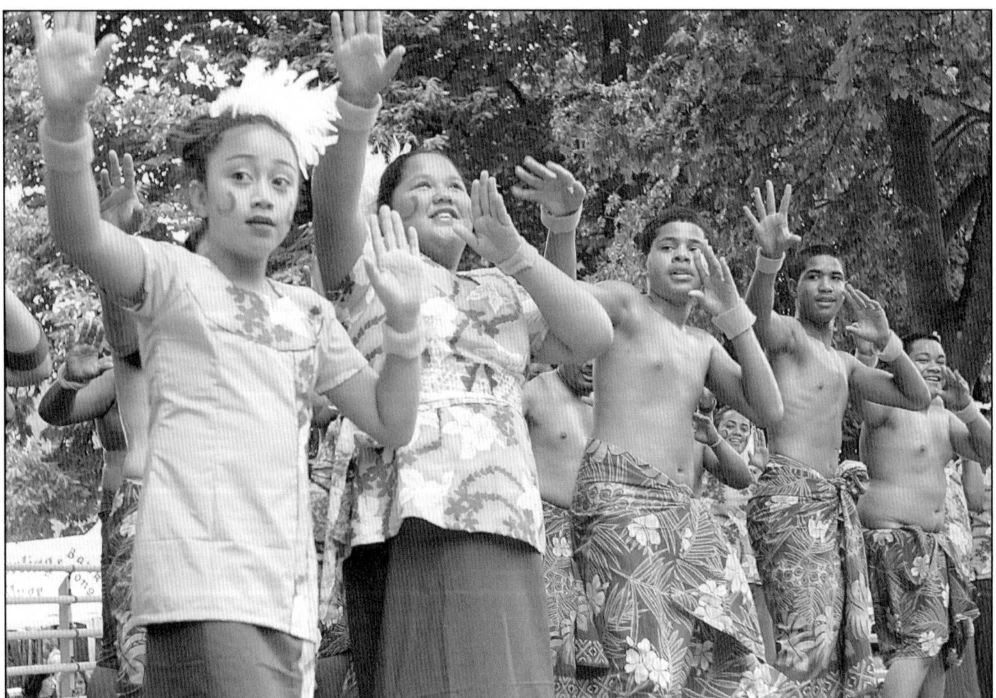

Seven

A Walk in the Park

Wright Park's appeal for more than 100 years has been its setting as a serene and verdant oasis in the midst of the city. Indeed, as soon as the City of Tacoma published the original plan of landscape designer Edward O. Schwagerl in 1890, the citizens and newspapers lauded it as "utilizing nature at nearly every point to make a beautiful and useful work of art." The statuary from Europe, the bandstand, paths, lake, and groves of trees planted with an eye to the future, and the graceful note of the conservatory added to Park Heights by the benevolence of William W. Seymour in 1908—all these features and embellishments were very much in keeping with the design aesthetics of late-19th-century public parks.

Missing from this original pastoral scene of Wright Park, however, was acreage set aside for sports or recreation, at least in the present understanding of those terms. To be sure, the park's natural contours precluded the possibility of any regulation-size fields or pitches, for there simply was not the space, or even level ground. The level grade that did exist was occupied by the course of Yakima Avenue bisecting the park from north to south. More to the point, though, was that the late-1800s concept of public parks held that they should be green and harmonious retreats from the city. However, in the early decades after 1900, public sentiment across the nation began to embrace the notion that parks should also increase the public good by providing locations for the growing interest in structured leisure time.

The emergence of this national recreation movement was made manifest all across Tacoma with a tremendous increase in organized activities in parks large and small. In Wright Park, the closure of Yakima Avenue in the late 1920s, due largely to traffic safety concerns, at last provided reasonably large and level expanses for the introduction of limited sports and recreation.

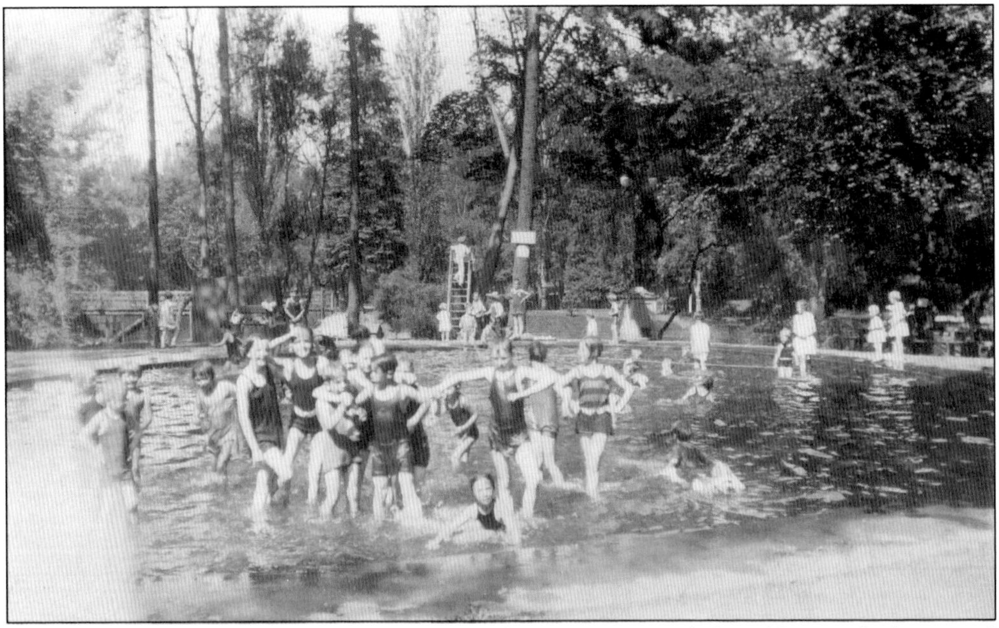

A *Tacoma Ledger* article during the summer of 1920 announced the addition of a large oval concrete wading pool as "a recent gift to the kiddies of Tacoma." Located close to South I Street in the northwest quadrant of Wright Park, it was a welcome respite from the summer heat. The lake and bridge are visible at the far left of this *c.* 1925 view.

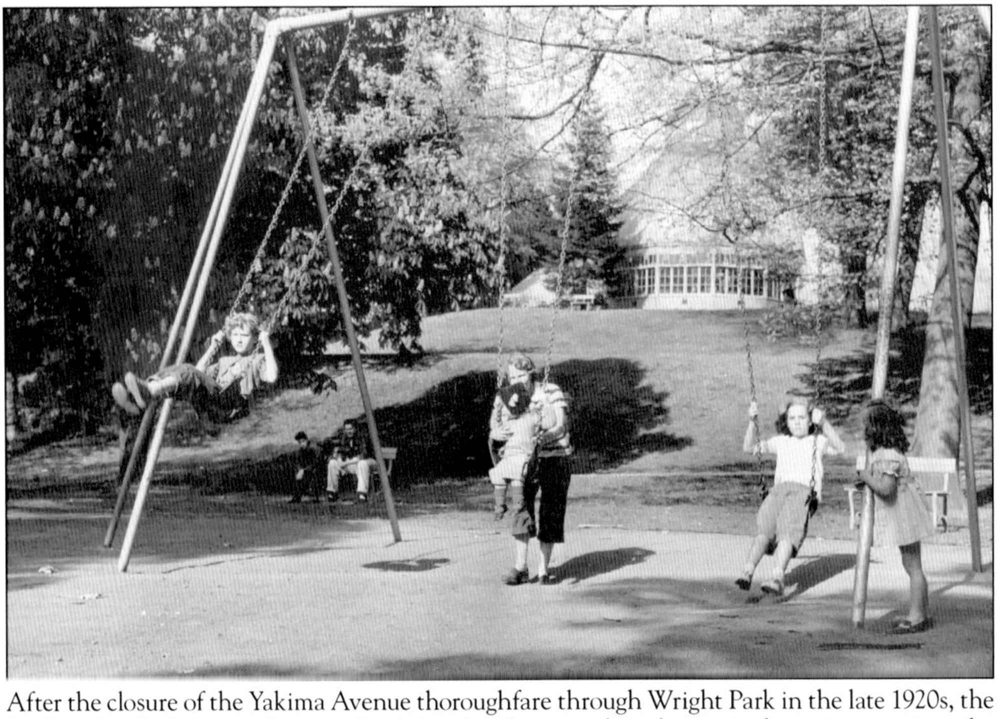

After the closure of the Yakima Avenue thoroughfare through Wright Park in the late 1920s, the level grade it had occupied was used to bring the playgrounds and organized activity areas into the central area of the park—a safer location away from the traffic on South I Street. Here children of the 1950s enjoy the swings located down the slope from the rear of the conservatory.

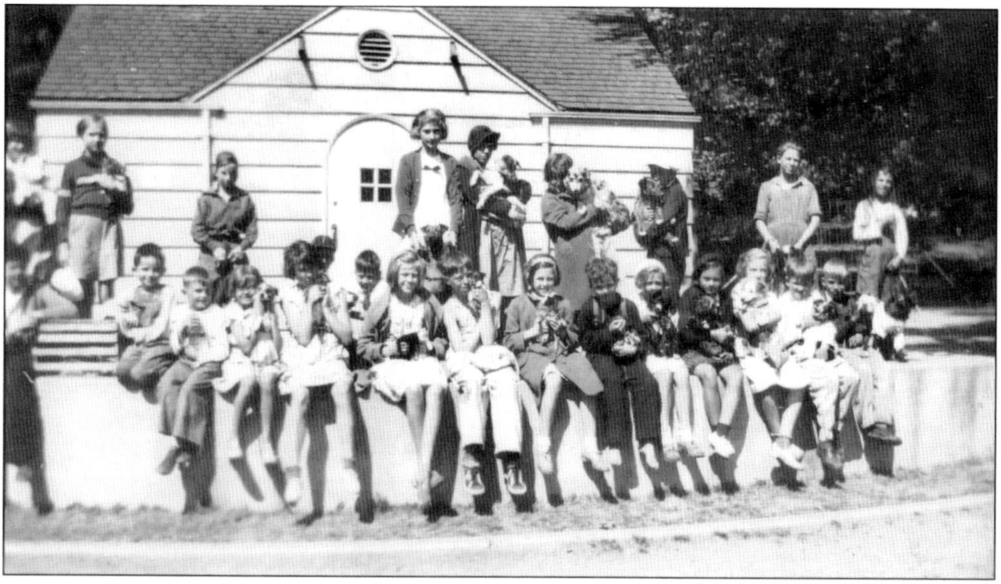

The Metropolitan Park District Board of Commissioners built the Shelter House in 1932 as a small recreation center; it too was located in the central, level area provided by the closure of Yakima Avenue. Above, unidentified children pose with their dogs in 1935. Pet parades and contests were popular activities during the Depression years, when fun needed to be free. Below, teenagers gather near the Wright Park Shelter House for a round of ping pong in the summer of 1940. Small field houses such as this existed in several Tacoma parks at this time.

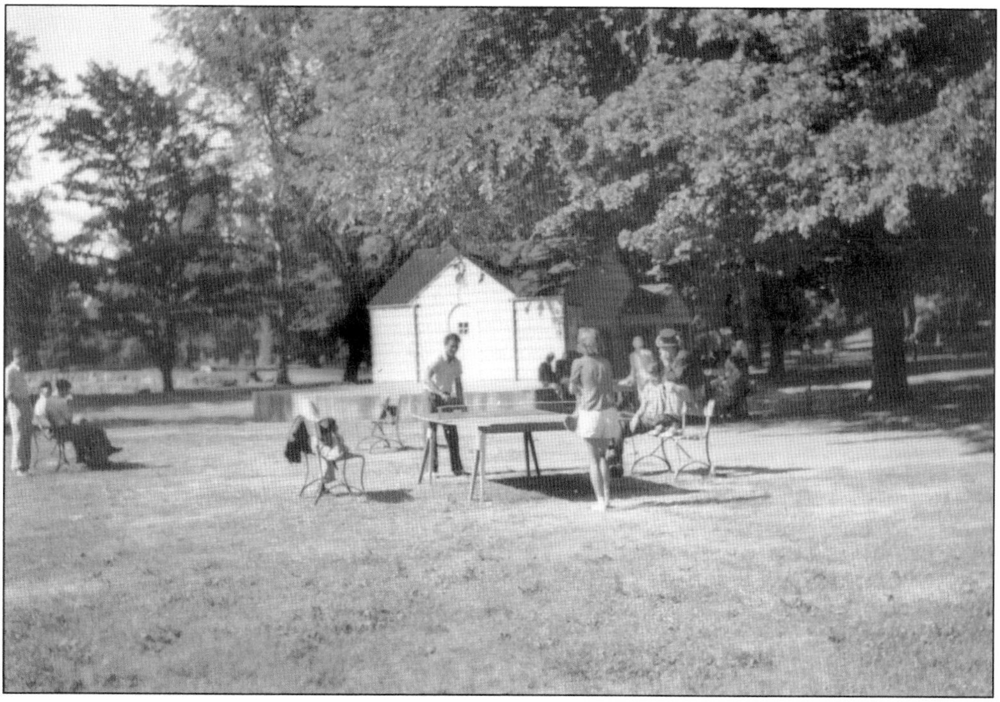

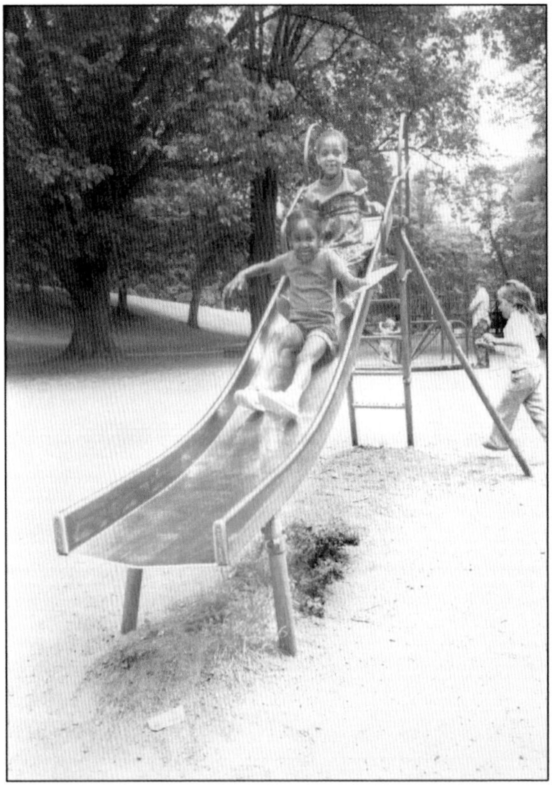

One of the main reasons cited for the closure of Yakima Avenue through Wright Park in the late 1920s was traffic safety near the children's playground area. The children of more recent decades have played in the area where horses, carriages, and early automobiles once drove. Interestingly, ideas about playground recreation and equipment evolve with time, and the passage of the 2005 citizen-approved Park Improvement Bond means that Wright Park's play areas are once again under scrutiny. Outdated swings and slides are slated for replacement by improved, 21st-century equipment, introducing the next era of the park's playground history.

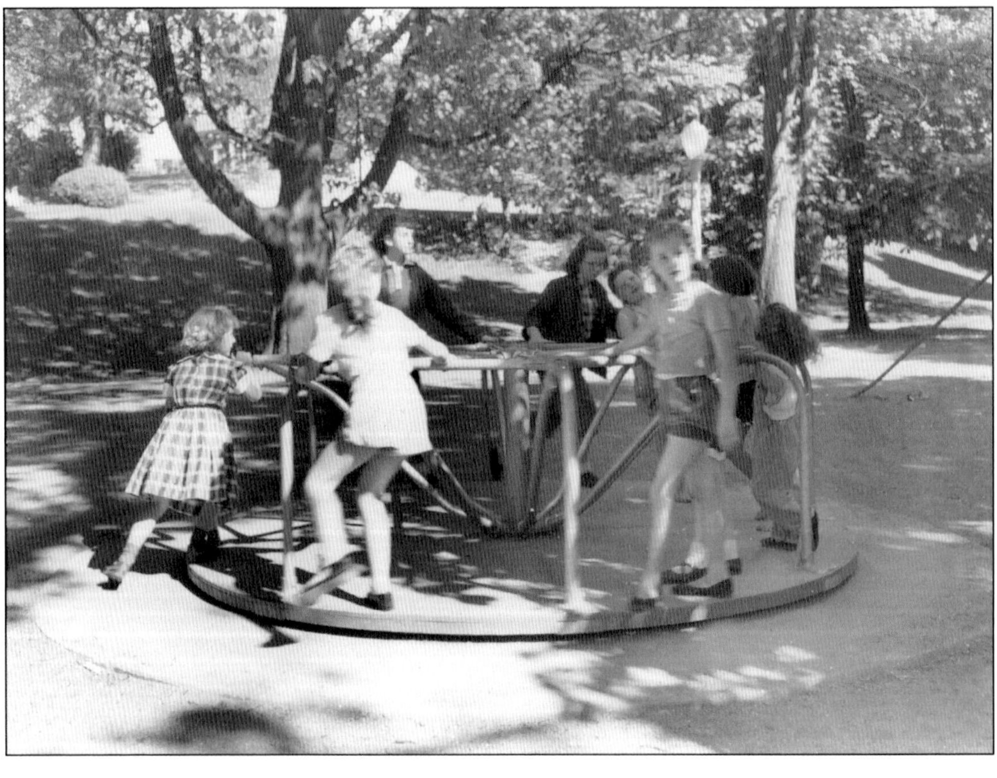

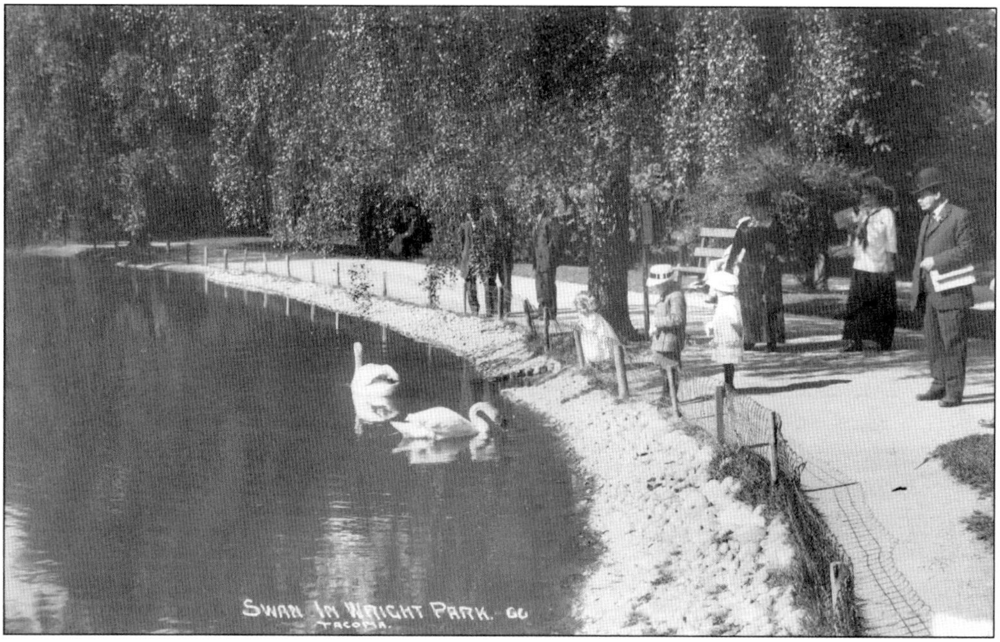

Generations of Tacoma children, such as those seen above around 1915, visited Wright Park to feed the swans and other aquatic birds that lived on the grounds near Bird Lake; they were doubtless met by more than one generation of swans since the original Victor and Victoria at the start of the 20th century. The lake was also popular for a variety of other pastimes as well. In the photograph below, Eugene Brown (left) and Jim Buirkhouse launch their model sailboats in Wright Park on a spring day. All audience members are unidentified except Kenneth Lober, the boy on the scooter. This photograph made the front page of the *Tacoma Times* on March 21, 1938. (Above courtesy ES; below courtesy TPL.)

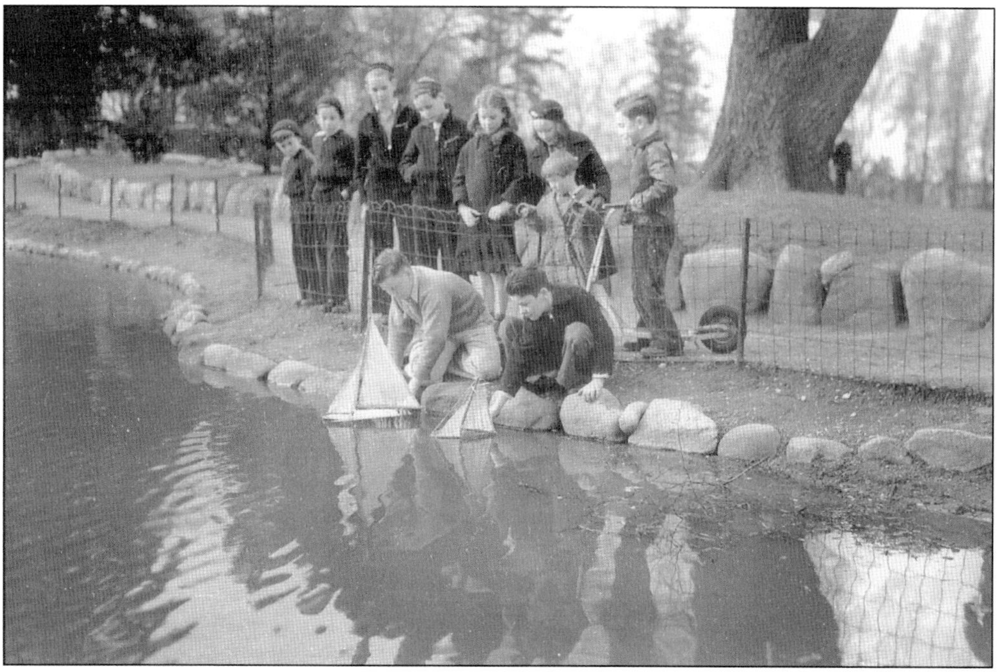

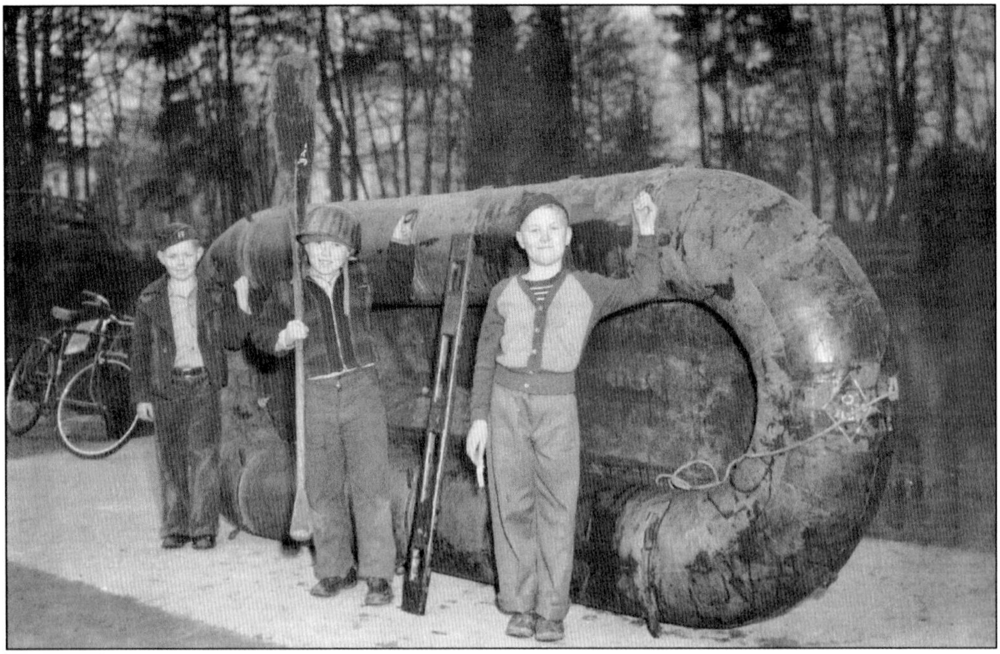

The lake in Wright Park offered more than a place to feed the birds and sail toy boats. This enterprising but unidentified trio must have had parental permission to head to the park so well-equipped for a large adventure, perhaps inspired by World War II news. Note their military helmet and hats and the obvious delight in their mission. (Courtesy TPL.)

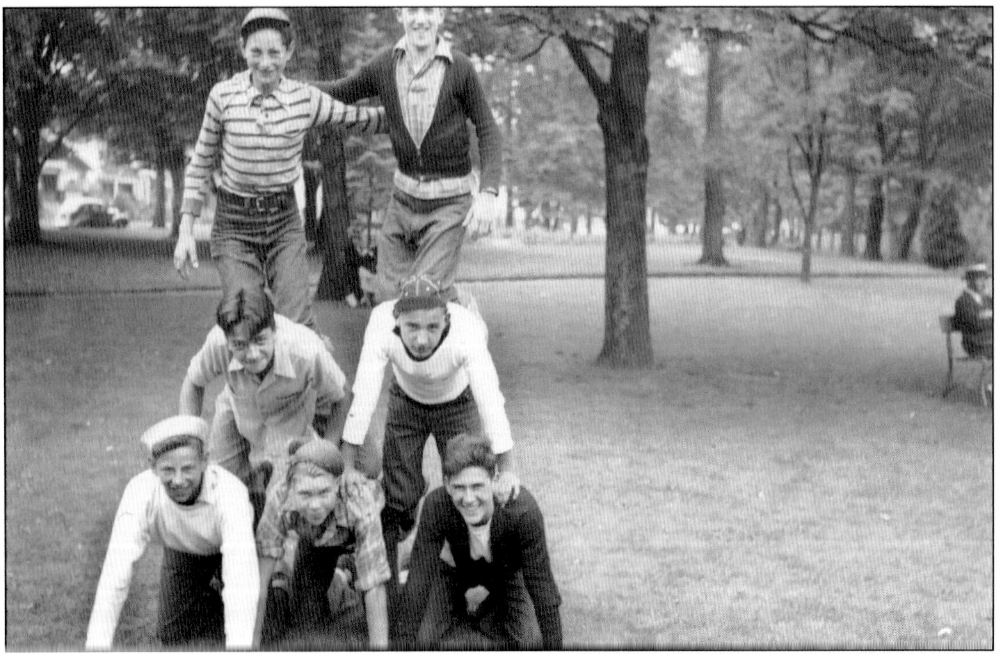

Jaunty young men form a pyramid in Wright Park in the summer of 1940, recording their winning status as "All Junior Olympic Champions" in football. Unfortunately, their names were not recorded in the album kept by one of the playground leaders. The Metropolitan Park District of Tacoma has operated an extensive series of recreation programs across the city since the 1920s.

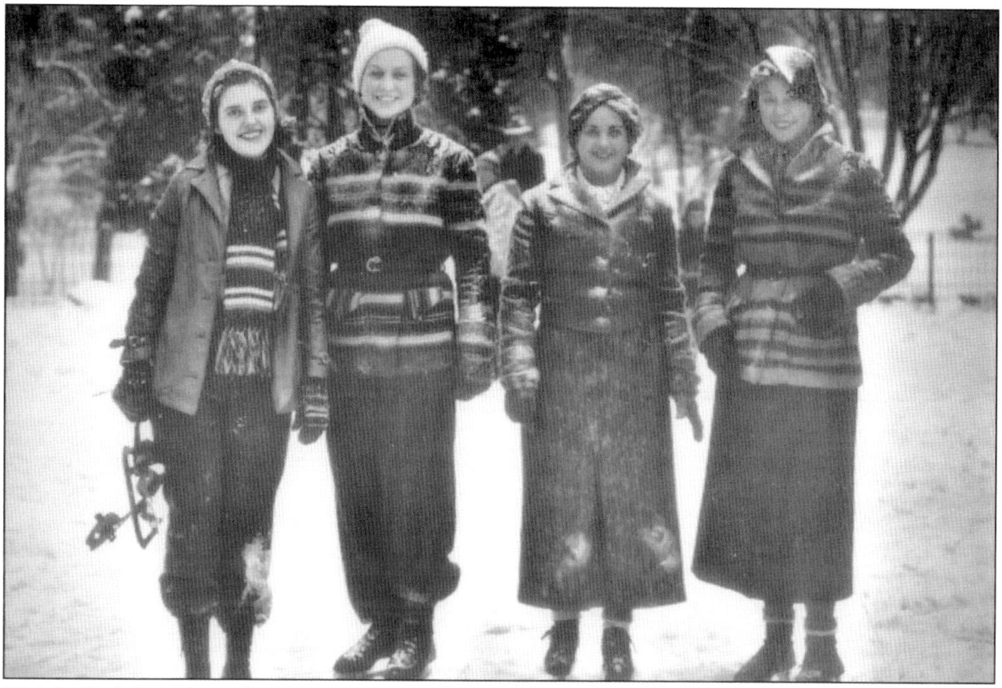

Wright Park has always been a popular wintertime destination for the neighborhood, particularly when temperatures have dipped low enough to provide winter sports and recreation. Many Tacoma residents of a certain age have fond memories of the lake in Wright Park freezing, thus permitting ice-skating. These photographs from the mid-1930s document two such anticipated occasions. Above, young ladies enjoy the ice in 1935. The 1937 skating party below includes, from left to right, Burrell Bresemann, Will LaPoint, Ray Hall, Don Heselwood, Shirley Quinn, Johanna Pitzl, Jack Alvord, and Ed Carlin. Bob Taylor stands behind the group. (Both courtesy TPL)

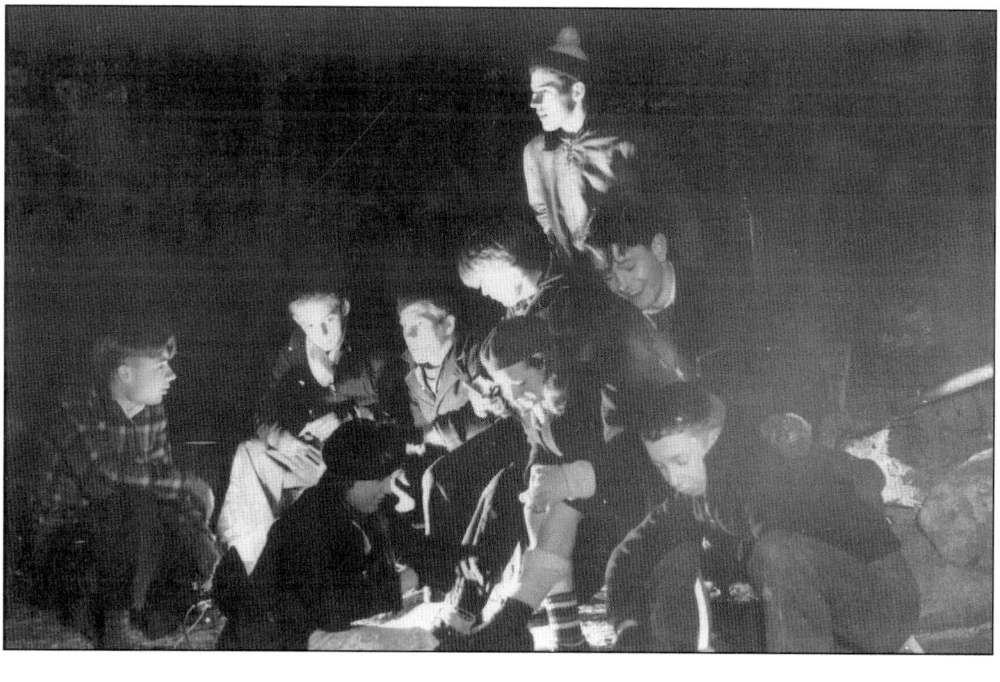

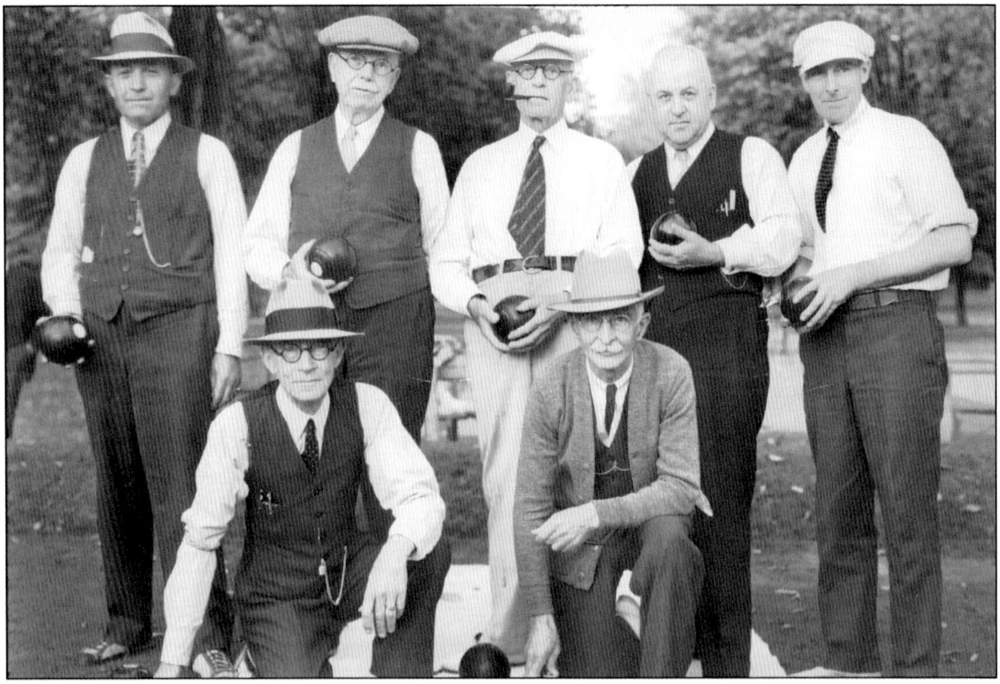

The Wright Park lawn bowling rinks, as the playing greens are called, date back to the establishment of the Tacoma Lawn Bowling Club in July 1929. The club petitioned the Metropolitan Park District for a regulation-size bowling green in 1933; it opened in 1936, with lighting for nighttime matches added in 1937. Alexander Drummond served as club president from 1929 to 1934. (Courtesy Tacoma Lawn Bowlers.)

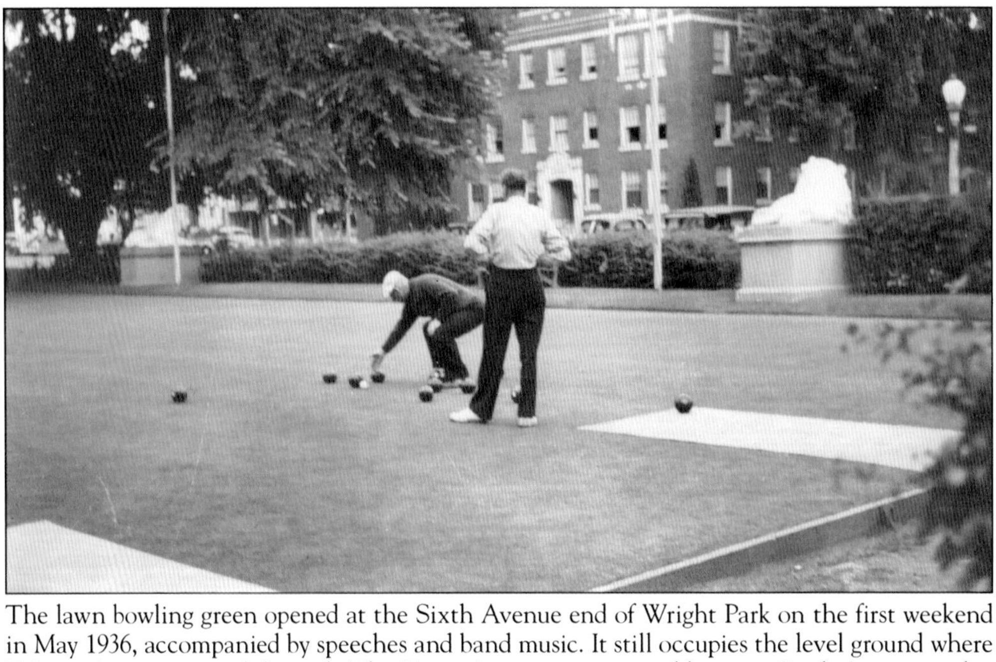

The lawn bowling green opened at the Sixth Avenue end of Wright Park on the first weekend in May 1936, accompanied by speeches and band music. It still occupies the level ground where Yakima Avenue entered the park. The Virges Apartments are visible across Sixth Avenue in this view. (Courtesy Tacoma Lawn Bowlers.)

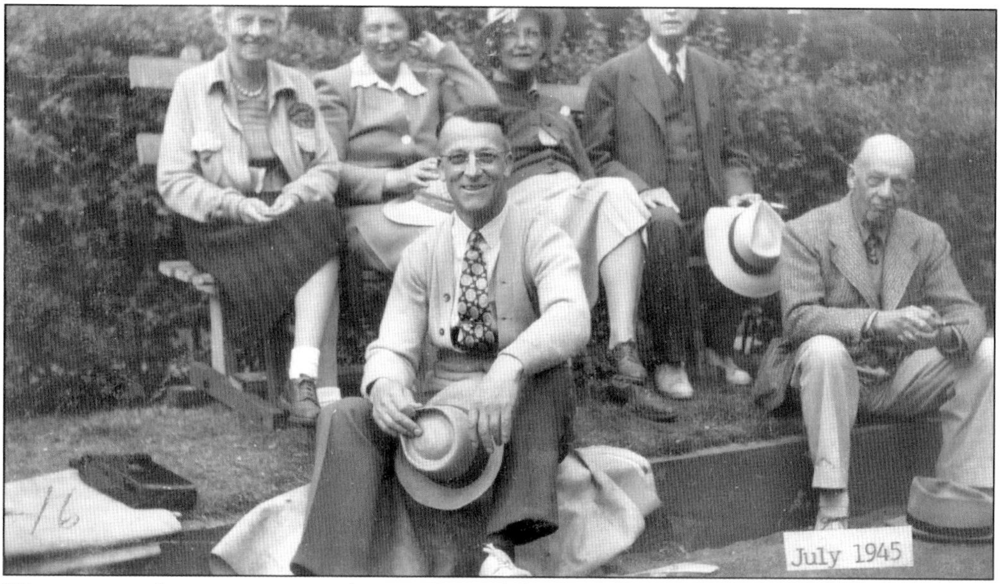

Women were also active among the members of the Tacoma Lawn Bowling Club. In July 1945, a photograph taken in Wright Park by Yale Henry records the victorious Mildred Geer (left), Grace McDonald (center), and Mrs. Sweeting. The women defeated the men seated on the curb of the green—Walter Heath (left), who seems happy about it, and W. L. McCormick, who does not. (Courtesy Tacoma Lawn Bowlers.)

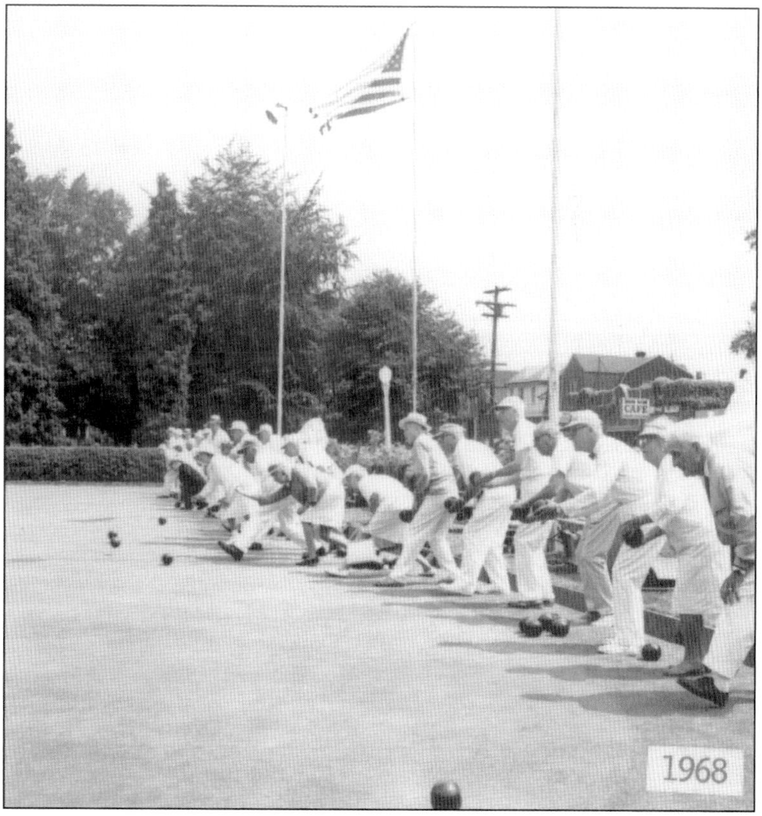

By the time of this 1968 photograph, members of the Tacoma Lawn Bowling Club were routinely wearing white clothing during matches. Here they almost obscure one of the pair of lion statues at the Yakima Avenue end of Wright Park. The Hob Nob Café, a neighborhood institution for decades, is visible across Sixth Avenue from the bowling green. (Courtesy Tacoma Lawn Bowlers.)

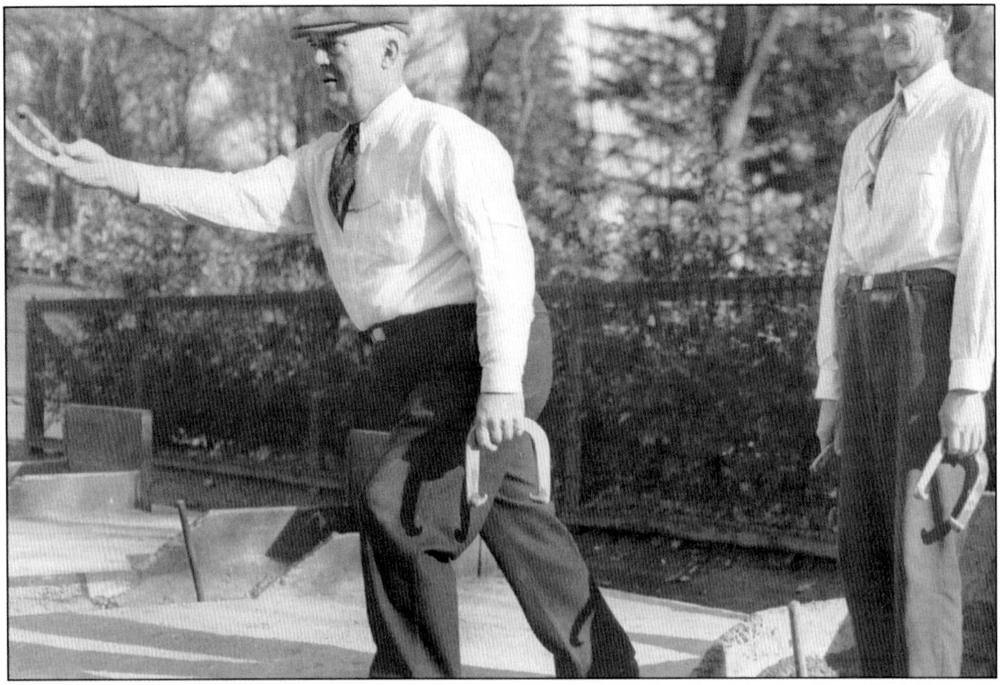

The sport of pitching horseshoes has a long history in Wright Park. The Metropolitan Park District and the Tacoma Horseshoe Pitchers Association installed courts in several of the city's parks and playgrounds in the 1920s. In 1938, eight were built in Wright Park along the former Yakima Avenue concourse. Above, two unidentified men tuck their neckties into their shirts and try out the new courts in March 1938. In 1949, the Washington State Horseshoe Pitching Tournament gathered 32 pitchers together in Wright Park for a crowd-gathering three-day competition. Afterward, contestants posed for a group portrait, seen below. (Both courtesy TPL.)

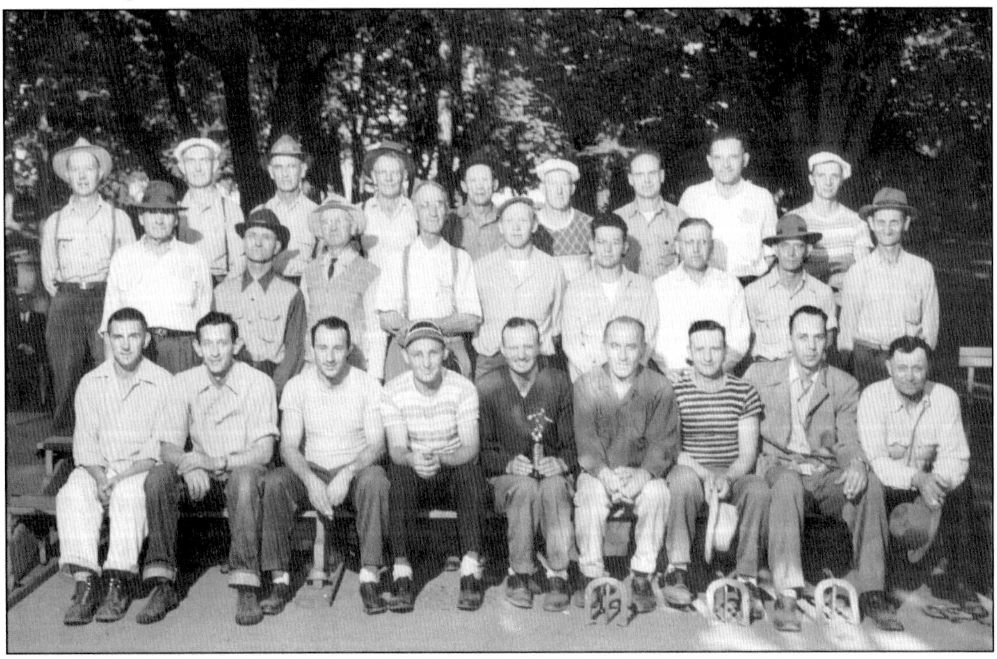

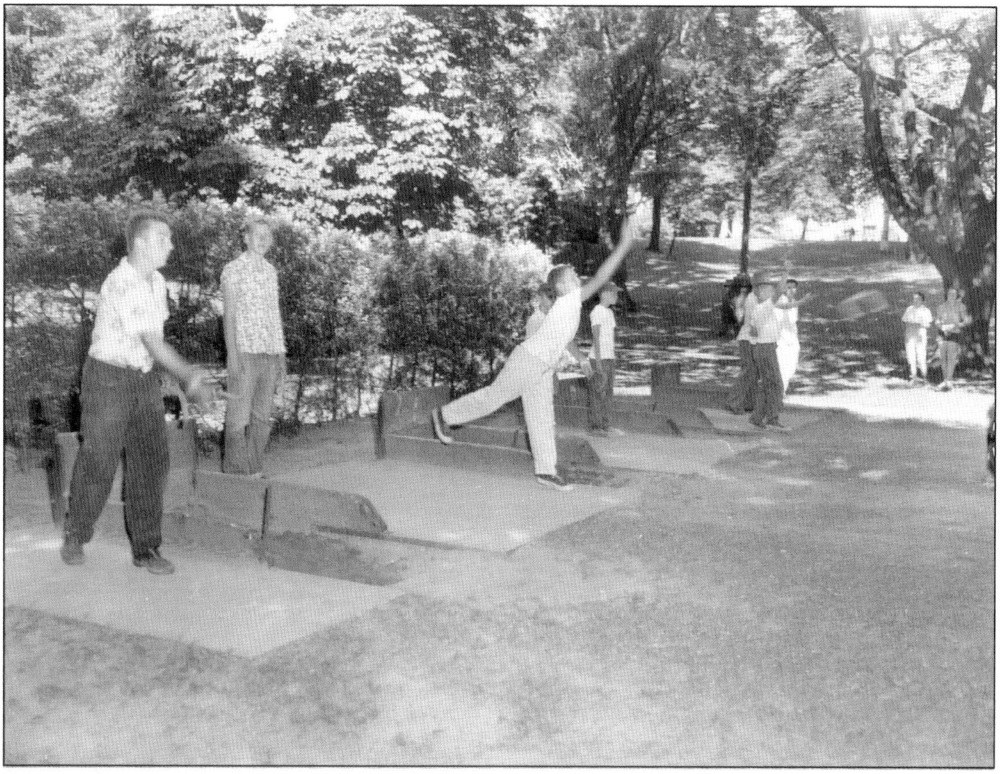

From its beginnings across Tacoma in the 1920s, horseshoe pitching has not always been strictly for adults. The Metropolitan Park District incorporated such competition into the wide range of activities offered in the summer recreation programs across the city. It was one of many organized outdoor options for youth in Wright Park during the 1950s, when these young Tacoma residents (above) were photographed in mid-pitch. Women and girls also played the game, though there is less of an official photographic record of their participation. The concentration of Ron Dixon (below) is readily apparent as he prepares to pitch at the annual Henry Gilbo Open, sponsored by the Tacoma Horseshoe Pitchers Association in Wright Park in May 1989. Dixon won the Class A competition.

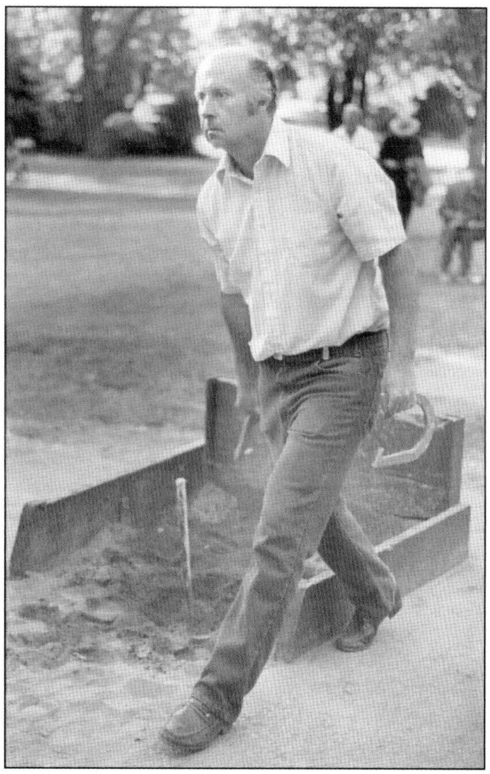

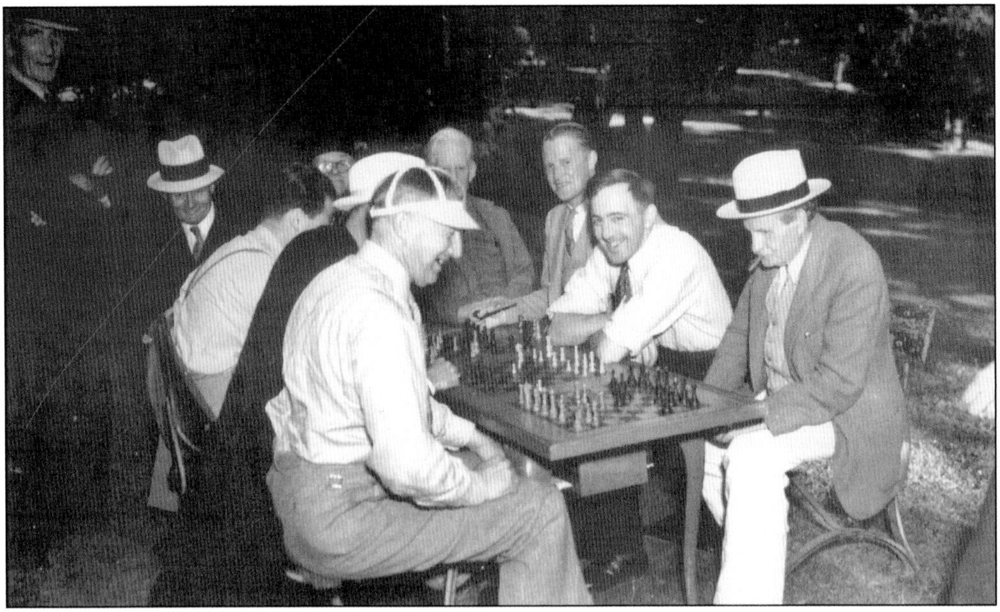

Competitive recreation in Wright Park over the decades has had cerebral as well as physical components. Here several men have met in Wright Park to play chess at a special three-game chess table in 1937. The decade of the 1930s, with the unemployment of the Great Depression, meant that these men may have had more spare time than they would have preferred. (Courtesy TPL.)

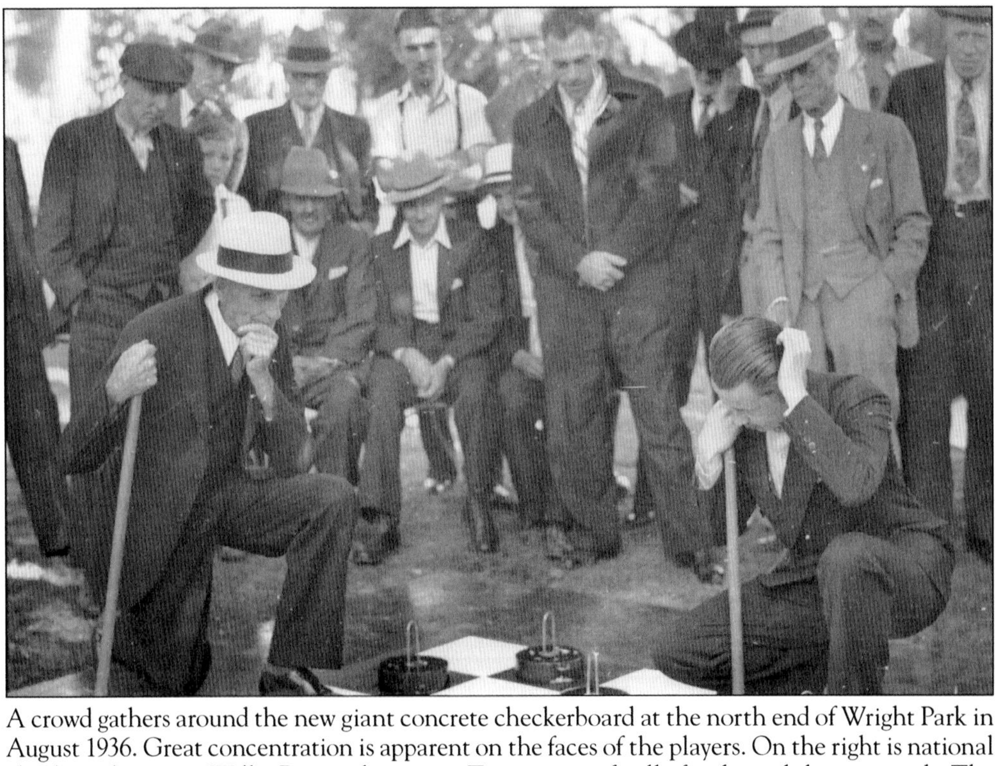

A crowd gathers around the new giant concrete checkerboard at the north end of Wright Park in August 1936. Great concentration is apparent on the faces of the players. On the right is national checkers champion Willie Ryan, who was in Tacoma specifically for this exhibition match. The checkerboard was 12 feet square, painted black and white with a green border. (Courtesy TPL.)

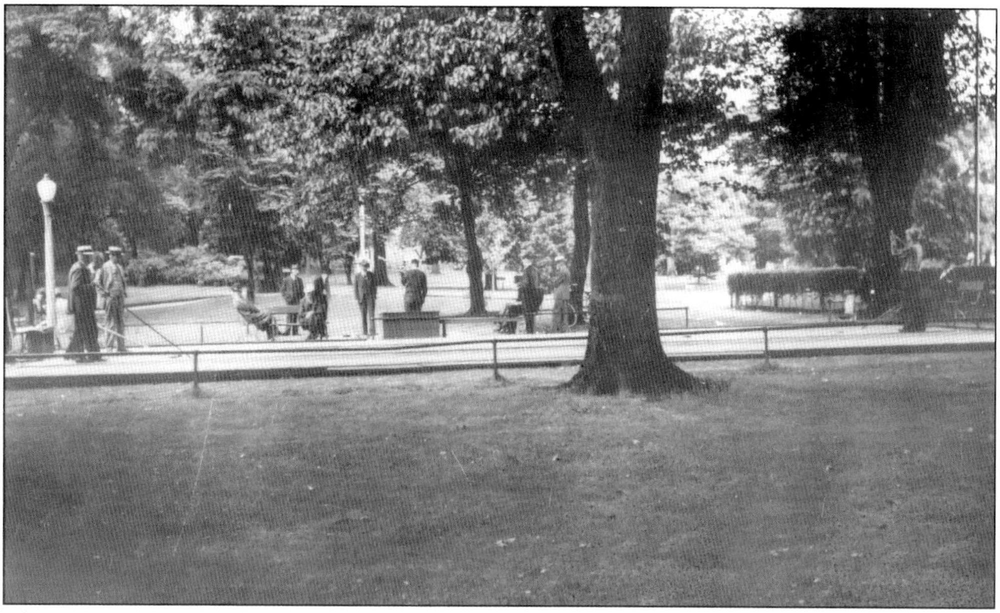

The construction of three shuffleboard courts was made possible by financial and material donations by Tacoma businesses. Courts were installed in July 1929, very soon after the closure of Yakima Avenue. The original boards were 50 feet long and 4 feet wide. Above, several men in suits, ties, and hats are poised for action with their cues in the 1930s. Below, two nattily dressed players discuss the strategy of using the shuffleboard cue and the disks on March 21, 1938—the first day of spring. (Below courtesy TPL.)

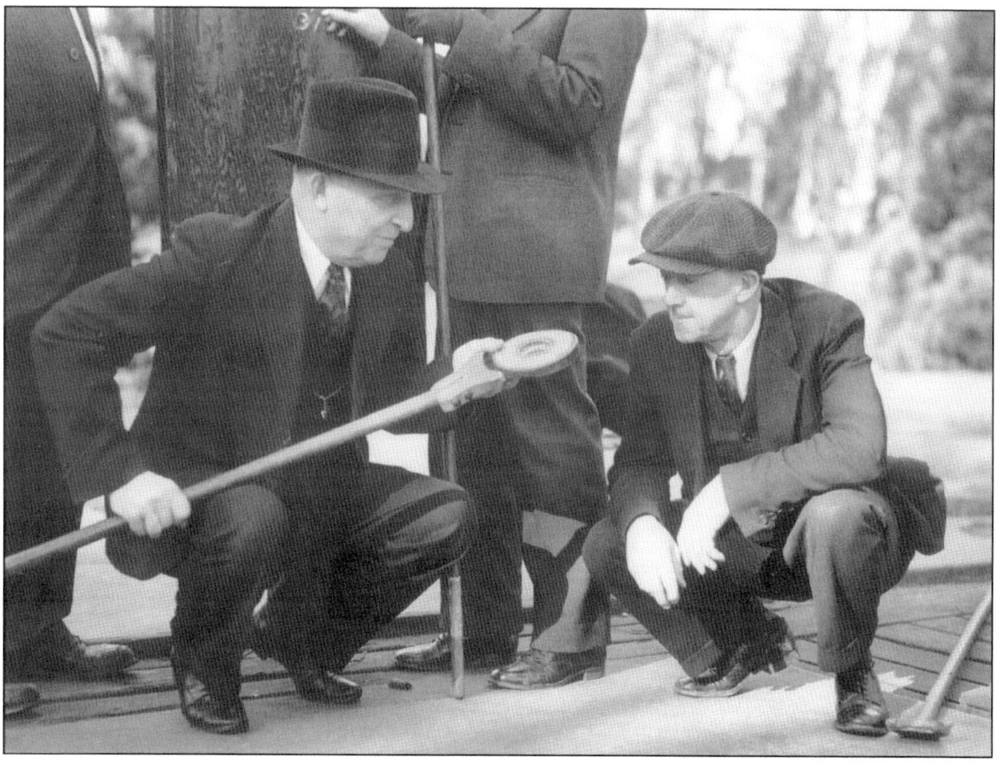

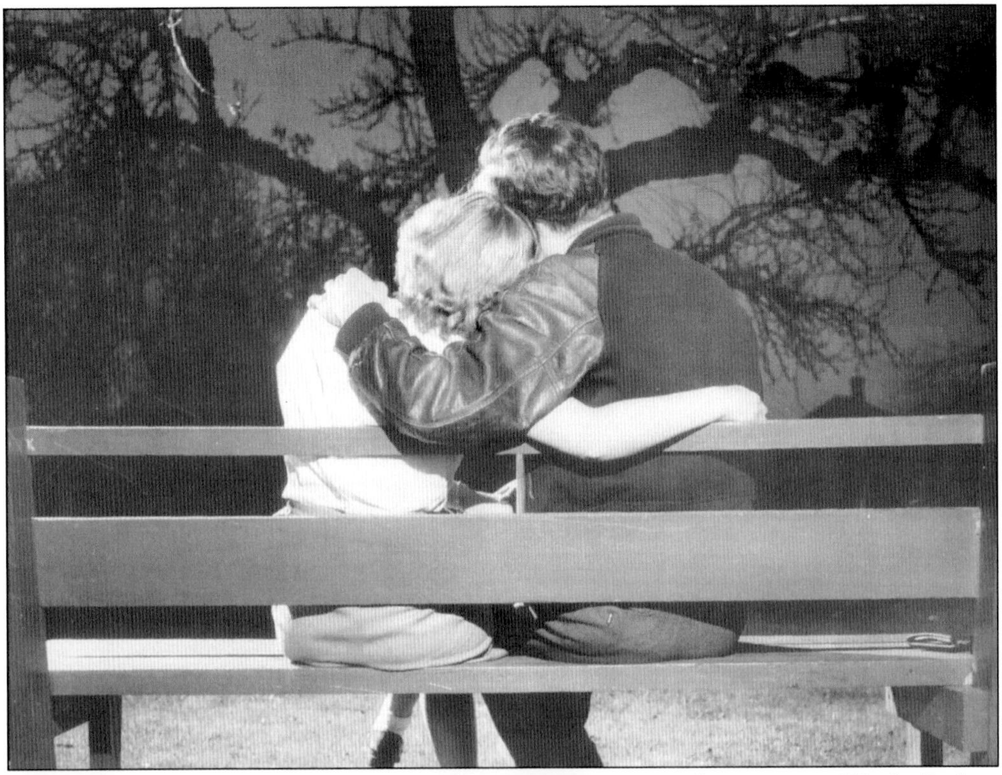

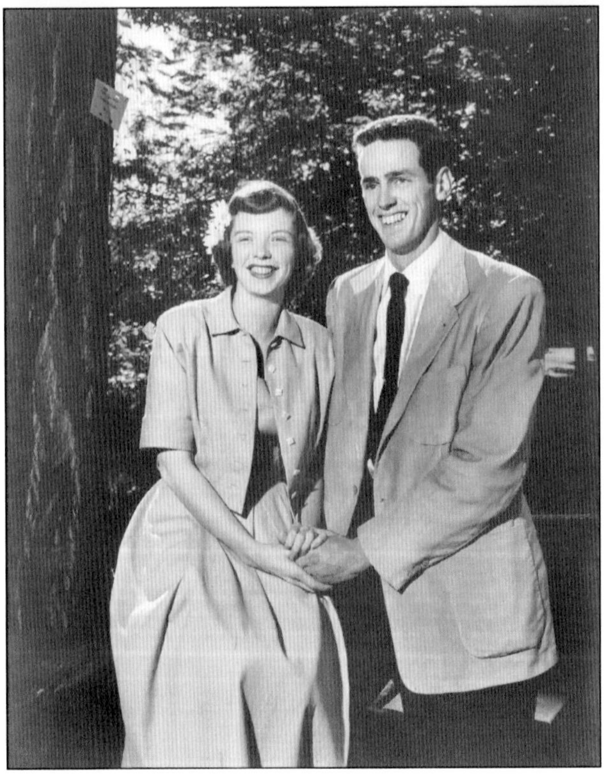

Not all activities in Wright Park were oriented toward sports teams, although courtship may certainly be described as such. No doubt many Tacoma residents have fond memories of shared moments in many parks across the city; the two illustrated here belong to Wright Park. Above, a young couple enjoys a mild spring evening in 1947. At left, Donna Thompson, a graduate of Lincoln High School and the University of Washington, and E. Wayne Mann Jr., a Stadium High School and College of Puget Sound graduate, pose for their spring 1950 engagement photograph in Wright Park. With all the houses of worship ringing its perimeter and the W. W. Seymour Conservatory available for ceremonies as well, Wright Park must appear as the background in many wedding albums. (Above courtesy TPL; left courtesy Wendy Mann Walters.)

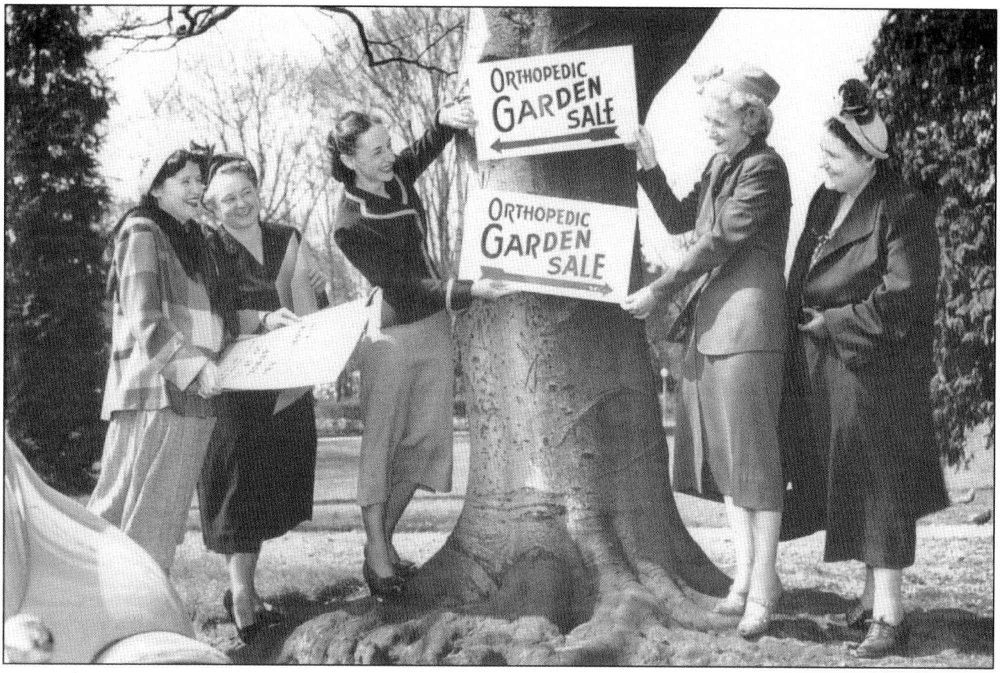

Over the decades, Wright Park frequently served as a desirable backdrop for a wide variety of publicity photographs taken by the city's commercial photographers. Here members of four guilds of the Tacoma Orthopedic Association pose in April 1950 to advertise a garden sale to raise funds for an eventual pediatric hospital in Tacoma. (Courtesy TPL.)

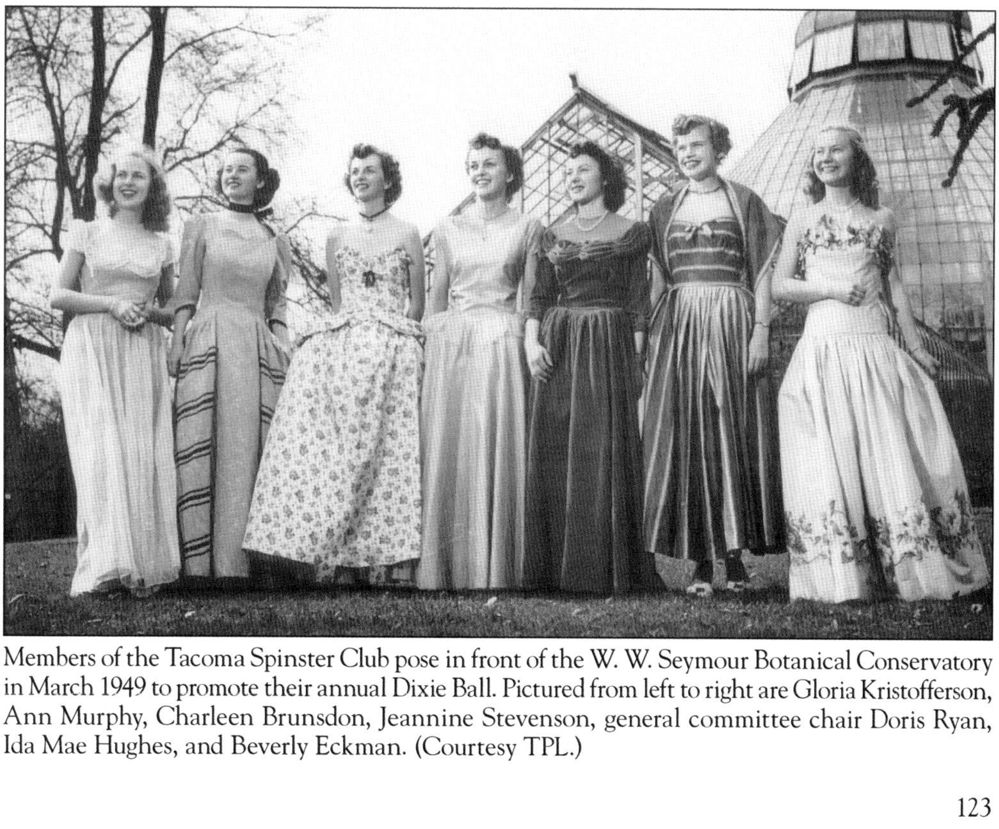

Members of the Tacoma Spinster Club pose in front of the W. W. Seymour Botanical Conservatory in March 1949 to promote their annual Dixie Ball. Pictured from left to right are Gloria Kristofferson, Ann Murphy, Charleen Brunsdon, Jeannine Stevenson, general committee chair Doris Ryan, Ida Mae Hughes, and Beverly Eckman. (Courtesy TPL.)

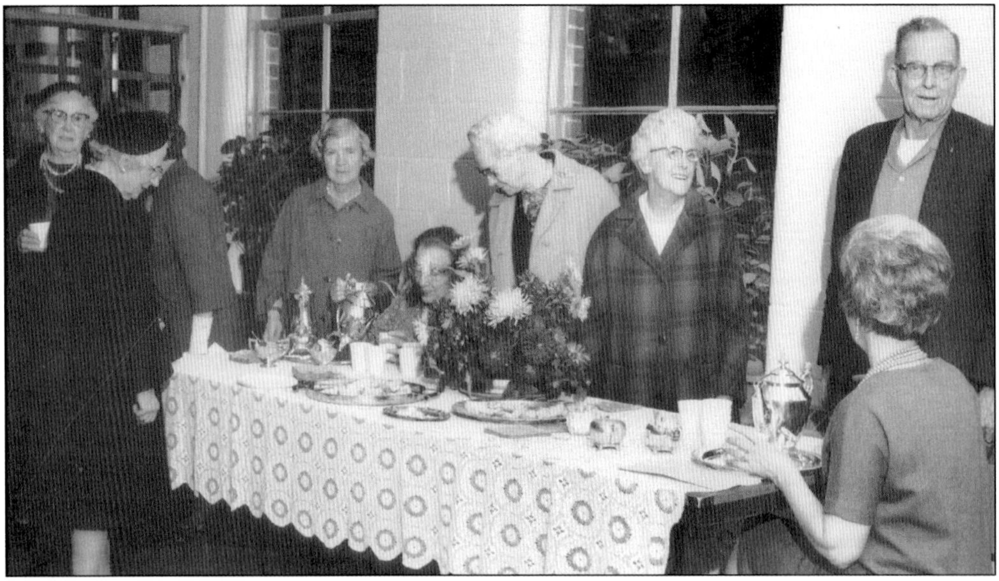

In 1953, the Metropolitan Park District constructed a senior citizens' activity room adjacent to the Wright Park maintenance building. In 1968, the activity room gained a kitchenette, and the Wright Park Senior Center began. The photograph above records the tea held on October 23, 1968, to mark the occasion. In 1980, the Wright Park Senior Center expanded to more than double its existing space for recreation, arts and crafts, and continuing education. Below, a park visitor demonstrates an outdoor fitness activity. In 1983, the Metropolitan Park District partnered with Wells Fargo Bank and Consolidated Hospitals (the forerunner of MultiCare Health System) to install a Senior Walking Course in Wright Park, giving the older population of the surrounding neighborhood expanded opportunities for outdoor health and recreation activities. (Above courtesy TPL.)

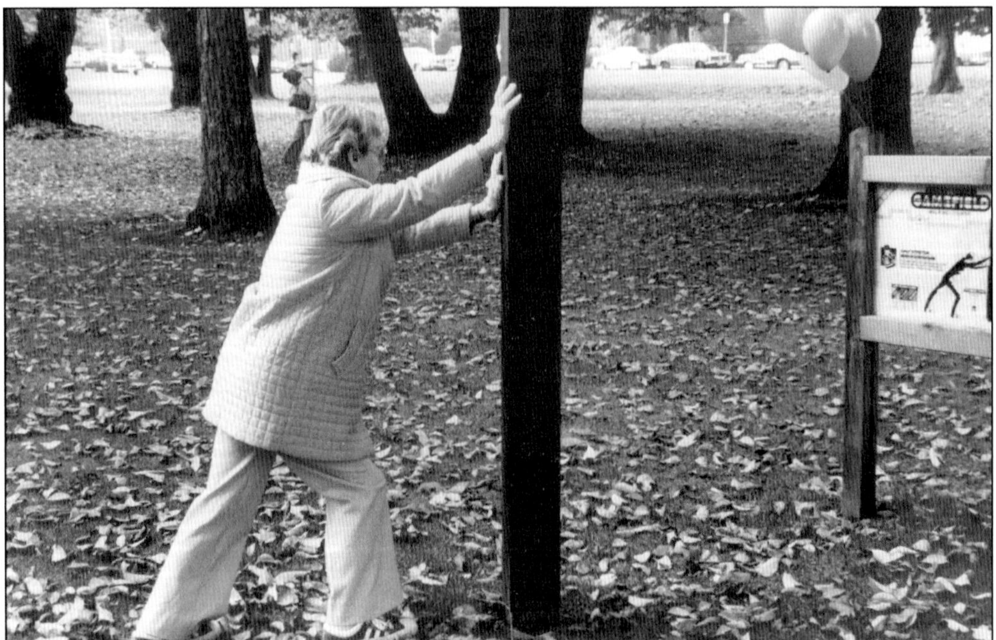

Sports in Wright Park have been as team-oriented or as individual as the visitor. A 1933 newspaper advertisement by Rhodes Brothers—a downtown Tacoma department store institution until its closure in 1974—appealed to women on both the fashion and health levels, and promoted Wright Park at the same time. Note that the sports attire cost as much as the sports equipment, even 75 years ago.

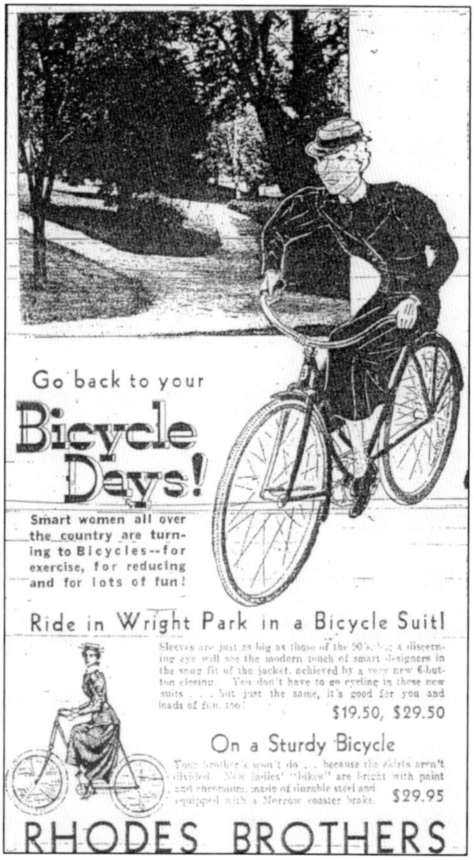

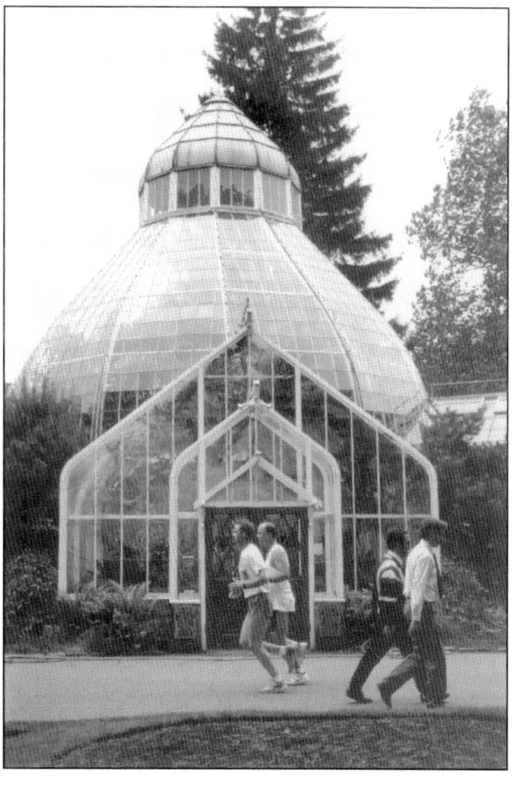

When the Tacoma Land Company and the young City of Tacoma established Wright Park between the years 1886 and 1890, early newspaper coverage extolled the virtues of the park for its healthful aspects and noted how frequently citizens walked its expanse, which was convenient to both downtown and residential areas. This 1980s photograph proves that the same remained true almost a century later.

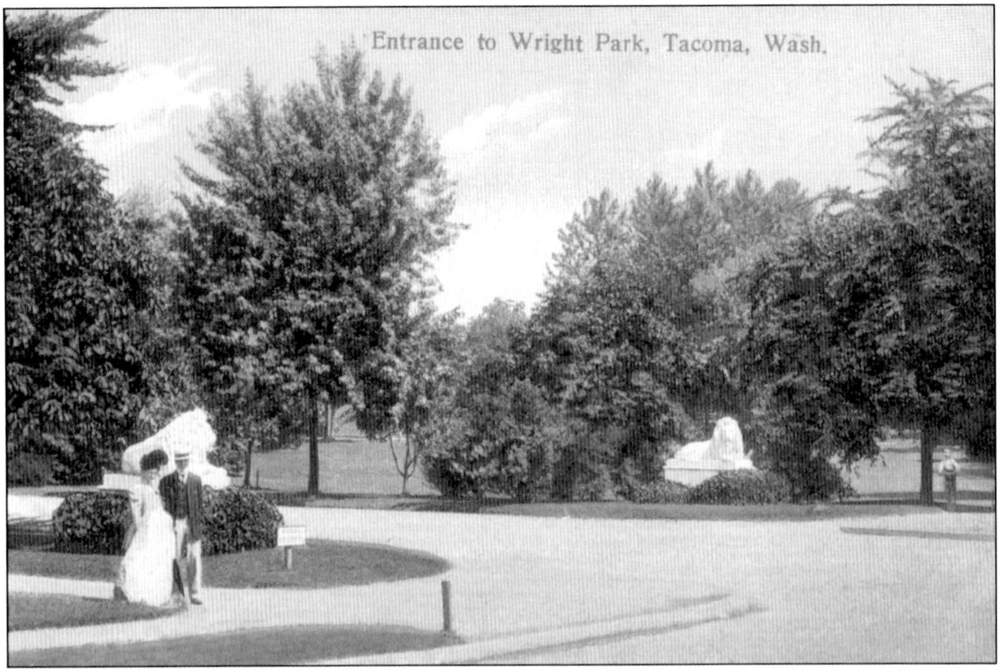

The Sixth Avenue entrance to Wright Park has been guarded by the two stately lions donated by Clinton Ferry for more than 116 years. Above, a stylish couple poses on the west side of Yakima Street when it was still a thoroughfare through the park. Below, modern-day parkgoers (left to right) Alexis Carr, Charles Carr, and Victoria Woodards enjoy the updated entrance. A 2005 citizen-approved capital park improvement bond included $4 million for upgrades to Wright Park. The guiding directive for the improvements was the historic character of the park. In the process, Ferry's lions were repaired and placed on sturdy marble mounts. Today's park visitors may dress differently, but they still enjoy the beauty of this lovely garden in the heart of the city.

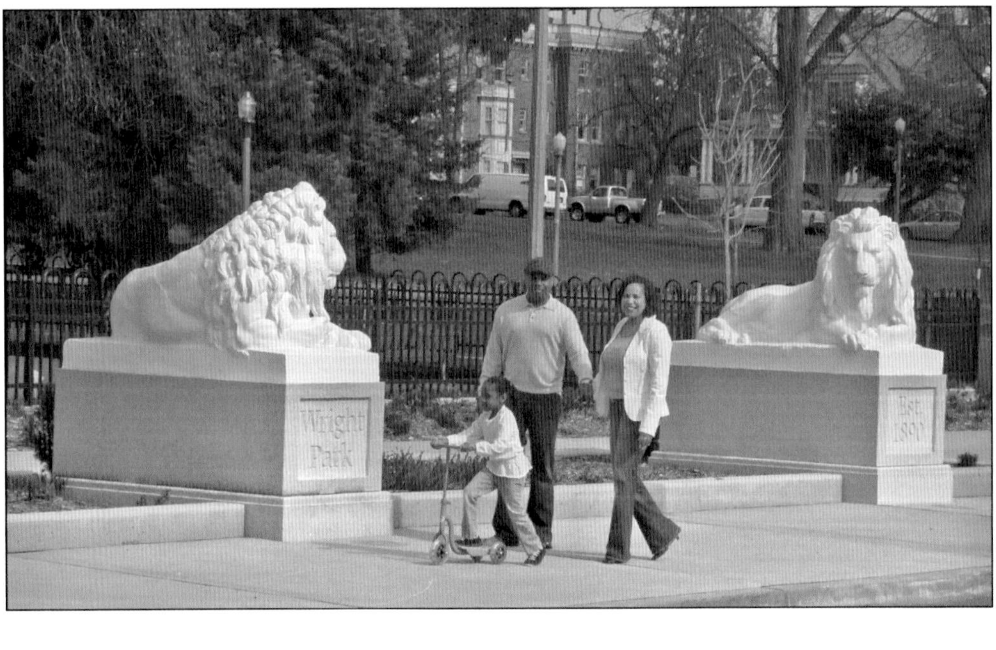

INDEX OF PHOTOGRAPHS

The authors are grateful to all who allowed the use of their photographs to bring the history of Wright Park to life. All photographs not credited are part of the collection of the Metropolitan Park District of Tacoma. Initials were used to identify items from the collections of the Annie Wright School (AWS), Eric Swanson (ES), MultiCare Health System (MHS), Tom Stenger (TS), Washington State Historical Society (WSHS), and the University of Washington Special Collections (UW).

The photographs of the Tacoma Public Library (TPL) Northwest Room are identified below:

Page 11 C156427-1 and G17.1-074
Pages 12 and 13 TPL-600
Page 14 General Collection
Page 16 TPL289 and TDS-005
Page 19 G66.2-020
Page 22 General Collection and G41.1-123
Page 23 DC-064
Page 24 General Collection
Page 26 G41.1-136
Page 28 and 29 General Collection
Page 31 DC-065
Page 42 972-7 and A7101-1
Page 43 D32041-15 and D32041-14
Page 44 D30233-1
Page 62 A-671 and D141770-15
Page 65 A9320#12
Page 66 A50067-1 and T52#2
Page 67 BU-2 and BU-0458
Page 70 2870
Page 73 D24549-8 andD9614-4
Page 74 General Collection
Page 77 G41.1-126
Page 78 General Collection
Page 83 General Collection
Page 84 D618-1
Page 86 D11501-1
Page 87 G41.1-151
Page 94 1032
Page 100 G41.1-127 and G66.1-117
Page 101 G40.1-026
Page 102 D22401-2 and 3
Page 103 D22720-1 and 3
Page 104 D66209-1 and D7905-6
Page 105 D41853-9
Page 106 D153835-1R and D163163-5
Page 113 D7139-6
Page 114 1997
Page 115 930-3 and D740-1
Page 118 D7139-8 and D44908-1
Page 120 D871-1 and D695-3
Page 121 D7139-9
Page 122 D27051-16
Page 123 D49085-1 and D41354-2
Page 124 D155053-3